# ITALIAN GRAMMAR

## Anna Proudfoot

TEACH YOURSELF BOOKS

Anna Proudfoot was born in Scotland, but she has spent long periods in Italy since her childhood. She graduated from Bedford College (University of London) in 1972 and since then has taught Italian in higher, further and adult education in London, Cambridge, Oxford and the USA. Her main interests are in developing materials for adult learners. She is currently the senior lecturer in Italian at Oxford Polytechnic where she also runs Oxford Polyglot, a language training unit providing language training for local businesses.

Acknowledgement: Extract from *Volevo i pantaloni* by Lara Cardella (Edizioni Oscar Originals) reproduced by permission of Hamish Hamilton.

Long-renowned as the authorative source for self-guided learning – with more than 30 million copies sold worldwide – the *Teach Yourself* series includes over 200 titles in the fields of languages, crafts, hobbies, sports, and other leisure activities.

*British Library Cataloguing in Publication Data*
Proudfoot, Anna
  Italian Grammar—(Teach Yourself Series).
  I. Title   II. Series
  458.2

*Library of Congress Catalog Card Number:* 92–80856

First published in UK 1992 by Hodder Headline Plc, 338 Euston Road, London NW1 3BH

First published in US 1992 by NTC Publishing Group, 4255 West Touhy Avenue, Lincolnwood (Chicago), Illinois 60646 – 1975 U.S.A.

Typeset by Hewer Text Composition Services, Edinburgh.
Printed in England by Cox & Wyman Ltd, Reading, Berkshire.

Impression number   14   13   12   11   10   9   8   7   6   5   4
Year                               1999   1998   1997   1996   1995   1994

# Contents

# ── INTRODUCTION ──

This book is designed as a reference guide for all those studying Italian on their own or in a class, and particularly for those using the new communicative approach, who feel they need some grammar back-up. You do not need a specialised knowledge of grammar terms to use this book, because everything is explained in a non-technical way.

The book is divided into units, each one covering a basic communicative function, such as Asking for and giving personal information, Talking about location and Describing the past. In each unit you will find the constructions you need to carry out the particular language function covered, with the essential vocabulary and important grammar points.

For each unit, the contents pages list both the language functions and the grammar points covered, so that you can see at a glance what is included in each unit.

If, on the other hand, you want to check specific grammar points, just look up the **Index** on page 217.

## *How To Use This Book*

Each of the Units in this book stands alone so if you want to learn or revise all of your Italian grammar, you can work through the units in any order you like. If there is a particular language function that you need to use, you can look in the **Contents** to find out which unit deals with the function that interests you. Unit 16, for example, teaches you how to express your likes and dislikes and Unit 7 shows you how to talk about your daily routine.

Start by reading the list called **Le funzioni** which lists the language functions studied in the unit. The section **Le strutture** tells you which grammar constructions you are going to need in order to carry out those functions. The **Nota introduttiva** gives a few examples (with English translations) of these constructions, with a very brief explanation. When you have looked at these examples, you are ready to study the **Analisi della Grammatica**, in which all the grammar points listed in **Le**

**strutture** are dealt with one by one. There are detailed explanations of each point, illustrated by lots of examples.

The **In contesto** section shows you how these language functions are used in the context of everyday life, with examples taken from both spoken language (short dialogues) and written language (newspaper articles, and so on). Look carefully at how these points are used in different contexts. You can use the dialogues and passages as a base and create some more of your own.

Once you feel confident about using the language points you have just learnt, you can expand your knowledge by reading the section **In aggiunta**. This section gives alternative ways of expressing the functions you have been studying, and mentions additional language points.

Any grammar points not covered directly in the units will be found in the **Grammatica** section which includes a list of the most common irregular verbs.

The **Italian–English vocabulary** lists all Italian words you will find in the book, and the **Index** lists specific grammar points in alphabetical order.

# 1

## Asking for and giving personal information

**Le funzioni**

In this unit, you will learn to:
Say who you are / what your name is ● Say where you are from / what nationality you are ● Say what your occupation is ● Ask other people for similar information

**Le strutture**

Subject pronouns **io**, **tu**, **lui**, etc. (*I, you, he*) ● Verb **essere** (present tense) *to be* ● Verb **chiamarsi** (present tense) *to be called* ● Adjectives of nationality

## Nota introduttiva

To give or ask for personal information you need to learn the subject pronouns (Italian words for *I, you, he, she,* etc.), the verb **chiamarsi**, *to be called*, and the verb **essere**, *to be*. Look at these examples before going on.

| | |
|---|---|
| Mi chiamo Anna. | *My name's Anna.* |
| Sono inglese. | *I'm English.* |
| Sono di Oxford. | *I'm from Oxford.* |
| Lei è italiana? | *Are you Italian?* |
| È di Roma? | *Are you from Rome?* |

# ———— Analisi della grammatica ————

## 1 Io, tu, lui, lei: *I, you, he, she*

You don't normally use the subject pronouns (the equivalent of the English *I, you, he, she,* etc.) in Italian, because the ending of the verb shows which person is being talked about. The pronouns can, however, be used for emphasis, for example:

(a) when you want to distinguish between *he* and *she*, which have the same verb form:

> **Lui** è inglese.       *He is English.*
> **Lei** è italiana.      *She is Italian.*

(b) when you want to emphasise a difference or contrast:

> **Io** sono italiana.    *I'm Italian (woman).*
> **Lui** è inglese.       *He is English.*

(c) or, especially when using the polite form, to make a question sound less abrupt:

> **Lei** è italiana?      *Are you Italian?*

Here are the form of subject pronouns generally used in this situation:

| Singular | | Plural | |
|---|---|---|---|
| io | *I* | noi | *we* |
| tu | *you (familiar)* | voi | *you* |
| lui | *he* | loro | *them* |
| lei | *she* | Loro | *you (polite)* |
| Lei | *you (polite)* | | |

## 2 Tu *or* Lei? *Both mean 'you'*

Italian has two forms of address meaning *you,* in the singular: **tu** (the familiar form) used with friends, family, children and animals; and **Lei** (the polite form, written with a capital 'l') used in business situations such as in a shop or a bank, with new acquaintances (until invited to use **tu**) and with people older than you or worthy of respect such as mothers-in-law. **Lei** uses the same form of the verb as **lui** (*he*) or **lei** (*she*).

There is also a polite form of address for more than one person (**Loro**) which uses the same form of verb as **loro** (*they*) but this is less common. A waiter, shop assistant or hotel receptionist may use **Loro** when addressing more than one client. But it would not be impolite to use the **voi** form.

## 3 Essere *(to be)*

You use the verb **essere** when giving information about yourself, such as where you are from or what nationality you are (the verb within a sentence is the word which describes the action, such as *to be*: *I am, you are, he is*, etc. See unit 5).

Italian verbs come into three main groups: ending in **-are**, in **-ere** and in **-ire**. Usually the verbs follow a pattern according to their group, but **essere** (*to be*) does not follow such a pattern. Here are all the forms of the verb **essere** with the subject pronouns you could use:

| Singular | | | Plural | | |
|---|---|---|---|---|---|
| (io) | sono | *I am* | (noi) | siamo | *we are* |
| (tu) | sei | *you are* | (voi) | siete | *you are* |
| (lui) | è | *he is* | (loro) | sono | *they are* |
| (lei) | è | *she is* | (Loro) | sono | *you are (polite)* |
| (Lei) | è | *you are (polite)* | | | |

## 4 Chiamarsi *(to be called)*

The Italian for *my name is* is **mi chiamo** (Lit: *I call myself*). To say this, you need the verb **chiamarsi** (*to call oneself*). (This is a reflexive verb, see unit 7 for a full explanation.)

| Singular | | |
|---|---|---|
| (io) | mi chiamo | *I am called* |
| (tu) | ti chiami | *you are called* |
| (lui) | si chiama | *he is called* |
| (lei) | si chiama | *she is called* |
| (Lei) | si chiama | *you are called (polite)* |

| Plural | | |
|---|---|---|
| (noi) | ci chiamiamo | *we are called* |
| (voi) | vi chiamate | *you are called* |
| (loro) | si chiamano | *they are called* |
| (Loro) | si chiamano | *you are called (polite)** |

*As for **essere** the Loro form, polite plural of *you*, is shown here. It is always the same as **loro** they and is not shown hereafter.

For more verbs that end in **-are (mangiare, parlare**, etc.) see units 5 and 6. For more reflexive verbs (actions you do to or for yourself and which require reflexive pronouns) see unit 7.

Italians don't say *What are you called?*; they say *How are you called?* (**Come ti chiami?**).

## 5 Nationality

An adjective tells you about someone or something. You use an adjective with the verb **essere** (*to be*) to say what nationality someone is:

Sara è italiana.          *Sara is Italian.*

In Italian, the adjective has to agree with the person (or object) it describes, i.e. it must have a masculine or feminine, singular or plural ending to match the gender (or sex) and the quantity of the person (people) or thing (-s). (In Italian, objects are either masculine or feminine, as are people! Singular means there is one person or thing, and plural means that there are more than one.) For a further explanation of gender agreement, see unit 2.

There are two types of adjective in Italian:

(a) Those ending in **-e** (same for masculine or feminine) whose plural ends in **-i**:

Gerald è inglese.          *Gerald is English.*
Geraldine è inglese.          *Geraldine is English.*
Gerald e Geraldine sono inglesi.          *Gerald and Geraldine are English.*

(b) Those ending in **-o** (masc.) or **-a** (fem.) whose plural ends in **-i** (masc.) or **-e** (fem.):

Mario è italiano.          *Mario is Italian.*

| Maria è italiana. | *Maria is Italian.* |
| Mario e Piero sono italiani. | *Mario and Piero are Italian (men).* |
| Maria e Teresa sono italiane. | *Maria and Teresa are Italian (women).* |
| Mario e Maria sono italiani. | *Mario and Maria are Italian (man and woman).* |

You will notice that when there is one male and one female subject, the adjective becomes masculine for both of them!

## In contesto

### Lei: the polite form of 'you'

When starting a conversation with someone you don't know, you use the **Lei**, or polite form, for *you*:

| **Lei è italiana?** | *Are you Italian?* |
| **No. Sono inglese, di Londra. E Lei?** | *No. I'm English, from London. And you?* |
| **Io sono italiano. Sono di Roma. Come si chiama Lei?** | *I'm Italian. I'm from Rome. What's your name?* |
| **Mi chiamo Anne Smith. E Lei come si chiama?** | *My name's Anne Smith. And what's your name?* |
| **Mi chiamo Franco Rossi.** | *My name's Franco Rossi.* |

### Tu: the informal form of 'you'

Two young people starting up a conversation might address each other informally, using the **tu** form, from the start:

| **Sei italiana?** | *Are you Italian?* |
| **No. Sono inglese, di Oxford. E tu?** | *No, I'm English, from Oxford. And you?* |
| **Io sono italiano. Sono di Milano. Come ti chiami?** | *I'm Italian. I'm from Milan. What's your name?* |
| **Mi chiamo Tracy. E tu come ti chiami?** | *My name's Tracy. And what's your name?* |
| **Mi chiamo Franco.** | *My name's Franco.* |

And here is how you would talk about your friends:

| | |
|---|---|
| **Lui si chiama George. È inglese.** | *He's called George. He's English.* |
| **E lei?** | *And (what about) her?* |
| **Lei si chiama Georgina. È inglese.** | *She's called Georgina. She's English.* |
| **E loro?** | *And them?* |
| **Loro si chiamano Henry e Henrietta. Sono inglesi.** | *They're called Henry and Henrietta. They're English.* |

---
## In aggiunta
---

### 1 Professions or occupations

You can extend the conversation by asking someone his or her profession or occupation:

| | |
|---|---|
| Lei è professore? | *Are you a teacher?* |
| No. Sono medico. E Lei? | *No. I'm a doctor. What about you?* |
| Io sono avvocato. | *I'm a lawyer.* |
| Giovanni è medico. | *Giovanni's a doctor.* |
| Giovanna è medico. | *Giovanna's a doctor.* |
| Carlo è avvocato. | *Carlo's a lawyer.* |
| Carla è avvocato. | *Carla's a lawyer.* |

You don't use the Italian equivalent of *a* when saying what someone does. You say **Carlo è avvocato.** (Lit. *Carlo is lawyer.*)

Linguistically speaking, in Italian, it doesn't make much difference whether you are a man or a woman – you will still be **medico** or **avvocato**.

However, some nouns denoting professions do have a female equivalent, for example:

| Masculine | Feminine | |
|---|---|---|
| maestro | maestra | *teacher* |
| sarto | sarta | *tailor/dressmaker* |
| cuoco | cuoca | *cook* |
| infermiere | infermiera | *nurse* |
| cameriere | cameriera | *waiter, waitress* |
| ragioniere | ragioniera | *accountant* |
| professore | professoressa | *lecturer, teacher* |
| dottore | dottoressa | *doctor* |
| studente | studentessa | *student* |

| Masculine | Feminine | |
|-----------|----------|---|
| attore | at**trice** | *actor, actress* |
| scrittore | scrit**trice** | *writer* |
| direttore | diret**trice** | *director* |

Some nouns denoting occupation don't change their endings. Here are some examples:

| dentista | *dentist* | giornalista | *journalist* |
|----------|-----------|-------------|--------------|
| turista | *tourist* | ciclista | *cyclist* |
| artista | *artist* | cantante | *singer* |
| pianista | *pianist* | insegnante | *teacher* |
| autista | *driver* | | |

## 2 Marital status

You can also use the verb **essere** to give information on marital status:

Giovanni è sposato     *Giovanni is married.*
Maria è sposata.     *Maria is married.*
Giovanni e Maria **sono**     *Giovanni and Maria are married.*
    sposati.

Although the words **celibe** *bachelor*, and **nubile** *spinster* exist, Italians would say:

Non è sposato.     *He isn't married.*
Non è sposata.     *She isn't married.*

## 3 Questions

In Italian a statement can be turned into a question in two ways:

(a) change the order, putting the subject (such as **tu**, **Lei**) after the verb:

Statement:   Lei è inglese.
Question:    È inglese Lei?

(b) raise the voice at the end of the sentence:

Lei è inglese? ↑

## 4 *Negative sentences*

Negative sentences (statements or questions) are formed simply by adding **non** immediately before the verb:

| | |
|---|---|
| Sono inglese. | *I'm English.* |
| **Non** sono inglese. | *I'm not English.* |
| | |
| Sei studente? | *Are you a student?* |
| **Non** sei studente? | *Aren't you a student?* |
| | |
| Lei è italiana? | *Are you Italian?* |
| Lei **non** è italiana? | *Aren't you Italian?* |

It's not difficult to say *no*!

| | |
|---|---|
| Sei italiana? | *Are you Italian?* |
| **No,** non sono italiana. | *No, I'm not Italian.* |

# 2

# Identifying people and things

**Le funzioni**

In this unit, you will learn how to:
Ask for something ● Ask or say who someone is ● Ask or say what something is

**Le strutture**

Nouns (an object, a person or an animal) ● The indefinite article **un**, **uno**, **una**, **un'** (English: *a*, *an*) ● plurals ● Chi è? ● Cosa è?

## Nota introduttiva

Study these examples of things you might want to ask for in Italy:

| | |
|---|---|
| Un cappuccino, per favore. | *A coffee, please.* |
| Una cioccolata, per piacere ... e una spremuta, due paste e due cappuccini. | *A hot chocolate please ... and a fresh fruit juice, two cakes and two cappuccinos.* |

You might want to know what something is:

| | |
|---|---|
| Che cosa è? | *What is it?* |
| È un gettone telefonico. | *It's a telephone token.* |
| Che cosa è? | *What is it?* |
| È una cabina telefonica. | *It's a telephone kiosk.* |

Or what several things are:

| | |
|---|---|
| Che cosa sono questi? | *What are these?* |
| Sono gettoni telefonici. | *They're telephone tokens.* |

Or who somebody is:

| | |
|---|---|
| Chi è? | *Who is he?* |
| È un turista. | *He's a tourist.* |
| Chi è? | *Who is she?* |
| È una studentessa. | *She's a student.* |

Or who some people are:

| | |
|---|---|
| Chi sono? | *Who are they?* |
| Sono turisti inglesi. | *They're English tourists.* |

———— **Analisi della grammatica** ————

## 1 Nouns

A noun is a person, an animal, an object or an abstract thing. In Italian, objects, as well as people, have genders: these are masculine or feminine (see unit 1).

There are several ways of saying *a* or *an*, **un, uno, una, un'** (indefinite article): these depend on whether the noun is masculine or feminine, and if the noun starts with a vowel or a consonant. When deciding which form to use, you can normally get a clue by looking at the end of the word.

### (a) Nouns that end in -o

Nouns that end in **-o** are usually masculine. Their indefinite article is, as a general rule, **un**, but if they start with **s-** plus another consonant, **gn, ps, z** or (usually) **pn** or **x** it is **uno**:

| | |
|---|---|
| **un** cappuccino | *a cappuccino* |
| **un** espresso | *an espresso* |
| **uno s**puntino | *a snack* |
| **uno z**oo | *a zoo* |
| **uno ps**ichiatra | *a psychiatrist* |

*Exceptions*: a few nouns end in **-o**, but are feminine. For example,

| | |
|---|---|
| **una** mano | *a hand* |

### (b) Nouns that end in -a

Nouns that end in **-a** are usually feminine and their indefinite article is **una**, but if they start with a vowel (a, e, i, o, u) it is **un'**:

| | |
|---|---|
| **una** cioccolata | *a hot chocolate* |
| **una** pasta | *a cake* |
| **una** spremuta | *a fresh fruit juice* |
| **un'** aranciata | *an orangeade* |

*Exceptions*: a few nouns end in **-a**, but are masculine. For example:

| | |
|---|---|
| **un** programma | *a programme* |
| **un** cinema | *a cinema* |

There are several words for professions which end in **-a** and can be *either* masculine (with **un, uno**) or feminine (with **una**, or **un'**). For example:

| | |
|---|---|
| **un** artista | *a (male) artist* |
| **un'** artista | *a (female) artist* |
| **un** pianista | *a (male) pianist* |
| **una** pianista | *a (female) pianist* |
| **uno** specialista | *a (male) specialist* |
| **una** specialista | *a (female) specialist* |

## (c) Nouns that end in -e

Some nouns that end in **-e** are masculine (these take **un** or **uno**) and some are feminine (these take **una** or **un'**).

| | |
|---|---|
| **un** giornale | *a newspaper* |
| **uno** studente | *a student (male)* |
| **una** lezione | *a lesson* |
| **un'** automobile | *a car* |

You may be surprised to learn that – grammatically speaking – in Italian, there isn't always a male and a female of a species:

**una** giraffa (*giraffe*) is always female.
**un** ippopotamo (*hippopotamus*) is always male.

In order to provide the missing half, you say:

| | |
|---|---|
| **una** giraffa maschio | *a male giraffe* |
| **un** ippopotamo femmina | *a female hippopotamus* |

Some animals – as in English – have a different name for the male and the female of the species:

| | |
|---|---|
| un cane (*dog*) | una cagna (*bitch*) |
| un gallo (*cock*) | una gallina (*hen*) |

Here are the different types of nouns set out in table form, with **un, uno, una, un'** as appropriate.

| un cappuccino (*cappuccino*)<br>un bar (*café*) | una cioccolata (*hot chocolate*) |
|---|---|
| un aperitivo (*aperitif*) | un' aranciata (*orangeade*) |
| uno spuntino (*snack*) | una spremuta (*fresh fruit juice*) |
| un giornale (*newspaper*) | una chiave (*key*) |

Foreign words (i.e. not originally Italian, but now used in the Italian language) are usually masculine and take **un** or **uno**:

| **un** bar | *a café* |
|---|---|
| **un** sandwich | *a sandwich* |
| **un** club | *a club* |
| **un** toast | *a toasted sandwich* |

But not always:

| **una** brioche | *a brioche* (from French) |
|---|---|

For more examples of nouns that do not fit the patterns shown above, refer to the Grammar Section on page 173.

## 2 Plurals

### (a) Nouns that end in -o

Masculine nouns that end in **-o**, end in **-i** in the plural:

| un cappuccino | *a cappuccino* |
|---|---|
| due cappuccini | *two cappuccinos* |
| uno spuntino | *one snack* |
| due spuntini | *two snacks* |

So does this feminine noun:

| una mano | *one hand* |
|---|---|
| due mani | *two hands* |

This is an irregular plural:

| un uomo | *a man* |
|---|---|
| due uomini | *two men* |

### (b) Nouns that end in -a

Feminine nouns ending in **-a**, end in **-e** in the plural:

| una cioccolata | *a chocolate* |
| due cioccolate | *two hot chocolates* |
| una spremuta | *a fresh fruit juice* |
| due spremute | *two fresh fruit juices* |

Masculine nouns that end in -**a**, end in -**i** in the plural:

| un programma | *a programme* |
| due programmi | *two programmes* |

Where both genders exist, masculine nouns in the plural end in -**i**, (**artisti**) and feminine nouns in the plural end in -**e**, (**artiste**), for example:

| un artista | *a (male) artist* |
| due artisti | *two (male) artists* |
| uno stilista | *a (male) fashion designer* |
| due stilisti | *two (male) fashion designers* |

| un' artista | *a (female) artist* |
| due artiste | *two (female) artists* |
| una stilista | *a (female) fashion designer* |
| due stiliste | *two (female) fashion designers* |

### (c) Nouns that end in -e

Masculine nouns ending in -**e**, end in -**i** when they are plural:

| un giornale | *a newspaper* |
| due giornali | *two newspapers* |
| uno studente | *a student* |
| due studenti | *two students* |

So do the feminine nouns:

| una lezione | *a lesson* |
| due lezioni | *two lessons* |
| un' automobile | *a car* |
| due automobili | *two cars* |

### (d) Words that don't change in the plural:

(i) Words of 'foreign' origin:

| un bar | *a café* | due bar | *two cafés* |
| un sandwich | *a sandwich* | due sandwich | *two sandwiches* |
| una brioche | *a brioche* | due brioche | *two brioches* |

(ii) Words ending in a vowel with an accent:

| una città | *a city* | due città | *two cities* |
|-----------|----------|-----------|--------------|
| un caffè | *a coffee* | due caffè | *two coffees* |
| un tè | *a tea* | due tè | *two teas* |

For further examples of nouns that don't fit the patterns shown above see page 173.

## 3 Chi è?: *who is it?*

To ask who someone is you use **chi** (*who*) and **è** (*he, she, it is*).

| Chi è? | *Who is it?* |
|--------|--------------|
| **Chi è?** | *Who is he?* |
| È un turista. | *He's a tourist.* |
| **Chi è?** | *Who is it?* |
| È Giorgio. | *It's Giorgio.* |

And for more than one person:

| Chi sono? | *Who are they?* |
|-----------|-----------------|
| **Chi sono?** | *Who are they?* |
| Sono due turisti. | *They're two tourists.* |
| **Chi sono?** | *Who are they?* |
| Sono Henry e Henrietta. | *They're Henry and Henrietta.* |

## 4 Che cosa è?: *what is it?*

To ask what something is, you say:

| | Che cosa è? | *What is it?* (Lit. *What thing is it?*) |
|---|-------------|------------------------------------------|
| OR | Cosa è? | *What is it?* |
| | Che cosa è? | *What is it?* |
| | È un elenco telefonico. | *It's a telephone directory.* |
| | Che cosa è? | *What is it?* |
| | È un gettone telefonico. | *It's a telephone token.* |

Sometimes **cosa** is abbreviated, especially in speech, to:

| Che cos'è? | *What is it?* |
|------------|---------------|
| Cos'è? | *What is it?* |

For more than one thing, you say:

| | Che cosa sono? | *What are they?* |
|---|----------------|------------------|
| OR | Cosa sono? | *What are they?* |

| | |
|---|---|
| **Cosa sono?** | *What are they?* |
| Sono tagliatelle. | *They're noodles.* |
| **Cosa sono?** | *What are they?* |
| Sono biscotti. | *They're biscuits.* |

## In contesto

### 1 In a bar

| | |
|---|---|
| **Un cappuccino e una brioche, per favore.** | *A cappuccino and a brioche, please.* |
| **Sì, certo.** | *Yes, of course.* |
| **Un' aranciata e una limonata, per favore.** | *An orangeade and a lemonade, please.* |
| **Subito, signora.** | *Straightaway (madam).* |
| **Due caffè e un tè, per favore.** | *Two coffees and a tea, please.* |
| **Sì, signore. Altro?** | *Yes, sir. Anything else?* |
| **Due cornetti.** | *Two croissants.* |

### 2 What is it?/What are they?

| | |
|---|---|
| **Che cos'è?** | *What is it?* |
| **È una brioche.** | *It's a brioche.* |
| **Cos'è?** | *What is it?* |
| **È un aperitivo.** | *It's an aperitif.* |
| **Che cosa sono?** | *What are they?* |
| **Sono paste.** | *They're cakes.* |
| **Cosa sono?** | *What are they?* |
| **Sono fusilli.** | *They're pasta spirals.* |

### 3 Who is he?/Who are they?

| | |
|---|---|
| **Chi è?** | *Who is he?* |
| **È Luigi.** | *He's Luigi.* |
| **Chi è Luigi?** | *Who's Luigi?* |
| **È uno studente.** | *He's a student.* |

| | |
|---|---|
| **Chi sono?** | *Who are they?* |
| **Sono Henry e Henrietta.** | *They're Henry and Henrietta.* |
| **Chi sono Henry e Henrietta?** | *Who are Henry and Henrietta?* |
| **Sono due turisti.** | *They're two tourists.* |

---

**un caffè:** an (espresso) coffee
**un cappuccino:** a (cappuccino) coffee
**una brioche:** is generally eaten for breakfast or tea.
**un cornetto:** the nearest you can get to a croissant in Italy; can be plain or filled with jam or pastry cream filling, and eaten for breakfast. This is nothing to do with ice-cream: **un cono** is the Italian word for an ice-cream cone!

---

## In aggiunta

### 1  Questo: *this*

To make it clear who or what you are referring to, you can point, and/or add **questo** to your question or your reply. **Questo** means *this* or *this thing* or *this person*, indicating something or someone near you. It has different forms (**questo, questa, questi, queste**) according to whether the object or person referred to is singular or plural, masculine or feminine.

**Masculine singular**

| | |
|---|---|
| Questo è un aperitivo. | *This is an aperitif.* |
| Cos'è questo? | *What's this?* |
| È un aperitivo. | *It's an aperitif.* |

**Feminine singular**

| | |
|---|---|
| Questa è una bibita. | *This is a drink.* |
| Cos'è questa? | *What is this?* |
| È una bibit. | *It's a drink.* |

**Masculine plural**

| | |
|---|---|
| Questi sono gnocchi. | *These are gnocchi.*\* |
| Cosa sono questi? | *What are these?* |
| Sono gnocchi. | *They're gnocchi.* |

## Feminine plural

| | |
|---|---|
| Queste sono caramelle. | *These are sweets.* |
| Cosa sono queste? | *What are these?* |
| Sono carmelle. | *They're sweets.* |

Questo can also be used to indicate a person:

| | |
|---|---|
| Chi è questo? | *Who is this (man)?* |
| È Luigi. | *It's Luigi.* |
| Chi è questa? | *Who is this (woman)?* |
| Questa è una turista americana. | *This is an American tourist.* |
| Chi sono questi? | *Who are these (people)?* |
| Sono Henry e Henrietta. | *They're Henry and Henrietta.* |
| Chi sono queste? | *Who are these (women)?* |
| Queste sono turiste americane. | *These are American tourists.* |

While you will usually be able to tell whether a person is masculine or feminine, and therefore whether to use **questo** or **questa** it is less easy with an object. It's safest to assume an object is masculine and use **questo** (**questi** if it's plural):

| | |
|---|---|
| Chi è **questo**? | *Who is this (man)?* |
| È un professore. | *He's a teacher.* |
| Chi è **questa**? | *Who is this (woman)?* |
| È un' amica. | *She's a friend.* |
| Cos'è **questo/questa**? | *What's this?* |
| È una spremuta d'arancia. | *It's a fresh orange juice.* |

**Questo** can also be found alongside a noun and used as an adjective. See unit 5.

**\*Gnocchi** are very small dumplings made out of semolina or potato, and covered in a sauce. They are usually eaten as a first course as a change from pasta.

While **pasta** means pasta (i.e. spaghetti, tagliatelle, etc.) it can also mean a little cake that you eat all to yourself!

# 3

# – Asking about availability –

**Le funzioni**

In this unit you will learn how to:
Ask if something exists • Say that something exists • Ask if
something is available • Say that something is available

**Le strutture**

**C'è, ce n'è; ci sono, ce ne sono** • **Alcuni, alcune** • **Dei, delle,
degli** • **Qualche**

---

## Nota introduttiva

---

Before going on, study these examples:

**C'è** un telefono qui vicino?  *Is there a telephone near here?*
Sì, **ce n'è** uno al Bar Roma. *Yes, there's one at the Roma café.*

**Ci sono** tortellini oggi?  *Are there tortellini today?*
Sì. **Ce ne sono.**  *Yes. There are (some).*

**Ci sono** turisti a Lecce?  *Are there any tourists in Lecce?*
Sì, **ce ne sono** alcuni.  *Yes, there are a few.*
**Ci sono** anche degli  *Are there foreigners too?*
  stranieri?
**Ci sono** dei tedeschi, e  *There are Germans, and a few*
  qualche inglese.  *English.*

# —— Analisi della grammatica ——

## 1 C'è: *there is*

In unit 1, you learnt **essere** (*to be*). If you put it together with **ci** (*there*) you get **c'è** (*there is*) which is short for **ci è**. To ask whether there is a telephone, or a toilet, etc. use:

C'è ...          *There is* ...

You make it sound like a question by raising your voice at the end, as you learnt in unit 1.

C'è? ↑          *Is there?* ↑

The plural version is:

Ci sono ...          *There are* ...
Ci sono ... ?          *Are there?*

**Examples:**

**C'è** una toilette?      *Is there a toilet?*
Sì, **c'è** una toilette.      *Yes, there's a toilet.*

**C'è** un medico?      *Is there a doctor?*
Sì, **c'è** un medico.      *Yes, there's a doctor.*

**Ci sono** pesche oggi?      *Are there any peaches today?*
Sì, oggi **ci sono** pesche.      *Yes, there are peaches today.*

Instead of repeating the object (C'è un telefono? Sì, c'è un telefono.) you can combine **c'è** (*there is*) with **ne** (*of them*) and **uno** or **una** (*one*): note that when **ci** plus **ne** plus **è** are combined the **ci** becomes **ce**. E.g:

C'è un medico?      *Is there a doctor?*
Sì, **ce n'è** uno.      *There is one of them.*

**Ci sono** can also be combined with **ne**:

Ci sono delle guide?      *Are there any guides?*
Sì, **ce ne sono** due.      *There are two of them.*

— 19 —

**Examples:**

| | |
|---|---|
| C'è un telefono? | *Is there a telephone?* |
| Sì, **ce n'è** uno. | *Yes, there is one (of them).* |
| C'è una toilette? | *Is there a toilet?* |
| Sì, **ce n'è** una. | *Yes, there is one.* |
| **Ci sono** pesche? | *Are there peaches?* |
| Sì, **ce ne sono**. | *Yes, there are (some of them).* |

*One* will be **uno** or **una** depending on whether the object or person is masculine or feminine.

To say that there aren't any:

| | |
|---|---|
| C'è un telefono? | *Is there a telephone?* |
| No. **Non c'è**. | *No. There isn't one.* |
| Ci sono studenti qui? | *Are there any students here?* |
| No. **Non ce ne sono.** | *No. There aren't any.* |

**Ne** is used with the plural (non ce **ne** sono), but tends to be used in the singular only with a number or other indication of quantity.

*Some* can be expressed, in Italian, in several ways (see below).

## 2 Dei, delle, degli: *some, any*

You can use **dei, delle, degli** (*some, any*) the forms of which vary to match the noun they go with, i.e. masculine or feminine (see unit 2). For masculine nouns, use **dei**, or **degli** if the noun starts with a vowel, **s** plus a consonant, **z, gn, ps** and **pn**, or **x**. For feminine nouns the correct form is **delle**. Here are some examples:

| | |
|---|---|
| Ci sono **dei** biscotti al cioccolato. | *There are some chocolate biscuits.* |
| Ci sono **delle** paste. | *There are some cakes.* |
| Ci sono **degli** zucchini. | *There are some courgettes.* |
| Ci sono **degli** alberghi. | *There are some hotels.* |
| Ci sono **delle** melanzane? | *Are there any aubergines?* |
| Sì, ci sono **delle** melanzane bellissime oggi. | *Yes, there are some beautiful aubergines today.* |

## 3 Alcuni, alcune: *some, a few*

Another way of expressing *some* is to use **alcuni** (for masculine nouns) or **alcune** (for feminine nouns). **Alcuni** suggests the idea of *a few* rather than *several* and can be used as an adjective (describing a noun) or as a pronoun (on its own) meaning *a few things* or *a few people*:

| | |
|---|---|
| Ci sono **alcuni** problemi. | *There are a few problems.* |
| Ci sono **alcune** cose da fare prima di partire. | *There are a few things to do before leaving.* |

The construction **ce ne sono** can also used with **alcuni**; in this case **alcuni** stands on its own, without a noun:

| | |
|---|---|
| Ci sono dei libri italiani? | *Are there any Italian books?* |
| Ce ne sono **alcuni**. | *There are a few (of them).* |

## 4 Qualche: *some*

**Qualche** is similar in meaning to **alcuni**; it means *a few* or *some*, but, although the meaning is plural, it is always used with a noun in the singular form.

It can only be used with nouns that can be counted and not with uncountable nouns like *sugar* for which there is another way of saying *some* (see 5 below).

| | |
|---|---|
| C'è **qualche** programma interessante stasera? | *Are there any interesting programmes on TV tonight?* |
| C'è **qualche** amico di Marco a casa. | *There are a few friends of Marco's at home.* |

## 5 Un po' di: *a little*

Finally, with 'uncountable' nouns such as *sugar, coffee* and *wine* you use **un po' di** (short for **un poco**): although you can also use **del** (see 2 above) in its singular forms.

| | |
|---|---|
| **un po' di** vino | *a little wine* |
| **un po' di** caffè | *a little coffee* |
| **del** zucchero | *some sugar* |

# In contesto

## Dialogo 1

| | |
|---|---|
| C'è un autobus? | *Is there a bus?* |
| Sì, ce n'è uno alle cinque. | *Yes, there's one at five o'clock.* |
| Dov' è la fermata? | *Where's the bus stop?* |

## Dialogo 2

| | |
|---|---|
| C'è una banca qui vicino? | *Is there a bank near here?* |
| No. Non c'è. | *No. There isn't one.* |
| C'è un ufficio cambio allora? | *Is there a bureau de change then?* |
| Sì, ce n'è uno in centro. | *Yes, there's one in the town centre.* |

## Dialogo 3

| | |
|---|---|
| Ci sono le fragole oggi? | *Are there strawberries today?* |
| Sì, oggi ci sono le fragole con la panna. | *Yes, today there are strawberries with cream.* |
| Ci sono anche i fichi? | *Are there figs too?* |
| No, mi dispiace, oggi non ce ne sono. | *No, I'm sorry. There aren't any today.* |

## Dialogo 4

| | |
|---|---|
| C'è un po' di vino bianco in frigo, Maria. | *There's a little bit of white wine in the fridge, Maria.* |
| C'è anche del Chianti? | *Is there some Chianti too?* |
| Sì, ce n'è ancora un po'. | *Yes, there's still a little.* |

# In aggiunta

## 1 Placing something

To say where something is, you often use a preposition, such as *in, at, to*. For example:

| | |
|---|---|
| **in** centro | *in the town centre* |
| **a** Roma | *in Rome* |
| **in** Italia | *in Italy* |

Whether saying *to* or *in* a place, Italians use **a** with a town or city, and **in** with a country.

| | |
|---|---|
| **a** Londra | *in London/to London* |
| **in** Inghilterra | *in England/to England* |

More phrases denoting place can be found in the next unit.

## 2 No

To emphasise that there isn't or there aren't any, use – as well as **non** – the negative form **nessun** (*no*) which varies in the same way as **un, uno, una, un'**:

| | |
|---|---|
| Non c'è **nessuna** guida. | *There is no guide.* |
| Non c'è **nessun'** automobile disponibile. | *There are no cars available.* (Lit. *there is no car.*) |
| Non c'è **nessun** posto. | *There is no room.* |
| Non c'è **nessuno** scrittore interessante. | *There are no interesting writers.* |

In unit 19 you can find out what happens when you qualify statements such as the above with an additional specification. For example:

| | |
|---|---|
| Non c'è nessuno scrittore italiano **che mi piaccia.** | *There are no Italian writers **that I like.*** |

## 3 Anything or nothing, anybody or nobody

While **qualche** and **nessun** are adjectives and are used with a noun the pronouns **qualcosa** (*something, anything*), **qualcuno** (*someone*) and **nessuno** (*nobody*) can be used on their own:

| | |
|---|---|
| C'è **qualcosa** da mangiare? | *Is there anything to eat?* |
| C'è **qualcuno**? | *Is anyone there?* |
| Non c'è **nessuno**. | *There's nobody there.* |
| È venuto **qualcuno**. | *Someone came.* |

Likewise **niente** (*nothing*):

| | |
|---|---|
| Non c'è **niente** da mangiare. | *There is nothing to eat.* |

# 4

# — Talking about location —

**Le funzioni**

In this unit you will learn how to:
Ask where something or someone is ● Say where something/someone is

**Le strutture**

Definite article (**il, lo, la**, etc.) and plural of nouns ● **Dov'è, dove sono?** ● Prepositions (**in, a**) and combined preposition and article (**nel, al**, etc.)

## Nota introduttiva

Before going on study these examples:

| | |
|---|---|
| **Dov'è** il Bar Roma? | *Where is the Roma café?* |
| È **in** Via dei Sette Santi. | *It's in Via dei Sette Santi.* |
| **Dove sono** gli scavi? | *Where are the excavations?* |
| Sono **in** fondo a questa strada. | *They're at the bottom of this road.* |
| **Dov'è** il telefono? | *Where is the phone?* |
| È **nell'** angolo. | *It's in the corner.* |
| **Dove sono** gli elenchi telefonici? | *Where are the telephone directories?* |
| Sono **dietro il** banco. | *They're behind the counter.* |

# ———— Analisi della grammatica ————

## 1  Il, lo, la: *the*

In unit 2, you saw that **un** (*a, an*) varies according to the gender and quantity of the noun (person or thing). The same thing happens with **il**, **lo**, **la** (*the*), the definite article.

Look at these examples:

| | |
|---|---|
| **Singular** | |
| Dov'è **il** bar? | *Where is the café?* |
| Dov'è **la** stazione? | *Where is the station?* |
| Dov'è l'automobile? | *Where is the car?* |
| Dov'è **lo** stadio? | *Where is the stadium?* |
| Dov'è l'albergo? | *Where is the hotel?* |
| | |
| **Plural** | |
| Dove sono **i** bambini? | *Where are the children?* |
| Dove sono **le** ragazze? | *Where are the girls?* |
| Dove sono **gli** studenti? | *Where are the students?* |

### (a) Nouns ending in -o

Masculine nouns ending in **-o** require the article **il**, or **lo**, if they start with s plus another consonant, **gn**, **ps**, **z** and (usually) **pn** or **x**; and **l'** if they start with a vowel.

In the plural, masculine nouns will have the article **i**, but have **gli** if they begin with s plus a consonant, **gn**, **ps**, **z**, **pn** or **x**.

| Singular | | Plural | |
|---|---|---|---|
| **Il** ragazzo | *the boy* | **i** ragazzi | *the boys* |
| **lo** studente | *the student (masc.)* | **gli** studenti | *the students* |
| l'albergo | *the hotel* | **gli** alberghi | *the hotels* |

There are a few feminine nouns ending in **-o** and these need the article **la**. The plural of such nouns is also irregular:

| Singular | | Plural | |
|---|---|---|---|
| **la** mano | *the hand* | **le** mani | *the hands* |
| **la** radio | *the radio* | **le** radio | *the radios* |

## (b) Nouns ending -a

Most nouns ending in -a are feminine and are used with **la**, or **l'** if they start with a vowel; the article used with the plural form is **le**:

| Singular | | Plural | |
|---|---|---|---|
| **la** ragazza | *the girl* | **le** ragazze | *the girls* |
| **la** studentessa | *the student (fem.)* | **le** studentesse | *the students* |
| **l'**aranciata | *the orangeade* | **le** aranciate | *the orangeades* |

Some nouns ending in -a are masculine and their article is **il** or **lo**. The plural is regular with the article **i**:

| Singular | | Plural | |
|---|---|---|---|
| **Il** programma | *the programme* | **I** programmi | *the programmes* |

There are several words which denote professions and which end in -a (see unit 2). These can be either masculine (with **il**, **lo**, **l'**); or feminine (with **la**, **l'**).

In the plural, the masculine nouns end in -i, and are used with the article **i** or **gli**, while the feminine nouns end in -e and use the article **le**:

| Singular | | Plural | |
|---|---|---|---|
| **Il** pianista | *the pianist (male)* | **I** pianisti | *the pianists* |
| **la** pianista | *the pianist (female)* | **le** pianiste | *the pianists* |
| **lo** specialista | *the specialist (male)* | **gli** specialisti | *the specialists* |
| **la** specialista | *the specialist (female)* | **le** specialiste | *the specialists* |
| **l'**artista | *the artist (male or female)* | **gli** artisti | *the artists* |
| | | **le** artiste | *the artists* |

## (c) Nouns ending in -e

Some nouns ending in -e are masculine (with **il**, **lo** before the consonants listed above in (a), and **l'** before a vowel). Some are feminine (with **la** or **l'** before a vowel). The plural forms have the article **i** or **gli** for the masculine nouns and **le** for the feminine nouns:

| Singular | | Plural | |
|---|---|---|---|
| **Il** giornale | *the newspaper* | **I** giornali | *the newspapers* |
| **lo** studente | *the student* | **gli** studenti | *the students* |
| **la** lezione | *the lesson* | **le** lezioni | *the lessons* |
| **l'**automobile | *the car* | **le** automobili | *the cars* |

For nouns that do not fit this pattern see Grammar Section, page 173.

## 2  Dov'è? *or* Dove sono?: *Where is or where are?*

The word **dove** means **where**: it combines with **è** when you want to ask where something *is*, and **sono** to ask where several things *are*:

| | |
|---|---|
| **Dov'è** la banca? | *Where is the bank?* |
| **Dov'è** la cameriera? | *Where is the waitress?* |
| **Dove sono** i biscotti? | *Where are the biscuits?* |
| **Dove sono** le caramelle? | *Where are the sweets?* |
| **Dov'è** l'Ufficio Cambio? | *Where is the Bureau de Change?* |

## 3  A, in, da: *to, in, at*

When the prepositions **a**, **in**, **da** (see unit 3) are combined with the definite articles **il**, **lo**, **la**, etc. a range of forms is created. For example:

---

**a + il, (etc.)**

| | |
|---|---|
| al ristorante | *at/to the restaurant* |
| allo stadio | *at/to the stadium* |
| all'albergo | *at/to the hotel* |
| all'accademia | *at the academy* |
| alla spiaggia | *at/to the beach* |
| ai laghi | *at/to the lakes* |
| agli alberghi | *at/to the hotels* |
| agli sportelli | *at/to the ticket windows* |
| alle stelle! | *(up) to the stars!* |

**in + il, (etc.)**

| | |
|---|---|
| nel ristorante | *in the restaurant* |
| nello specchio | *in the mirror* |
| nell'ufficio | *in the office* |
| nell'acqua | *in the water* |
| nella camera | *in the bedroom* |
| nei giardini | *in the gardens* |
| nell'alberi | *in the trees* |
| negli scavi | *in the excavations* |
| nelle camere | *in the bedrooms* |

---

When a location is commonly mentioned, Italians miss out the article and use the simple form **in**, **a**, etc.

| in centro | *in the centre* |
| in giardino | *in the garden* |
| a casa | *at home* |
| a scuola | *at school* |

A preposition which has no equivalent in English is **da** which means *at the house of* or *at the shop/restaurant of*; e.g.

| da Carmelo | *at Carmelo's (house, shop, restaurant)* |
| da Maria | *at Maria's (house, shop, restaurant)* |

It is often used as a restaurant's name, such as **da Lorzenzo**, *at Lorenzo's*.

This is combined with the article to create the following:

---

**da + il, (etc.)**

| dal medico | *at the doctor's* |
| dallo psichiatra | *at the psychiatrist's* |
| dall'amica | *at the (female) friend's (house)* |
| dall'amico | *at the (male) friend's (house)* |
| dalla zia | *at the aunt's house* |
| dai ragazzi | *at the boys' house* |
| dagli americani | *at the Americans' house* |
| dagli studenti | *at the students' house* |
| dalle ragazze | *at the girls' house* |

---

# In contesto

## Dialogo 1

| Turista | **Scusi, dov'è l'albergo Rondinella?** | *Excuse me, where is the Hotel Rondinella?* |
| Passante | **L'albergo Rondinella? È in Piazza Treviso, vicino alla stazione.** | *Hotel Rondinella? It's in Piazza Treviso, near the station.* |
| Turista | **Dove sono i grandi magazzini?** | *Where are the department stores?* |
| Passante | **Sono in Viale Messina, vicino al duomo.** | *They're in Viale Messina, near the cathedral.* |

## Dialogo 2

| Carla | **Pronto, Giulio? Sono Carla.** | *Hello, Giulio? It's Carla.* |
|---|---|---|
| Giulio | **Pronto, Carla. Dove sei?** | *Hello, Carla. Where are you?* |
| Carla | **Sono in Via Roma ma sono senza macchina.** | *I'm in Via Roma but I'm without a car.* |
| Giulio | **Dov'è la macchina?** | *Where's the car?* |
| Carla | **La macchina è dal meccanico. C'è un piccolo problema.** | *The car is with the mechanic. There's a slight problem.* |
| Giulio | **Che problema c'è?** | *What problem is there?* |
| Carla | **Un piccolo incidente.** | *A little accident!* |

─────────── **In aggiunta** ───────────

## 1 Ecco!: *here is!*

An easy way to reply to *where* questions is to use the word **ecco** which means *here is; here are* or even *there is* or *there are*:

| Dov'è il telefono? | *Where is the telephone?* |
|---|---|
| **Ecco** il telefono! | *There's the telephone!* |
| Dove sono gli elenchi telefonici? | *Where are the telephone directories?* |
| **Ecco** gli elenchi! | *Here are the directories!* |

**Ecco** can also stand on its own, and can be used when someone hands you something (English: *There you are!*) or has just done something when it is often combined with the word **fatto** (*done*):

| **Ecco** fatto! | *That's that!* |
|---|---|

## 2 Ecco *plus* lo/la: *here he/she/it is*

**Ecco** can also be combined with **lo, la, li** or **le**; these are the equivalent of the English *it, them* and are pronouns (i.e. they are used in place of a noun, whether person or inanimate object). They are usually found linked directly to a verb (see unit 14) and are therefore known as direct object pronouns. The form will depend on whether the person or object they are replacing is masculine or feminine, singular or plural. Study these examples:

| Dov'è il barista? | *Where is the barman?* |
| Eccolo! | *Here he is!* |

| Dov'è la stazione? | *Where is the station?* |
| Eccola! | *There it is!* |

| Dove sono i bambini? | *Where are the children?* |
| Eccoli! | *Here they are!* |

| Dove sono le pile? | *Where are the batteries?* |
| Eccole! | *Here they are!* |

## 3  Mi, ti: *me, you*

These refer to people and are also direct object pronouns:

| mi | *me* |
| ti | *you (familiar)* |
| La | *you (polite)* |
| ci | *us* |
| vi | *you (plural)* |

These can also be used with a verb (see unit 14) or combined with **ecco**, for example:

| Eccomi! | *Here I am!* |
| Eccoci! | *Here we are!* |
| Ah, eccoLa! | *Ah, here you are!* |

# 5

# Stating choice and preference

---

**Le funzioni**

In this unit you will learn how to:
Ask how much something costs ● Express preferences ● Indicate the article you want

**Le strutture**

**Questo**, demonstrative pronoun/adjective ● **Quello**, demonstrative pronoun, and **quel**, demonstrative adjective ● *How much?*, **Quanto?** ● Verbs ending in **-are** such as **costare** ● Verbs ending in **-ere** such as **prendere** ● Numbers

---

## **Nota introduttiva**

Look at the examples:

**Questo**

| | |
|---|---|
| Quanto costa **questo**? | *How much does this cost?* |
| Quanto costano **questi** sandali? | *How much do these sandals cost?* |
| **Questi** costano centocinquantamila lire. | *These cost L.150,000 lire.* |
| Prendiamo **queste** due cartoline. | *We'll take these two postcards.* |

**Quello**

| | |
|---|---|
| Quanto costa **quello**? | *How much does that cost?* |
| Quanto costano **quelle** scarpe? | *How much do those shoes cost?* |

| Prendo **quel** borsellino in vetrina. | *I'll take that purse in the window.* |
| Prendo **quelli**. | *I'll take those ones.* |

--------- **Analisi della grammatica** ---------

## 1 Questo, quello: *this, that*

The English *this* and *that* are used to pinpoint the object or person being talked about; they are called demonstrative adjectives or pronouns. The Italian equivalents are **questo** (*this*) and **quello** (*that*).

## 2 Questo: *this*

**Questo** can be used as a pronoun, i.e. on its own in place of a noun, and meaning *this* (*one*), *these* (*ones*) (see unit 2).

**Questo** è difficile.  *This is difficult.*

**Questo** is used to indicate something or someone near to the speaker. When **questo** is used as an adjective, describing a person or thing, it changes its ending according to whether the person or thing is singular or plural, masculine or feminine:

---

**Singular**

| Questo museo è interessante. | *This museum is interesting.* |
| Questa borsetta è cara. | *This bag is expensive.* |

**Plural**

| Questi sandali sono comodi. | *These sandals are comfortable.* |
| Queste scarpe sono strette. | *These shoes are tight.* |

---

**Questo** used on its own still has to vary its ending according to the gender and number of the thing or person it is referring to. But if you don't know what something is called in Italian – far less the gender – just point and use **questo** (or **questi** if it's plural)!

**Questi** sono belli.  *These are beautiful.*

Quale gonna vuole misurare? *Which skirt do you want to try on?*
**Questa**. *This one.*

Quali scarpe vuole provare? *Which shoes do you want to try on?*
**Queste**. *These ones.*

**Quale** means *which*. The plural form is **quali**. If you want to know more, read the section **In aggiunta** at the end of this unit.

## 3  Quello: *that*

Use **quello** to pinpoint something which is not nearby (*that* or *those*, in English). Its forms vary in exactly the same way as the article **il** (*the*) according to whether the noun is masculine, feminine, singular or plural and according to the initial letter. Look at these examples of **quel** used as an adjective:

**Quel** ristorante è sporco. *That restaurant is dirty.*
**Quell'** albergo è di lusso. *That hotel is luxury class.*
**Quello** scontrino è sbagliato. *That receipt is wrong.*
**Quella** pensione costa poco. *That pensione is cheap.*
**Quell'** agenzia è chiusa. *That agency is closed.*
**Quei** sandali sono di plastica. *Those sandals are plastic.*
**Quegli** stivali sono brutti. *Those boots are ugly.*
**Quelle** scarpe sono di pelle. *Those shoes are leather.*

Like **questo**, **quello** can also be used on its own, as a pronoun. **Quello** can also be used as a pronoun meaning *that one*, **quelli**, *those ones*. Use **quello** (singular) or **quelli** (plural) if you are uncertain of the gender:

**Quello** è incredibile. *That (person or thing) is unbelievable.*
**Quelli** sono antipatici. *Those (people) are unpleasant.*
**Quella** è carina. *That (girl) is pretty.*
**Quelle** sono simpatiche. *Those (girls) are nice.*

## 4  Quanto: *how much, how many*

**Quanto** can be used as an adjective, with a person/object, meaning *how much* (e.g. sugar), *how many* (e.g. sandwiches). **Quanto** varies according to whether the noun is masculine, feminine, singular, or plural. It can also be used on its own, meaning *how much*, in which case it doesn't change:

| | |
|---|---|
| **Quanto** zucchero prendi? | *How much sugar do you take?* |
| **Quanta** pasta mangi? | *How much pasta do you eat?* |
| **Quanti** panini prendi? | *How many sandwiches are you having?* |
| **Quante** sigarette fumi al giorno? | *How many cigarettes do you smoke a day?* |
| **Quanto** costa? | *How much does it cost?* |
| **Quanto** ti fermi? | *How long are you staying?* (Lit. *How much time are you stopping?*) |

## 5   -are and -ere verbs

The pronoun (see unit 1) is not needed with the verb in Italian because the verb endings show who or what is doing the action., i.e. who or what is the subject of the sentence. The pronoun can, however, be used for emphasis and this form is supplied below in brackets.

Most Italian verbs follow one of three main patterns; they end in **-are**, **-ere** or **-ire**.

### (a) -are

Verbs are usually listed in a dictionary in the infinitive form. An example is **parlare** (*to talk*).

| (io) | **parlo** | *I speak* | (noi) | **parliamo** | *we speak* |
|---|---|---|---|---|---|
| (tu) | **parli** | *you speak* | (voi) | **parlate** | *you speak* |
| (lui) | **parla** | *he speaks* | (Loro) | **parlano** | *they speak* |
| (lei) | **parla** | *she speaks* | | | |
| (Lei) | **parla** | *you speak (polite form)* | | | |

### (b) -ere

An example within this group is **prendere** (*to take, to have* e.g. something to eat or drink)

| (io) | **prendo** | *I take* | (noi) | **prendiamo** | *we take* |
|---|---|---|---|---|---|
| (tu) | **prendi** | *you take* | (voi) | **prendete** | *you take* |
| (lui) | **prende** | *he takes* | (Loro) | **prendono** | *they take* |
| (lei) | **prende** | *she takes* | | | |
| (Lei) | **prende** | *you take (polite)* | | | |

## (c) -ire

There is a third group of verbs ending in **-ire**. You will meet these in unit 6. They do not vary much from the **-ere** verbs.

Unfortunately, some verbs don't follow a pattern; these are called irregular. For a list of these see the Grammar Section on page 196.

# 6 Numbers

### 1 to 20

| | | | | | | | |
|---|---|---|---|---|---|---|---|
| 0 | zero | 6 | sei | 12 | dodici | 18 | diciotto |
| 1 | uno | 7 | sette | 13 | tredici | 19 | diciannove |
| 2 | due | 8 | otto | 14 | quattordici | 20 | venti |
| 3 | tre | 9 | nove | 15 | quindici | | |
| 4 | quattro | 10 | dieci | 16 | sedici | | |
| 5 | cinque | 11 | undici | 17 | diciassette | | |

### 21 to 30

| | | | |
|---|---|---|---|
| 21 | ventuno | 26 | ventisei |
| 22 | ventidue | 27 | ventisette |
| 23 | ventitrè | 28 | ventotto |
| 24 | ventiquattro | 29 | ventinove |
| 25 | venticinque | 30 | trenta |

### 31 to 40 and up . . .

| | | | |
|---|---|---|---|
| 31 | trentuno | 60 | sessanta |
| 32 | trentadue | 70 | settanta |
| 33 | trentatrè | 80 | ottanta |
| 38 | trentotto | 90 | novanta |
| 40 | quaranta | 100 | cento |
| 50 | cinquanta | | |

### hundreds . . .

| | |
|---|---|
| 101 | centouno |
| 102 | centodue |
| 140 | centoquaranta |
| 142 | centoquarantadue |
| 200 | duecento, . . . etc. |

**thousands . . .**

| | |
|---|---|
| 1,000 | mille |
| 1,001 | mille (e) uno |
| 1,500 | millicinquecento |
| 1,550 | millecinquecentocinquanta |
| 1,555 | millecinquecentocinquantacinque |
| 2,000 | duemila |
| 10,000 | diecimila |

**millions . . .**

| | |
|---|---|
| 1,000,000 | un milione |
| 2,000,000 | due milioni |
| 1,500,255 | un milionecinquecentomiladuecentocinquantacinque |

**billions . . .**

| | |
|---|---|
| 1,000,000,000 | un miliardo |

In **ventuno** and **ventotto** the **i** is dropped from **venti**.

**Tre** does not have an accent on the last letter, but **ventitrè** does, as do all the compounds including **tre** from **ventitrè** upwards.

In **trentuno, trentotto** the **a** has been dropped from **trenta**; likewise all the other numbers ending in -a from 30 upwards.

**Cento** occasionally loses its final **-o** as in centottanta (**cento ottanta**); **centotto (cento otto)**.

The plural of **mille** is **mila**.

In English, you say **one** hundred, **one** thousand: in Italian you omit the *one*: **cento** and **mille**, but **un** milione **di** abitanti (*one million inhabitants*) (the **di** is omitted when other numbers follow).

Several digit numbers are generally written as one word. E.g.

*142*                                                    **Centoquarantadue**

**Ordinal numbers**

The ordinal numbers, *first, second,* etc., in Italian usually end in **-esimo** e.g. quindicesimo, ventesimo, centesimo. But the first ten are as follows, **primo, secondo, terzo, quarto, quinto, sesto, settimo, ottavo, nono, decimo.** These can be abbreviated to 10, 20 etc.

# In contesto

## Buying a handbag

| | | |
|---|---|---|
| Cliente | **Senta, quanto costa quella borsa marrone?** | *Excuse me, how much does that brown bag cost?* |
| Negoziante | **Questa? Costa L.250.000, signora. È firmata.** | *This one? It costs L.250.000, signora. It's a designer label.* |
| Cliente | **Oh. È troppo cara. Ce n'è un' altra meno cara?** | *Oh, it's too expensive. Is there another less expensive one?* |
| Negoziante | **Sì, signora. Questa, di pelle, è molto spaziosa e costa L.180.000.** | *Yes, signora. This one, in leather, is very roomy and costs L.180.000.* |
| Cliente | **Anche questa è bella, ma è un po' troppo grande. Avete un altro modello, magari più piccolo?** | *This one's nice too, but it's a bit too big. Do you have another style, perhaps smaller?* |
| Negoziante | **C'è questa, ma il prezzo è sempre lo stesso: L.180.000.** | *There's this one, but the price is still the same: L.180.000.* |
| Cliente | **Ecco. Questa è bella ed è meno grande. Prendo questa.** | *That's just right. This one's nice and it's less big. I'll take this one.* |
| Negoziante | **Va bene, signora.** | *All right, signora.* |

## Buying a present

| | | |
|---|---|---|
| Cliente | **Scusi, quanto costa quel borsellino?** | *Excuse me, how much does that purse cost?* |
| Negoziante | **Quale? Questo qui nero?** | *Which one? This black one here?* |
| Cliente | **No, quello più in alto.** | *No, that one higher up.* |
| Negoziante | **Ah, quello blu. Quello costa L.34.000.** | *Ah, that navy blue one. That costs L.34.000.* |
| Cliente | **Mmm. Molto caro. E quei guanti, invece?** | *Mmm. Very expensive. And those gloves?* |
| Negoziante | **Quali, signora? Quelli in alto?** | *Which ones, signora? Those ones up there?* |
| Cliente | **Sì, quelli neri.** | *Yes, those black ones.* |

*(Assistant takes gloves down from display)*

| | | |
|---|---|---|
| Negoziante | **Questi sono di camoscio. Costano L.70.000.** | *These are in suede (chamois). They cost L.70.000.* |
| Cliente | **Mmm. Sono cari.** | *Mmm. They're dear.* |
| Negoziante | **Ci sono questi, signora, che costano solo L.60.000. Sono sempre belli, ma il prezzo è più basso.** | *There are these, signora, which only cost L.60.000. They're nice too, but the price is lower.* |
| Cliente | **Sì, sono belli. Prendo questi, anche se sono un po' cari. Sono un regalo.** | *Yes, they're nice. I'll take these ones, even if they're a bit dear. They're a present.* |

## In aggiunta

## 1 Posizione: *position*

| | |
|---|---|
| qui | *here* |
| lì | *there* |
| in alto | *high up, up there* |
| in basso | *down there, at the bottom* |
| giù | *down (there)* |
| in vetrina | *in the (shop) window* |
| in mezzo | *in the middle* |
| a sinistra | *on the left* |
| a destra | *on the right* |

## 2 Quale: *which*

**Quale** is an adjective meaning *which*. It has singular form, **quale**, and a plural form, **quali**.

| | |
|---|---|
| Quale gelato vuoi? | *Which ice-cream do you want?* |
| Quali biscotti prendiamo? | *Which biscuits shall we get?* |

It can also be used to translate the English *what* in certain cases. See unit 10.

# 6

# – Talking about the present –

**Le funzioni**

In this unit you will learn how to:
Ask and talk about work ● Ask and talk about where someone lives
● Ask about time ● Talk about now, the present

**Le strutture**

Verbs ending in **-ire** . Recap verbs ending in **-are, -ere** ● Question
words: **dove?** (*where?*) **a che ora?** (*at what time?*) **come?** (*how?*)
● **Stare**: plus gerund

## Nota introduttiva

Study these examples of how to ask and answer questions about your
life and work:

| | |
|---|---|
| Dove abiti, Lucia? | *Where do you live, Lucia?* |
| Abito in centro. | *I live in the centre.* |
| | |
| Lavori in città, Marco? | *Do you work in town, Marco?* |
| Sì, lavoro in banca. | *Yes, I work in a bank.* |
| | |
| A che ora cominci a lavorare? | *What time do you start work?* |
| Comincio alle otto. | *I start work at 8am.* |
| A che ora finisci? | *What time do you finish?* |
| Finisco alle sette. | *I finish at 7pm.* |
| | |
| Come vai al lavoro? | *How do you get to work?* |
| | |
| Prendo l'autobus. | *I take the bus.* |
| | |
| Com'è il tuo lavoro? | *What is your work like?* |
| È interessante? | *Is it interesting?* |

Com'è Milano?             *What is Milan like?*

And how to talk about what you are doing right now:

Sto mangiando!            *I'm eating!*
Sto leggendo un libro.    *I'm reading a book.*

## —— Analisi della grammatica ——

### 1  -ire verbs

In unit 5, the verbs ending in **-are** and **-ere** were explained. Here you meet them again with a new type of verb, ending in **-ire**:

| **finire** (*to finish*) | | | | |
|---|---|---|---|---|
| (io) | **fin*isco*** | *I finish* | (noi) | **fin*iamo*** | *we finish* |
| (tu) | **fin*isci*** | *you finish* | (voi) | **fin*ite*** | *you finish* |
| (lui) | **fin*isce*** | *he finishes* | (loro) | **fin*iscono*** | *they finish* |
| (lei) | **fin*isce*** | *she finishes* | | | |
| (Lei) | **fin*isce*** | *you finish (polite)* | | | |

There is another type of verb ending in **-ire** which is much simpler:

| **dormire** (*to sleep*) | | | | |
|---|---|---|---|---|
| (io) | **dorm*o*** | *I sleep* | (noi) | **dorm*iamo*** | *we sleep* |
| (tu) | **dorm*i*** | *you sleep* | (voi) | **dorm*ite*** | *you sleep* |
| (lui) | **dorm*e*** | *he sleeps* | (loro) | **dorm*ono*** | *they sleep* |
| (lei) | **dorm*e*** | *she sleeps* | | | |
| (Lei) | **dorm*e*** | *you sleep (polite)* | | | |

You will see that there is not much difference between the three types of verb. Three of their parts have the same ending, i.e.:

| *I eat*, etc. | **mang*io*** | **prend*o*** | **dorm*o*** | **finisc*o*** |
| *You eat*, etc. | **mang*i*** | **prend*i*** | **dorm*i*** | **finisc*i*** |
| *We eat*, etc. | **mang*iamo*** | **prend*iamo*** | **dorm*iamo*** | **fin*iamo*** |

### 2  Dove?: where?

**Dove** means *where* (see unit 4). You can use it to ask where someone works or lives:

| Dove lavora Lei? | *Where do you work?* |
| Dove abitano i Rossi? | *Where do the Rossi family live?* |

**Dove**, meaning *where*, is abbreviated before **è** (*it is, is*):

| Dov'è il bar? | *Where is the bar?* |
| Dove sono i bambini? | *Where are the children?* |

Although not strictly necessary, the pronoun **Lei** is often used when asking a question in the polite form, to make the question sound less abrupt.

| **Dove dorme Lei?** | *Where do you (polite form) sleep?* |

## 3 A che ora . . . ?: what time . . . ?

**A che ora . . . ?** means literally *at what hour . . . ?*:

| **A che ora** comincia a lavorare? | *What time do you (polite) start work?* |
| **A che ora** chiude il negozio? | *What time does the shop close?* |
| **A che ora** parte il treno? | *What time does the train leave?* |

## 4 Come?: how?

**Come** used in a question means *how*:

| **Come** arrivi al lavoro? | *How do you get to work?* |
| **Come** arrivi in centro? | *How do you get to the centre?* |
| **Come** comincia il film? | *How does the film begin?* |
| **Come** finisce la storia? | *How does the story end?* |

**Come** is generally abbreviated before **è** to **com'è**.

For further uses of **come** see the Grammar Section on page 194.

## 5 Stare: (to be) plus gerund (-ing)

Occasionally you need to express something more immediate than the simple present tense conveys (*The boys are reading right now*). For this, use the verb **stare** along with a part of the verb called the gerund, e.g. **mangiando, leggendo, partendo** (the Italian equivalent of the **-ing** ending). E.g. **I ragazzi stanno leggendo.** *The boys are reading.*

The verb **stare** means *to be*, but can not take the place of **essere** all the time; it is used only in expressions such as **Come stai?** (*How are you?*) or with the gerund **Sto mangiando** (*I am eating*) or to express geographical location **Dove sta la casa?** (*Where is the house?*).

### (a) Stare

The verb **stare** is irregular. Here is its present tense:

| (io) | **sto** | *I am* | (noi) | **stiamo** | *we are* |
|------|---------|--------|-------|------------|----------|
| (tu) | **stai** | *you are* | (voi) | **state** | *you are* |
| (lui) | **sta** | *he is* | (loro) | **stanno** | *they are* |
| (lei) | **sta** | *she is* | | | |
| (Lei) | **sta** | *you are (polite)* | | | |

### (b) Gerund

The gerund is formed by taking the infinitive of the verb (e.g. **parlare**, *to speak*) removing the **-are** part and adding the ending **-ando**. Similarly, for **-ere** verbs we remove the **-ere** and add **-endo**; for **-ire** verbs we remove **-ire** and add **-endo**.

| parl**are** | (*to speak*) | parl**ando** | (*speaking*) |
|-------------|--------------|--------------|--------------|
| legg**ere** | (*to read*) | legg**endo** | (*reading*) |
| part**ire** | (*to leave*) | part**endo** | (*leaving*) |

A few verbs (such as those with a shortened infinitive) have irregular gerund forms:

| **fare** | (*to do*) | fac**endo** | (*doing*) |
|----------|-----------|-------------|-----------|
| **bere** | (*to drink*) | bev**endo** | (*drinking*) |

### (c) Stare plus the gerund

| Cosa **stai facendo?** | *What are you doing (right now)?* |
|---|---|
| **Sto mettendo** in ordine. | *I'm tidying up.* |

| **Sto mangiando.** | *I'm eating.* |
|---|---|
| **Sto scrivendo** una cartolina. | *I'm writing a postcard.* |

**Stare** plus the gerund cannot be used to talk about anything in the future, even if it's only tonight. For this you must use the plain present or the future.

| Cosa **fai** stasera? | *What are you doing tonight?* |
|---|---|

# In contesto

## Interview with a commuter

| | |
|---|---|
| Dove abita, signor Ruzzini? Abita a Firenze? | *Where do you live, Mr Ruzzini? Do you live in Florence?* |
| No, abito a Pisa, ma lavoro a Firenze. | *No, I live in Pisa, but I work in Florence.* |
| E viaggia ogni giorno? | *And do you travel every day?* |
| Sì. Parto alle sette e arrivo alle otto. | *Yes. I leave at 7am and I arrive at 8am.* |

## Interview with a working mother

| | |
|---|---|
| Signora Giannini, a che ora comincia a lavorare? | *Signora Giannini, what time do you start work?* |
| Comincio alle otto e trenta. | *I begin at 8.30am.* |
| A che ora finisce? | *What time do you finish?* |
| Finisco alle sette. | *I finish at 7pm.* |
| Torno a casa stanca morta. | *I get home dead tired.* |
| E suo marito? | *And your husband?* |
| Mio marito non lavora. Resta a casa con la bambina. | *My husband doesn't work. He stays at home with the child.* |
| E la sera? | *And in the evening?* |
| La sera guardiamo la TV. | *In the evening we watch TV.* |

## A dialogue between friends

| | | |
|---|---|---|
| Carla | Vieni al cinema, Marco? | *Are you coming to the cinema, Marco?* |
| Marco | Sì, vengo volentieri. | *Yes, I'll be happy to come.* |
| Carla | Sbrigati, allora, stiamo uscendo proprio adesso. | *Hurry up, then, we're just going out now.* |
| Marco | Sto venendo. Mi sto mettendo le scarpe. | *I'm coming. I'm just putting my shoes on.* |
| Carla | Sei sempre l'ultimo . . . | *You're always last . . .* |
| Marco | Stai scherzando! Tu sei la più lenta di tutti. | *You're joking. You're always the slowest of us all.* |

See unit 7 (page 45) for an explanation of reflexive verbs such as **sbrigarsi** and for the order/imperative forms of these verbs.

## In aggiunta

### 1 Expressions of time

| | |
|---|---|
| oggi | *today* |
| ieri | *yesterday* |
| domani | *tomorrow* |

| | |
|---|---|
| **Oggi ti amo più di ieri, ma meno di domani.** | *Today I love you more than yesterday, but less than tomorrow.* |

| | |
|---|---|
| stasera | *this evening* |
| stamattina | *this morning* |
| stanotte | *this night (last night)* |
| ieri sera | *yesterday evening* |
| ieri pomeriggio | *yesterday afternoon* |
| ieri notte | *last night* |
| domani mattina | *tomorrow morning* |
| domani pomeriggio | *tomorrow afternoon* |
| domani sera | *tomorrow evening* |

### 2 A or in (in a place)

To translate the preposition *in*, already seen in unit 4, Italians use **a** for a town and **in** for a country.

| | |
|---|---|
| Abito **a** Firenze. | *I live in Florence.* |
| Abito **in** Inghilterra. | *I live in England.* |

### 3 Double adjectives

| | |
|---|---|
| stanco morto | *dead tired* |
| ubriaco fradicio | *dead drunk (Lit. soaking drunk)* |
| bagnato fradicio | *soaking wet* |
| pieno zeppo | *packed out* |

# 7

## Talking about routine and habits

---

**Le funzioni**

In this unit you will learn how to talk about:
Regular actions ● Daily routine ● Something one does for oneself

**Le strutture**

Reflexive verbs ● Phrases of time ● Adverbs of frequency

---

## Nota introduttiva

Before looking at the grammar details study the following examples of reflexive verbs in use:

A che ora ti alzi, Gianna?    *What time do you get up, Gianna?*
Di solito mi alzo alle sei.    *Usually I get up at 6am.*

Signora, a che ora si alza    *What time do you get up in the*
   la mattina?    *morning, signora?*
Io mi alzo tardi, in genere    *I get up, usually, around 8am*
   verso le otto, e mi    *and make myself a coffee.*
   preparo un caffè.

---

## Analisi della grammatica

### 1 Reflexive verbs

In Italian, verbs expressing actions that one does *to* or *for* oneself are known as reflexive verbs – verbs referring back to the subject or person carrying out the action (see unit 1 – **chiamarsi**, *to be called*). Many of them refer to everyday actions. Looking up the verb in the dictionary you'll find it in the infinitive form (**-are**, **-ere**, or **-ire**) with the final **-e** dropped and the reflexive pronoun (**si**) attached to the end, i.e. **alzarsi, radersi, vestirsi**:

> **alzare** (*to get someone up*)   plus **si** = alzar**si** (*to get oneself up*)
> **lavare** (*to wash someone/ something*)   plus **si** = lavar**si** (*to wash oneself*)

To say what you do or what someone else does, you use the appropriate form of the verb, with the correct reflexive pronoun, *myself, yourself*, etc., before the verb:

| **alzarsi** (*to get up*) | | | | | |
|---|---|---|---|---|---|
| (io) | **mi** alzo | *I get up* | (noi) | **ci** alzi**amo** | *we get up* |
| (tu) | **ti** alz**i** | *you get up* | (voi) | **vi** alz**ate** | *you get up* |
| (lui) | **si** alza | *he gets up* | (loro) | **si** alz**ano** | *they get up* |
| (lei) | **si** alza | *she gets up* | | | |
| (Lei) | **si** alza | *you get up (polite)* | | | |

Many of the verbs expressing this type of action are **-are** verbs, but, of course, there are **-ere** or **-ire** verbs as well:

| **radersi** (*to shave*) | | | | | |
|---|---|---|---|---|---|
| (io) | mi rado | *I shave* | (noi) | ci rad**iamo** | *we shave* |
| (tu) | ti rad**i** | *you shave* | (voi) | vi rad**ete** | *you shave* |
| (lui) | si rade | *he shaves* | (loro) | si rad**ono** | *they shave* |
| (lei) | si rade | *she shaves* | | | |
| (Lei) | si rade | *you shave (polite)* | | | |

| **vestirsi** (*to dress*) | | | | | |
|---|---|---|---|---|---|
| (io) | mi vesto | *I get dressed* | (noi) | ci vest**iamo** | *we get dressed* |
| (tu) | ti vest**i** | *you get dressed* | (voi) | vi vest**ite** | *you get dressed* |
| (lui) | si veste | *he gets dressed* | (loro) | si vest**ono** | *they get dressed* |
| (lei) | si veste | *she gets dressed* | | | |
| (Lei) | si veste | *you get dressed (polite)* | | | |

Frequently, Italians use the reflexive pronoun, **mi**, **ti**, etc., where English would use the possessive, **my**, **your** etc., particularly when talking about articles of clothing or parts of the body:

| | |
|---|---|
| **Mi** metto la giacca per uscire. | *I put my jacket on to go out.* |
| **Si** lava i capelli tutti i giorni. | *She washes her hair every day.* |

Or even to express something one does *for* oneself:

| | |
|---|---|
| **Mi** preparo un caffè. | *I'll make myself a coffee.* |
| **Ti** prepari la valigia? | *Are you packing your suitcase?* |

When using a verb plus an infinitive construction (see unit 9 for more examples), you should remember that the reflexive pronoun will not always be **si**, but will change according to whoever it refers to:

truccarsi (*to put on one's make-up*)

| | |
|---|---|
| Devo truccar**mi** per andare alla festa. | *I must put my make-up on to go to the party.* |

vestirsi (*to get dressed*)

| | |
|---|---|
| I bambini preferiscono vestir**si** da soli. | *The children prefer to get dressed by themselves.* |

prepararsi (*to get ready*)

| | |
|---|---|
| Perché ci metti tanto a prepara**ti**? | *Why do you take so long to get ready?* |

**Ci** used with **mettere** in this way is an expression meaning to take time.


## 2 Saying exactly when

Here are some expressions used when making arrangements and talking about time in general:

| | |
|---|---|
| prima | *first* |
| prima di me | *before me* |
| poi | *then* |
| più tardi | *later* |
| dopo | *after* |
| alle tre | *at 3 o'clock* |
| verso le tre | *around, about 3 o'clock* |
| dalle nove in poi | *from 9 o'clock on* |
| dalle nove all'una | *from 9 to 1 o'clock* |

| lunedì | *on Monday* |
|--------|-------------|
| il lunedì | *every Monday* |
| ogni lunedì | *every Monday* |
| tutti i lunedì | *every Monday* |

## 3 Saying how often

The following are useful adverbs (a word which describes the verb of a sentence) when talking about how often you do something:

| in genere | *generally* |
|-----------|-------------|
| di solito | *usually* |
| normalmente | *normally* |
| generalmente | *generally* |

## In contesto

### A casa: at home

La mattina mio marito si alza prima di me e mi prepara il caffè. Io mi alzo dopo, mi lavo, mi vesto e poi mi preparo per uscire.

*In the morning my husband gets up before me and makes me a coffee. I get up after, I get washed, I get dressed, then I get ready to go out.*

Piero e Maddalena, perché non andate a farvi la doccia? Su, cercate di sbrigarvi! Poi mettetevi i vestiti puliti e pettinatevi un pochino.

*Piero and Maddalena, why don't you go and have a shower? Come on, try and hurry up, put your clean clothes on and comb your hair a bit.*

## In aggiunta

### 1 Position of pronouns

With the **tu, noi, voi** imperative forms used for orders or commands (see unit 9), the reflexive pronoun is joined to the *end* of the verb:

Vi mettete le scarpe.    *You put your shoes on.*
Mettetevi le scarpe!    *Put your shoes on!*

| | |
|---|---|
| Ti metti il vestito nuovo? | *Are you putting your new dress on?* |
| Mett**iti** il vestito nuovo. | *Put your new dress on.* |
| Ci prepariamo. | *We're getting ready.* |
| Prepariamo**ci**. | *Let's get ready.* |

## 2 How to form adverbs

An adverb is similar in purpose to an adjective, but instead of describing a person or a thing, it describes the way someone does something; in other words, it qualifies the verb.

| | |
|---|---|
| Gli italiani guidano **velocemente.** | *Italians drive fast.* |

It can also describe extent or measure, and so is often found qualifying an adjective, or even another adverb. In the examples that follow, **troppo** and **molto** are adverbs:

| | |
|---|---|
| Questa borsa è **troppo** grande. | *This bag is too big.* |
| Questo treno è **molto** volece. | *This train is very fast.* |
| Tu guidi **troppo** velocemente. | *You drive too fast.* |

There are two common ways in which adverbs are formed in Italian, with a few exceptions.

(a) Adjectives such as **rapido, educato** which end in -**o** change to the feminine form (rapid**a**) and add -**mente**, to become **rapidamente**, **educatamente**.

(b) Adjectives that end -**e** such as **facile, veloce, regolare** merely add -**mente** to form adverbs such as **velocemente**, **facilmente**, **regolarmente**. (Note that in the case of adjectives ending in -**le** or -**re**, the **e** is dropped.)

The exceptions to these two rules include some common adjectives such as **buono, cattivo** (*good, bad*), which have their own distinctive adverbs: **bene, male** (*well, badly*).

Italians often prefer to use a phrase rather than an adverb, even if the adverb exists. Some examples are:

| | |
|---|---|
| con attenzione | *with care (carefully)* |
| in modo educato | *in a polite way (politely)* |
| senza cura | *without care (carelessly)* |
| in maniera sgarbata | *in an impolite way (rudely)* |

# 8

# Talking about possibility and permission

**Le funzioni**

In this unit you will learn about:
Asking permission to do something ● Asking someone if he/she is able to do something ● Saying you can or can't do something ● Asking if something is allowed

**Le strutture**

**Posso?** ● **Può** and **mi può** ● Impersonal **si può? È possibile?**

## Nota introduttiva

| | |
|---|---|
| Può indicarmi la strada per Pisa? | *Can you show me the road to Pisa?* |
| Posso telefonare da qui? | *Can I telephone from here?* |
| Si può parcheggiare? | *Can one park?* |
| È possibile telefonare? | *Is it possible to phone?* |
| Sa dirmi quanto costa? | *Can you tell me how much it costs?* |

## Analisi della grammatica

### 1   Potere: *to be able to*

This verb means *to be able to* (*I can*). It is an irregular verb, i.e. it does not follow the pattern of verbs we have seen so far. The complete verb in the present tense looks like this:

| (io) | **posso** | *I can* | (noi) | **possiamo** | *we can* |
|------|-----------|---------|-------|--------------|----------|
| (tu) | **puoi** | *you can* | (voi) | **potete** | *you can* |
| (lui) | **può** | *he can* | (loro) | **possono** | *they can* |
| (lei) | **può** | *she can* | | | |
| (Lei) | **può** | *you can (polite)* | | | |

**Potere** is used to say what you are able, or not able, to do, to ask permission and to ask other people if they can do something:

Non posso sopportare il caldo.    *I can't bear the heat.*

Possiamo prendere l'autobus?    *Can we get the bus?*

Non posso mangiare le fragole,    *I can't eat strawberries, because* perché sono allergica.         *I'm allergic.*

Posso mangiare questa mela?    *Can I eat this apple?*

Posso telefonare in Inghilterra?   *Can I phone England?*

Può darmi l'elenco telefonico?    *Can you give me the telephone*                                            *directory?*

Può cambiare questo biglietto    *Can you change this L.100.000* da L.100.000?                           *note?*

Può indicarmi la strada per    *Can you show me the road for* Roma?                                 *Rome?*

There are two ways of asking the last question above:

Mi può indicare la strada per Roma?    *and*

Può indicarmi la strada per Roma?

## 2 Si può . . . ?: *can one . . . ?*

This is a way of asking if *one* can do something; it does not mention a specific person:

Si può parcheggiare qui?    *Can one park here?*

Si può entrare?    *Can one come/go in?*

Si può telefonare in    *Can one phone England?* Inghilterra?

**È possibile?** can replace **si può?**

È possibile parlare con il    *Is it possible to speak to the* direttore?                      *manager?*

È possibile andare in    *Is it possible to go by car?* macchina?

—————————— **In contesto** ——————————

## Asking the way: using Lei

| | | |
|---|---|---|
| Turista | Scusi, può indicarmi la strada per Piazza Danoni? | *Excuse me, can you tell me the way to Piazza Danoni?* |
| Passante | Sì, ma Piazza Danoni è molto lontana da qui. | *Yes, but Piazza Danoni is a long way from here.* |
| Turista | Posso prendere l'autobus? | *Can I take the bus?* |
| Passante | Sì. C'è il 22. | *Yes. There's the 22.* |
| Turista | Può indicarmi la fermata? | *Can you show me (where) the bus stop (is)?* |
| Passante | Ecco. La fermata è proprio lì di fronte. | *Over there. The bus stop is right opposite.* |
| Turista | Grazie. Senta, si può fare il biglietto in autobus? | *Thanks. Listen, can one buy a ticket on the bus?* |
| Passante | No, ma è possibile fare i biglietti alla tabaccheria qui vicino. | *No, but it's possible to buy tickets at the tobacconist's just near here.* |

## Asking a friend to lend you money

| | | |
|---|---|---|
| Carlo | Anna, puoi prestarmi diecimila lire? | *Anna, can you lend me ten thousand lire?* |
| Anna | No, non posso. Non ho abbastanza soldi da poter prestarli. | *No, I can't. I haven't got enough money to be able to lend it.* |
| Carlo | Allora non posso mangiare oggi, perché non è possibile mangiare con cinquemila lire. E un problema. | *Well, I can't eat today then, because it's not possible to eat with five thousand lire. It's a problem.* |
| Anna | L'unico problema è che tu non sai gestire i soldi. Ne sei sempre senza. | *The only problem is that you don't know how to manage your money. You never have any.* |

For further uses of **ne** see the Grammar Section page 182.

—————————— **In aggiunta** ——————————

## 1 Sapere: *knowing how to*

Sometimes the real meaning of *I can* is I know how to (**sapere**), and not *I can because circumstances permit* (**potere**):

| | |
|---|---|
| **So** nuotare bene. | *I know how to swim well. (I can swim well)* |
| **Sai** cucinare? | *Can you cook?* |

**Sapere** is also used to express the idea of knowing a piece of information:

| | |
|---|---|
| **Sai** a che ora parte l'autobus? | *Do you know what time the bus leaves?* |
| **Sa** dirmi a che ora parte il treno? | *Can you tell me what time the train leaves?* |

## 2 *Where to omit* potere

In sentences where in English, you would use the word *can*, the verb **potere** is often omitted, in Italian:

| | |
|---|---|
| Non sento niente. | *I can't hear anything.* |
| Non vediamo nessuno. | *We can't see anyone.* |

## 3 *Other tenses and moods*

**Potere** when used in the *conditional* (see unit 20) means *could*, for example:

| | |
|---|---|
| Potresti farmi un favore? | *Could you do me a favour?* |
| Potrei passare domani. | *I could pass by tomorrow.* |

And in the *past conditional* (see unit 21):

| | |
|---|---|
| Avresti potuto avvertirmi. | *You could have warned me.* |
| Avrei potuto farne a meno. | *I could have done without it.* |

In the *perfect* tense (see unit 11):

| | |
|---|---|
| Non ho potuto telefonargli. | *I couldn't ring him.* |
| Non potevo aspettare. | *I couldn't wait.* |

**Potere** is normally used with **avere** in the perfect tense, but when followed by a verb used with **essere**, it can also use **essere** instead. In this case the past participle (**potuto**) has to agree with the subject in number and gender:

Non sono potuto venire.      *I couldn't come.*
   (Non ho potuto venire)
Non siamo potuti andare.      *We couldn't go.*
   (Non abbiamo potuto andare)

## 4 Other ways of saying 'to be able to'

### (a) Essere in grado di: *to be able to, to be up to.*

**Essere in grado di** is followed by the preposition **di**. Here are two examples:

Non **è in grado di** fare      *He is not up to this work.*
   questo lavoro.
**Sei in grado di** darmi una      *Are you able to give me a reply?*
   risposta?

### (b) Farcela: *to manage to, to be able to.*

**Farcela** is an idiomatic expression composed of **fare** plus **ci** plus **la** which is followed by the preposition **a**. Here are two examples:

Non ce la faccio più.      *I can't cope./I can't go on./I can't manage.*
Ce la fai a portare quel tavolo? *Can you manage to carry that table?*

## 5 I can't bear it

**Non ne posso più** is an expression meaning: *I can't bear it, I can't stand it any longer.*

Non ne possono più.      *They can't stand it any more.*

# 9
# Giving orders and instructions

**Le funzioni**

In this unit you will learn about:
Requesting, ordering or giving instructions ● Reading written
instructions

**Le strutture**

Imperative (command) form: **tu, lei, noi, voi** and **loro** ● Written
instructions using the infinitive ● Negative forms of the imperative

## Nota introduttiva

A command, order or instruction is expressed in Italian by a different
verb form – the imperative. Study these examples before going on to the
grammar explanation.

### Giving instructions in the familiar 'tu' form

| | |
|---|---|
| Prend**i** un caffè, Marco! | *Have a coffee, Marco.* |
| Mang**ia** un panino! | *Eat a roll!* |

### Giving instructions in the polite 'Lei' form

| | |
|---|---|
| Sent**a**! Scusi! Come arrivo alla stazione? | *Listen. Excuse me. How do I get to the station?* |
| Prend**a** Via Manzoni. | *Take Via Manzoni.* |
| Al primo semaforo gir**i** a sinistra. | *At the first traffic lights turn left.* |

### Giving instructions, exhortations in the 'noi' form

Andiamo al cinema! C'è un film di Fellini. | *Let's go to the cinema! There's a Fellini film.*

No, torniamo a casa e guadiamo la televisione! | *No, let's go home and watch television!*

### Giving instructions in the 'voi' form

Bambini, andate a giocare in giardino! | *Children, go and play in the garden!*

Non andate fuori scalzi, mettetevi le scarpe! | *Don't go out with bare feet, put your shoes on!*

### Giving instructions in the polite 'loro' form:

Signorine, si accomodino! | *Ladies, please sit down.*

### Instructions on a packet

**Aprire** con cautela. | *Open with care.*

**Lavare** attentamente. | *Wash carefully.*

### Instructions (negative)

**Non aprire** la porta, Giorgio! | *Don't open the door, Giorgio!*

**Non entri**, signora Bianchi! | *Don't go in, signora Bianchi!*

**Non facciamo** tardi. | *Let's not be late.*

**Non andate** lontano, bambini! | *Don't go far off, children!*

**Non si** preoccupino, signore! | *Don't worry, ladies.*

## ——— Analisi della grammatica ———

## 1 *Imperative* tu

When giving an instruction to someone you are on friendly terms with, use the **tu** form. The ending will either be **-a** for the **-are** verbs, or **-i** for the **-ere** and **-ire** verbs (the same as the normal **tu** form of these verbs).

| Infinitive | Imperative | Meaning |
|---|---|---|
| Mangiare | Mangia! | *Eat up!* |
| Prendere | Prendi una caramella! | *Take a sweet!* |
| Sentire | Senti questo! | *Listen to this!* |
| Pulire | Pulisci la bocca! | *Clean your mouth!* |

## 2 *Imperative* Lei

When giving an instruction to someone you are on formal terms with, use the **Lei** (polite *you*) form. There are two types of ending: for **-are** verbs it is **-i** and for **-ere** and **-ire** it is **-a**.

| Infinitive | Imperative | Meaning |
|---|---|---|
| Scus**are** | Scus**i**! | *Excuse me!* |
| Port**are** | Mi port**i** il menù! | *Bring me the menu!* |
| Prend**ere** | Prend**a** un biscotto! | *Take a biscuit!* |
| Sent**ire** | Sent**a**! | *Listen!* |
| Fin**ire** | Fin**isca** pure! | *Please finish!* |

## 3 *Imperative* noi

Rather than a command, this is a way of suggesting doing something when the speaker is a part of the group. The form of the imperative is the same as the normal **noi** form of the present tense.

| Infinitive | Imperative | Meaning |
|---|---|---|
| Parlare | Parl**iamo** italiano! | *Let's talk Italian!* |
| Prendere | Prend**iamo** un gelato! | *Let's have an ice-cream!* |
| Sentire | Sent**iamo** questo! | *Let's hear this!* |
| Finire | Fin**iamo** domani! | *Let's finish tomorrow!* |

## 4 *Imperative* voi

This is the form of imperative or order used to more than one person, unless there is a reason to use the extremely polite form **Loro**. The form is exactly the same as the normal **voi** form of the present tense:

| Infinitive | Imperative | Meaning |
|---|---|---|
| Giocare | Gioc**ate** in giardino, bambini! | *Play in the garden, children!* |
| Mettere | Mett**ete** gli stivali, ragazzi! | *Put your boots on, kids!* |
| Dormire | Dorm**ite** bene, bimbi! | *Sleep well, children!* |
| Finire | Fin**ite** i compiti! | *Finish your homework!* |

## 5 *Imperative* Loro

**Loro** (the polite plural form of *you*) is most often used by shop assistants, waiters, hotel employees, and so on, when addressing more than one customer. You are unlikely to need to use it yourself unless planning on spending a working summer in Italy. The English equivalent would be *Sir and Madam* or *Ladies and Gentlemen*, but would not normally be used:

| Infinitive | Imperative | Meaning |
|---|---|---|
| Ascoltare | Ascolt**ino**, signori! | *Listen, ladies and gentlemen!* |
| Scendere | Scend**ano**, signori! | *Please get out (e.g. of the coach) ladies and gentlemen!* |
| Dormire | Dorm**ano** bene, signori! | *Sleep well!* |
| Finire | Finis**cano** pure di mangiare, signori! Non c'è fretta. | *Please finish eating! There's no hurry.* |

## 6 *Giving instructions (using the infinitive)*

Recipes, instruction manuals and other written instructions often use the infinitive (the *to* form of the verb):

> **Tagliare** la cipolla e **mettere** in un tegame.    *Chop the onion and place in a frying pan.*
> **Moderare** la velocità!    *Reduce your speed!*

## 7 *Telling someone not to do something*

For the **Lei, noi, voi** or **loro** forms, add **non** before the verb:

> **Non** esca, signora!    *Don't go out, signora!*
> **Non** andiamo da Maria!    *Let's not go to Maria's!*
> **Non** girate a sinistra!    *Don't turn left!*
> **Non** si preoccupino!    *Don't worry!*

You can also add **non** to instructions given in the infinitive:

> **Non parlare** con il conducente!    *Don't speak to the driver!*

But for the **tu** form, you use **non** and the infinitive (the **-are, -ere, -ire** forms):

**Non mangiare** troppo! *Don't eat too much!*
**Non prendere** tutto! *Don't take all (of it)!*
**Non dormire** fino a tardi! *Don't sleep in!*

## In contesto

### Spoken instructions

#### Asking directions and giving directions, using the *Lei* form

| | | |
|---|---|---|
| Turista | **Senta, scusi!** | *Excuse me!* |
| Passante | **Dica!** | *Yes?* |
| Turista | **Come arrivo alla stazione?** | *How do I get to the station?* |
| Passante | **Dunque . . . vada diritto per questa strada, al primo semaforo giri a sinistra, continui ancora un po', e in fondo a quella strada volti a destra . . . attraversi la piazza e la stazione è proprio di fronte.** | *Well now . . . go straight ahead along this road, at the first traffic lights turn left, go on a bit further, and at the bottom of that road, turn right . . . cross the square and the station is right opposite.* |
| Turista | **Ah, grazie. Lei è molto gentile.** | *Oh, thank you. You're very kind.* |

#### Giving instructions, using the *tu* form

| | | |
|---|---|---|
| Paolo | **Mamma, ho fame.** | *Mummy, I'm hungry.* |
| Mamma | **Prendi questi soldi, vai al bar e compra una merendina per te e per tuo fratello. Corri, perché è tardi.** | *Take this money, go the café and buy a cake for you and your brother. Hurry, because it's late.* |
| Paolo | **Grazie, mamma.** | *Thanks, mummy.* |
| Mamma | **Mi raccomando! Non perdere i soldi e non mangiare la merendina di tuo fratello.** | *Don't forget! Don't lose the money and don't eat your brother's cake.* |

## Getting your friends to do something, using the *noi* form of imperative

| | | |
|---|---|---|
| Carlo | **Dove andiamo stasera, ragazzi?** | *Where shall we go tonight, guys?* |
| Anna | **Andiamo da Gianluca a mangiare la pizza!** | *Let's go to Gianluca's for a pizza.* |
| Carlo | **No, lì non è buona la pizza. Proviamo invece da Zio Peppino, sul lungomare!** | *No, the pizza's no good there. Let's try Zio Peppino's on the sea front.* |
| Anna | **Sbrigiamoci, è tardi. Prendiamo la macchina e via!** | *Let's get a move on, it's late. Let's take the car and go.* |

## Giving instructions, using the *voi* form

| | | |
|---|---|---|
| Mamma | **Bambini, andate a fare un bagno.** | *Children, go and have a swim.* |
| Bambini | **Sì, mamma.** | *Yes, mummy.* |
| Mamma | **Non andate lontano. State qui vicino, così vi vedo.** | *Don't go far out. Stay near here, that way I can see you.* |
| Bambini | **Sì, mamma.** | *Yes, mummy.* |
| Mamma | **E non perdete il pallone in acqua.** | *And don't lose the ball in the water.* |
| Bambini | **No, mamma.** | *No, mummy.* |
| Mamma | **E ora uscite, è ora di andare a casa.** | *And now come out, it's time to go home.* |

## Polite command using the *loro* form of imperative

| | |
|---|---|
| **Signorine, buona sera. Si accommodino!** | *Good evening, Ladies! Sit down!* |
| **Grazie!** | *Thanks.* |
| **Si siedano, qui, accanto alla finestra!** | *Sit down here, near the window.* |
| **Grazie, c'è un bel panorama.** | *Thanks, there's a lovely view.* |

## Written instructions using the infinitive

### How to make a telephone call

Staccare il ricevitore, e inserire i gettoni. Comporre il numero. Alla fine della telefonata riattacare il ricevitore e attendere la restituzione dei gettoni.

*Remove the receiver and insert the tokens. Dial the number. At the end of the call, hang up and wait for the tokens to be returned.*

### A recipe

Tagliare due fette di pane. Spalmare il burro sulle fette di pane. Stendere una fetta di prosciutto su una fetta di pane e coprire con l'altra fetta di pane. Mangiare subito.

*Cut two slices of bread. Spread the butter on the slices of bread. Spread a slice of ham on one of the slices of bread and cover with the other slice of bread. Eat straightaway.*

## ——————— In aggiunta ———————

## 1 Irregular imperatives

Many verbs have an imperative form which does not follow the pattern shown above. Usually only the **tu** form is irregular. Some of the most common are:

| Infinitive | tu | Lei | voi | Loro |
|---|---|---|---|---|
| andare (*to go*) | va' | vada | andate | vadano |
| fare (*to go*) | fa' | faccia | fate | facciano |
| stare (*to be*) | sta' | stia | state | stiano |
| dare (*to give*) | da' | dia | date | diano |
| dire (*to say*) | di' | dica | dite | dicano |
| essere (*to*) | sii | sia | siate | siano |
| avere (*to have*) | abbi | abbia | abbiate | abbiano |

The **Lei** form of the imperative is the 3rd person (*he, she, you*) of the present subjunctive which is a special verb form used with specific expressions and meanings (see unit 17). (See the verbs on page 196.)

The one-syllable imperatives shown above are often spelt differently: **va, fà, sta, dà, dì**. Perhaps because they sound so abrupt, there is a tendency for the first four to be replaced by the normal non-imperative **tu** forms: **vai, fai, stai, dai**.

## 2 Pronouns: before or after?

The direct object pronouns (such as **mi, ti, lo, la**) explained in unit 14 normally come before the verb (**lo** prendo, **li** mangiamo) but, although this rule still applies in the case of **Lei** and the **loro** forms of the imperatives, the **tu, noi** and **voi** forms have the pronouns, including **ci** and **ne**, joined to the end:

| | |
|---|---|
| **Lo** mangi! | *Eat it! (polite form)* |
| **Lo** mangino, signori! | *Eat it! (polite plural form)* |
| Mangia**lo**! | *Eat it!* |
| Mangiate**lo**! | *Eat it!* |
| Mangiamo**lo**! | *Let's eat it!* |

The same thing happens in the case of the reflexive pronouns (**mi, ti, si,** etc.). Although normally before the verb, they come after when the verb is the imperative form (see unit 7).

| | |
|---|---|
| **Ti** alzi? | *Are you getting up?* |
| Alza**ti**! | *Get up!* |

There is a further complication in the case of the one-syllable **tu** imperatives (**da', fa', sta', di', va'**) which *double the initial consonant* of all the object pronouns except **gli**:

| | |
|---|---|
| **Dammi** diecimila lire! | *Give me ten thousand lire!* |
| **Dammelo**! | *Give it to me!* |
| **Vattene**! | *Go away!* |
| **Fammi** un piacere! | *Do me a favour!* |
| **Dimmi** cosa pensi! | *Tell me what you think!* |
| **Dagli** cinquecento lire. | *Give him five hundred lire.* |

# 10

## — Expressing possession —

**Le funzioni**

In this unit you will learn about:
Asking to whom something belongs ● Saying to whom it belongs
● Asking what other people have or own

**Le strutture**

Possessive adjectives, **mio, tuo, suo, nostro, vostro, loro, proprio**
● Possessive pronouns **mio, il mio,** etc. ● **Di** expressing ownership
● **Di chi è?** asking to whom something belongs

## Nota introduttiva

Before going on, look at these examples:

| | |
|---|---|
| La **tua** casa è grande. | *Your house is big.* |
| La **mia** è piccola. | *Mine is small.* |
| | |
| È **tua** questa giacca? | *Is this jacket yours?* |
| No, non è **mia**. | *No. It's not mine.* |
| | |
| **Di chi è** questa bicicletta? | *Whose is this bike?* |
| È **di** Franco. | *It's Franco's.* |
| | |
| Lei **ha** una macchina inglese? | *Do you have an English car?* |
| No, **ho** una macchina tedesca. | *No. I have a German car.* |
| | |
| **Qual** è la Sua macchina? | *Which is your car?* |
| **Quella** verde. | *That green one.* |
| | |
| **Qual** è il Suo indirizzo? | *What is your address?* |

# ——— Analisi della grammatica ———

## 1 Mio, tuo, suo: *my, your, his, etc.*

To say to whom something belongs, in Italian, use the words **mio**, **tuo**, **suo**, etc. (*my, your, his,* etc.); these are called possessive adjectives. Like all adjectives, **mio**, **tuo**, **suo**, **nostro** and **vostro** change according to whether the person or thing they are describing is singular or plural, masculine or feminine.

### (a) *Mio*: my

Here are all the forms of **mio**:

| | |
|---|---|
| il **mio** cane | *my dog* |
| la **mia** bicicletta | *my bicycle* |
| i **miei** calzini | *my socks* |
| le **mie** calze | *my stockings* |

You will notice that, in Italian, with the word **mio** (*my*) you use the definite article **il**, **la**, etc. (*the*). However, when you talk about relatives, you *don't* need the definite article, unless there is more than one.

| | |
|---|---|
| **mia** madre | *my mother* |
| **mio** padre | *my father* |
| i **miei** fratelli | *my brothers* |
| le **mie** sorelle | *my sisters* |

When there is an adjective or a suffix (something extra joined to the end of a word) you also have to use the article:

| | |
|---|---|
| **mia** sorella | *my sister* |
| la **mia** sorella più | *my younger sister* |
| la **mia** sorellina | *my little sister* |

### (b) *Tuo*: your

To say *your* (when you are on familiar terms and use **tu** with the person spoken to) you use **tuo** in its different forms:

| | |
|---|---|
| il **tuo** passaporto | *your passport* |
| la **tua** amica | *your friend* |
| i **tuoi** figli | *your children* |
| le **tue** scarpe | *your shoes* |

### (c) *Suo*: his

To say *his* or *her*, you use **suo** in its different forms:

| il **suo** amico | *his/her friend* |
| la **sua** collega | *his/her colleague* |
| i **suoi** amici | *his/her friends* |
| le **sue** cose | *his/her things* |

**Suo** can also mean *your* (when speaking to someone using the polite or **Lei** form); sometimes when **suo** means *your*, it is written with capital **S** just as the **Lei** form is often written with a capital **L**:

| È venuto Suo marito? | *Did your husband come?* |

Sometimes when you use **suo** it is not clear whether it means *his* or *her*.

| Ho visto Giorgio stasera. Era con Sandra. Il **suo** amico era appena tornato da Londra. | *I saw Giorgio tonight. He was with Sandra. His/Her friend had just got back from London.* |

To avoid confusion between *his* and *her*, you can if necessary replace **suo**, or add to it, with the words **di lui** (*of him*) or **di lei** (*of her*):

| Ho visto Giorgio oggi. Era con Sandra. L'amico **di lui** era appena tornato da Londra. | *I saw Giorgio today. He was with Sandra. His friend had just got back from London.* |

### (d) *Nostro:* our

To say **our** you use the different forms of **nostro**:

| il **nostro** treno | *our train* |
| la **nostra** amica | *our friend* |
| i **nostri** mariti | *our husbands (one each)* |
| le **nostre** case | *our houses* |

### (e) *Vostro:* your

To say **your** (plural) you use the different forms of **vostro**:

| il vostro errore | *your mistake* |
| la vostra macchina fotografica | *your camera* |
| i vostri biglietti | *your tickets* |
| le vostre valigie | *your suitcases* |

### (f) *Loro:* their

To say *their*, use **loro**. This is an exception to the rules above, because **loro** never changes whatever the gender or number of the object or person it describes, and it always takes the definite article (**il**, etc.).

| il **loro** cane | *their dog* |
| la **loro** casa | *their house* |
| i **loro** amici | *their friends* |
| le **loro** cose | *their things* |

**Loro** can also mean *your* (when you are addressing people using the polite plural form **loro**), but again its use in this respect is limited to waiters, etc. addressing clients.

## 2   Il mio, il tuo, il suo: *mine, yours, his, etc.*

When wanting to express ownership without naming the object, use the possessive pronouns **il mio, il tuo, il suo**, etc. (*mine, yours, his/hers*, etc.) rather than the adjective **mio** (*my*). The article **il, lo, la**, etc. and the form of **mio, tuo, suo, nostro, vostro** still have to agree with the object or person possessed in gender (masc. or fem.) and number (singular or plural):

| Questo libro è nostro. | *This book is ours.* |
| **Il vostro** dov'è? | *Where's yours?* |
| **Il nostro** è in macchina. | *Ours is in the car.* |

| Mio marito mi aiuta molto in cucina. | *My husband helps me a lot in the kitchen.* |
| **Il mio** non sa dov'è. | *Mine doesn't know where it is.* |

| La macchina di Giorgio è pericolosa. | *Giorgio's car is dangerous.* |

| Non prendiamo **la sua**, allora, prendiamo **la tua**. | *Let's not take his then, let's take yours.* |

When the possessive is used with **essere** alone, as in the examples below, the definite article (**il**, etc.) is often omitted. One of the first phrases Italian children learn is **È mio!** (*It's mine!*)

| Di chi è questo libro? | **È mio.** | *It's mine.* |
| Di chi è questa borsa? | **È tua.** | *It's yours.* |
| Di chi è questa macchina? | **È sua.** | *It's his.* |
| Di chi sono questi sandali? | **Sono nostri.** | *They're ours.* |
| | **Sono vostri.** | *They're yours.* |
| But: | **Sono i loro.** | *They're theirs.* |

Whether or not the article (**il**, etc.) is used, the **mio, tuo, suo** still changes according to the object: (.i.e. if it's masc. or fem., singular or plural).

The phrase **i tuoi** with no noun used can often indicate *your family*, while **i miei** means *my family*, and so on.

## 3 Proprio: *one's own*

**Proprio** means *one's own* and is used in place of the other possessive adjectives when the subject referred to is impersonal, i.e. *one* or *everyone* or similar:

Non tutti hanno la **propria** macchina.

*Not everyone has their own car.*

Ognuno ama il **proprio** paese. *Everyone loves his own country.*

It can also be used with one of the other possessives, to reinforce or emphasise the idea of *one's own*:

Marco è contento di vivere la sua **propria** vita.

*Marco is happy to live his own life.*

## 4 Di: *of (expressing ownership)*

The English phrase *It's Franco's* has to be expressed in Italian by using **di** (*of*) followed by the person's name:

Questa maglia è **di Franco**. *This sweater is Franco's.*
Queste scarpe sono **di Anna**. *These shoes are Anna's.*

If you want to ask to whom something belongs, you use **di** (*of*) and **chi** (*who*):

**Di chi** è questa borsetta? *Whose is this handbag?*
È di Gianna. *It's Gianna's.*

**Di chi** sono questi soldi? *Whose are these coins?*
Sono di Piero. *They're Piero's.*

## 5 Del: *of the (expressing belonging)*

If, instead of a name, there is a noun such as **ragazzo** or **amico**, the **di** combines with the definite article **il**, **la**, etc. to create forms similar to those of **nel**, **al**, **dal** (seen in unit 4), **del**, **dello**, and **della**. The plural forms are the same as those given in unit 3 when expressing *some*.

Di chi è questa bicicletta? *Whose is this bicycle?*
È **del** mio amico. *It's my friend's.*

Di chi sono queste scarpe? *Whose are these shoes?*
Sono **della** ragazza francese. *They're the French girl's.*

| | |
|---|---|
| Di chi sono questi asciugamani? | *Whose are these towels?* |
| Sono **dell'** albergo. | *They're the hotel's.* |
| Di chi sono questi libri? | *Whose are these books?* |
| Sono **dello** studente inglese. | *They're the English student's.* |

---

# In contesto

---

## *Other people's belongings*

| | | |
|---|---|---|
| Carlo | **Di chi è questa felpa?** | *Whose is that sweatshirt?* |
| Franco | **È mia. La tua è più sporca.** | *It's mine. Yours is dirtier.* |
| Carlo | **Come? La mia felpa? È molto pulita.** | *What? My sweatshirt? It's very clean.* |
| Franco | **E questa di chi è? E tua?** | *And this one, whose is this? Is it yours?* |
| Carlo | **No. Quella è di Mario. La mia è più grande.** | *No. That one's Mario's. Mine is bigger.* |

## *Family relations*

| | | |
|---|---|---|
| Mario | **Mia zia si chiama Isabella. Mio zio si chiama Teodoro.** | *My aunt is called Isabelle. My uncle is called Teodoro.* |
| Anna | **E i tuoi cugini?** | *And your cousins?* |
| Mario | **Mio cugino si chiama Aurelio, e la mia cugina più piccola si chiama Esmeralda.** | *My cousin is called Aurelio and my younger cousin is called Esmeralda.* |
| Anna | **Che nomi strani!** | *What funny names!* |
| Mario | **Sì, i miei cugini sono molto originali.** | *Yes, my cousins are very unusual.* |

## *At a party*

| | | |
|---|---|---|
| Anna | **Chi è quel bell'uomo biondo?** | *Who is that lovely fair-haired man?* |
| Maria | **È un nostro amico svedese.** | *He's a Swedish friend of ours.* |
| Anna | **È sposato?** | *Is he married?* |
| Maria | **Sì. Sua moglie è a Stoccolma,** | *Yes. His wife's in Stockholm,* |

|       | però. Lui invece, è ospite a casa nostra per un paio di giorni. | *however, But he's a guest in our house for a couple of days.* |
|-------|------------------------------------------------|------------------------------------------------|
| Anna  | **Mmm. Me lo presenti?**                       | *Mmm. Will you introduce me to him?*           |
| Maria | **Sì, volentieri. E poi, anche se non c'è sua moglie ci sono tutti i loro figli!** | *Yes, of course. Anyway, even if his wife isn't here, there are all their children!* |

## ———— In aggiunta ————

### 1 Replacement of possessive with reflexive pronoun

Italians tend to miss out the possessive *my* in expressions such as *I put my shoes on* and say instead *I put* the *shoes on* to myself.

> **Mi** metto le scarpe.       *I put my shoes on.*
> **Si** mette la giacca.       *He puts his jacket on.*

For all the forms of these reflexive pronouns (*myself, yourself*, etc.) see unit 7.

### 2 Missing out 'of'

In English you say *two of my friends*, but in Italian you omit the *of*, as in this example:

> **due miei amici**

Similarly *a friend* of *mine* is translated in Italian as:

> **un mio amico**

### 3 Verb avere, expressing ownership

You have already met the verb **avere** (*to have*); this can be used to talk about possessions:

> Ha un cane, signor Bianchi?      *Do you have a dog, Mr Bianchi?*
> Sì. Il mio cane si chiama Lillo.  *Yes. My dog is called Lillo.*
>
> Hai una giacca?                   *Do you have a jacket?*

No, non ho una giacca. Quella non è mia. È di Carla.
*No. I haven't got a jacket. That one's not mine. It's Carla's.*

Ah, è di Carla? Perché l'ha lasciata qui a casa nostra?
*Oh, it's Carla's? And why did she leave it here in our house?*

## 4 Omission of possessive

Italians tend to omit the possessive where the idea of ownership or possession is taken for granted:

Carla è partita con il marito. *Carla left with her husband.*

*(It is assumed that Carla left with her own husband.)*

I bambini hanno alzato le mani. *The children raised their hands.*

*(It is assumed that they raised their own hands.)*

È arrivato lo zio. *Uncle's arrived.*

*(Again it is thought unnecessary to add that it is our uncle.)*

## 5 Quale . . . ? what . . . ? and, which . . . ?

**Quale** means *which*. In unit 5 you saw how it is used as an adjective.

**Quale** borsa vuole? *Which bag do you want?*

You can also use it on its own when asking for information (such as someone's particulars) where in English you might use *what*. Before è (*it is*) it can be abbreviated, but should *not* be followed by an apostrophe:

---

### Singular

**Qual** è il Suo cognome? *What is your surname?*
**Qual** è la tua data di nascita? *What is your date of birth?*
**Qual** è la tua macchina? *Which is your car?*

### Plural

**Quali sono** i tuoi figli? *Which are your children?*
**Quali sono** le tue scarpe? *Which are your shoes?*
**Quali sono** i tuoi amici più cari? *Who are your closest friends?*

---

# 11

# Talking about events in the past

**Le funzioni**

In this unit you will learn how to:
Talk about events in the past • Talk about events in the past and which relate to the present • Talk about events which are still going on

**Le strutture**

The perfect tense and **avere** • The perfect tense and **essere** • Phrases of time • Reflexive verbs in the perfect tense • Negative sentences in the perfect tense • Use of the present tense with **da**

## Nota introduttiva

Look at these examples:

| | |
|---|---|
| Sabato, **sono andato** al mare e **ho mangiato** un gelato. E tu dove sei stato?* | *On Saturday, I went to the seaside and I ate an ice-cream. And where did you go?* |
| Io **sono andato** al bar e **ho bevuto** una birra. | *I went to the bar and I drank a beer.* |
| Siamo stati in America **per dieci anni.** | *We were in America for 10 years.* |
| Vivo in Inghilterra **da dieci anni.** | *I have lived in England for 10 years.* |
| Non lo vedo **da cinque** giorni. | *I haven't seen him for five days.* |

Hai **mai** visto una casa cosi brutta?     *Have you ever seen such an ugly house?*

**\*Stare** (*to be*) in this context is similar in meaning to the verb **andare** (*to go*) as is often the case in English too.

## ———— Analisi della grammatica ————

### 1 Perfect tense

In the examples above the passato prossimo (perfect tense) is used. It is used when talking about an action which is now over (finished, perfect) but which has some connection with present events. The passato prossimo can translate the English perfect tense, e.g. *I have eaten* or the past definite, e.g. *I ate* according to the circumstances:

(a) When no specific occasion is mentioned:

    **Sei** mai **stato** in Italia?     *Have you ever been to Italy?*

(b) A specific occasion or time:

    Sì. Ci **sono stato** due anni fa.     *Yes. I went there two years ago.*

(c) The action took place over a longer period of time but is complete:

    **Siamo vissuti** a Roma per 10 anni.     *We lived in Rome for 10 years.*

### 2 Perfect tense using avere

To form the passato prossimo, you use the present tense of the verb **avere** (*to have*) with the part of the verb known as the past participle (e.g. in English: *eaten, gone, jumped*):

    **Ho mangiato** un gelato.     *I ate/have eaten an ice-cream.*
    **Abbiamo dormito** per due ore.     *We slept/have slept two hours.*

The verb **avere** (*to have*) changes according to *who* carried out the action: **ho, hai, ha**, etc. The participle (**mangiato, dormito**) does not change.

Here is the passato prossimo of the verb **mangiare** (*to eat*):

| **Singular** | | |
|---|---|---|
| (io) | **ho mangiato** | *I have eaten* |
| (tu) | **hai mangiato** | *you have eaten* |
| (lui) | **ha mangiato** | *he has eaten* |
| (lei) | **ha mangiato** | *she has eaten* |
| (Lei) | **ha mangiato** | *you have eaten (polite)* |
| **Plural** | | |
| (noi) | **abbiamo mangiato** | *we have eaten* |
| (voi) | **avete mangiato** | *you have eaten* |
| (loro) | **hanno mangiato** | *they have eaten* |

## 3 Past participle

In English, in addition to regular past participles which follow a pattern such as *jumped (to jump)*, *hated (to hate)*, *loved (to love)*, there are many forms of past participle which do *not* follow a pattern, such as *eaten (to eat)*, *gone (to go)*, *ate (to eat)*. In Italian, the past participles of all **-are** verbs have a regular ending form **-ato**:

| mangiare | *to eat* |
|---|---|
| ho mangi**ato** | *I have eaten, I ate* |

| parl**are** | *to speak* |
|---|---|
| ho parl**ato** | *I have spoken, I spoke* |

The past participle of the **-ire** verbs always ends in **-ito**:

| dorm**ire** | *to sleep* |
|---|---|
| ho dorm**ito** | *I have slept, I slept* |

But the past participle of the **-ere** verbs ends with any one of a number of forms. It might take an **-uto** form like:

| dov**ere** | *to have to* |
|---|---|
| ho dov**uto** | *I had to* |

Or, it might be a shorter form like:

| mett**ere** | *to put* |
|---|---|
| ho m**esso** | *I have put, I put* |

There is no rule to help you learn all these forms, you just have to remember them! Here are **avere** and **essere** along with some of the more common **-ere** verbs, and their past participles:

| avere | *to have* | **avuto** |
|-------|-----------|-----------|
| essere | *to be* | **stato***  |
| chiudere | *to close* | **chiuso** |
| decidere | *to decide* | **deciso** |
| dovere | *to have to* | **dovuto** |
| leggere | *to read* | **letto** |
| perdere | *to lose* | **perso** *or* **perduto** |
| potere | *to be able to* | **potuto** |
| prendere | *to take* | **preso** |
| rimanere | *to remain* | **rimasto***  |
| rispondere | *to reply* | **risposto** |
| scendere | *to get down* | **sceso***  |
| scrivere | *to write* | **scritto** |
| tenere | *to hold* | **tenuto** |
| vedere | *to see* | **visto** *or* **veduto** |
| vivere | *to live* | **vissuto*** (optional) |
| volere | *to want to* | **voluto** |

The past participles marked * are those that form the passato prossimo with **essere** instead of **avere**. See below.

## 4 Perfect tense using essere

Some verbs – mainly those expressing movement – use **essere**. They still need a past participle to express the idea of *eaten* or *gone* but use **essere** (*to be*) with it instead of **avere** (*to have*). Like adjectives, (see unit 1) the past participle must change its ending depending on whether the subject (the person or thing that has carried out the action) is masculine or feminine, singular or plural:

| | |
|---|---|
| Carlo è andato in banca. | *Carlo went to the bank.* |
| Anna è andata al bar. | *Anna has gone to the café.* |
| Carlo e Anna sono andati al bar. | *Carlo and Anna have gone to the café.* |
| Anna e Franca sono andate al cinema. | *Anna and Franca have gone to the cinema.* |

Here is a list of the most common verbs that normally use **essere** in the perfect tense:

| essere | to be |
| stare | to be |
| venire | to come |
| andare | to go |
| partire | to leave, to depart |
| tornare | to return |
| uscire | to go out |
| entrare | to enter |
| salire | to go up |
| scendere | to go down |
| rimanere | to remain, to stay behind |
| restare | to remain, to stay behind |
| nascere | to be born |
| morire | to die |
| diventare | to become |
| divenire | to become |

The list above contains mainly verbs associated with movement: going or staying. There are other verbs that are used with **essere** rather than **avere**. Here are a few of the most common (or the most useful):

| dimagrire | to get thin | **Sono** dimagrito/-a. |
| ingrassare | to get fat | **Sono** ingrassato/-a. |

### (a) Impersonal verbs

These can be called 'it' verbs because they are used impersonally:

| sembrare | to seem | Mi è sembrato stanco. |
| costare | to cost | Quanto è costato? |
| volere ci | to take (time) | Ci è voluta un' ora. |
| piacere | to please | Ti è piaciuto il film? |

And lots more – see unit 18 for other examples of impersonal verbs.

### (b) Taking essere or avere

There are some verbs which can be used with **essere** or **avere** depending on their meaning:

| cominciare | to begin |
| finire | to finish |
| continuare | to continue |
| aumentare | to increase |
| diminuire | to decrease |
| migliorare | to improve |
| passare | to pass, pass by |
| scendere | to descend, take down |

**passare**

| | |
|---|---|
| **Sono** passata da Gianluca. | *I went by Gianluca's.* |
| **Ho** passato il menù alla mia amica. | *I passed the menu to my friend.* |

**scendere**

| | |
|---|---|
| **Sono** scesi dalla macchina. | *They got out of the car.* |
| **Hanno** sceso le scale. | *They came down the stairs.* |
| But; **Sono** scesi per le scale. | *They went down (by) the stairs.* |

## 5 Saying how long ago

To say how long ago you did something, you use **fa** (*ago*) and the appropriate length of time:

| | |
|---|---|
| due giorni **fa** | *two days ago* |
| una settimana **fa** | *a week ago* |
| un mese **fa** | *a month ago* |
| un anno **fa** | *a year ago* |
| poco tempo **fa** | *a short time ago* |
| pochi giorni **fa** | *a few days ago* |

To talk about the past few days or weeks you use **scorso** (*last*), which ends with **-o** or **-a** depending on whether the noun is masculine or feminine.

| | |
|---|---|
| la settimana **scorsa** | *last week* |
| il mese **scorso** | *last month* |
| l'anno **scorso** | *last year* |
| l'estate **scorsa** | *last summer* |

Some of the more common time phrases referring to the past are:

| | |
|---|---|
| ieri | *yesterday* |
| l'altro ieri | *day before yesterday* |
| oggi | *today* |
| stamattina | *this morning* |
| ieri mattina | *yesterday morning* |
| ieri sera | *yesterday evening* |

And the days of the week are:

| | | | |
|---|---|---|---|
| lunedì | *Monday* | mercoledì | *Wednesday* |
| martedì | *Tuesday* | giovedì | *Thursday* |

| venerdì | *Friday* | domenica | *Sunday* |
|---------|----------|----------|----------|
| sabato  | *Saturday* | | |

The months of the year:

| gennaio | *January* | luglio | *July* |
|---------|-----------|--------|--------|
| febbraio | *February* | agosto | *August* |
| marzo | *March* | settembre | *September* |
| aprile | *April* | ottobre | *October* |
| maggio | *May* | novembre | *November* |
| giugno | *June* | dicembre | *December* |

## 6 Perfect tense of reflexive verbs

Reflexive verbs (see unit 7) in the perfect tense need **essere** to form the past participle. The reflexive pronoun (*myself, yourself,* etc.) normally comes before the verb (although a reflexive verb in the infinitive has the -**si** tacked on to the end).

| alzarsi | *to get up* | **mi** sono alzato |
|---------|-------------|--------------------|
| sedersi | *to sit down* | **mi** sono seduto |
| vestirsi | *to get dressed* | **mi** sono vestito |

As with the other verbs that use **essere**, the past participle (**alzato**, **vestito**, etc.) has to agree with the subject (masc. or fem., singular or plural):

| Giuliano **si** è alzato alle sette. | *Giuliano got up at 7am.* |
|---|---|
| Maria Grazia **si** è alzata alle otto. | *Maria Grazia got up at 8am.* |
| I ragazzi **si** sono alzati tardi. | *The boys got up late.* |
| Le ragazze **si** sono alzate presto. | *The girls got up early.* |

## 7 Negatives

When the sentence in the perfect tense is negative, take care over the positioning of the **non** and the other negative words. Italian negatives usually come in pairs (this is called a double negative) with the **non** before the verb and the other negative word somewhere after. Look at these examples:

Here the second negative comes after the **avere** or **essere**, but before the participle:

**Non** ho **mai** visitato Palermo.   *I have never visited Palermo.*
**Non** abbiamo **ancora**        *We haven't eaten yet.*
mangiato.

Here the second negative word comes after the *whole* verb:

**Non** ho visto **nessuno** oggi.   *I haven't seen anyone today.*
**Non** ho fatto **niente** ieri.     *I didn't do anything yesterday.*

For further examples of negative words, see the Grammar Section on page 192.

## 8 Present tense plus da

When the event in question is still going on, Italians use the present tense with **da**:

Studio l'italiano **da** cinque   *I have been studying Italian for*
anni.                  *five years. (Lit. I study Italian*
                      *since five years.)*

Sono sposata **da** dieci anni.   *I have been married for 10 years.*
Non la vedo **da** tanto tempo.   *I haven't seen her for so long.*

──────────── **In contesto** ────────────

### What did you do today?

Carlo   **Ciao Mario, cos'hai fatto di**   *Hi, Mario, what have you*
       **bello?**                     *done – anything nice?*
Mario   **Niente di speciale. Sono**   *Nothing special. I went to*
       **andato a scuola, ho fatto due**   *school, did two hours' classes*
       **ore di lezione e poi sono**   *and then went home. And*
       **tornato a casa. E tu?**   *you?*
Carlo   **Ah, io ho incontrato Teresa,**   *Ah, I met Teresa. We went*
       **siamo andati al bar, ci siamo**   *to the café, sat down at a*
       **seduti ad un tavolo fuori e**   *table outside, and had some-*
       **abbiamo preso qualcosa da**   *thing to drink. That way we*
       **bere. Così ci siamo rilassati**   *relaxed a bit. For two months*
       **un po'. È da due mesi che**   *now I haven't done anything*
       **non faccio altro che studiare.**   *except study.*

## What did you do on holiday?

| | | |
|---|---|---|
| Teresa | **Ben tornati dalle vacanze! Com'è andata? Tutto bene?** | *Welcome back from holiday! How did it go? Everything OK?* |
| Maria | **Sì . . . è stata una vacanza un po' diversa dal solito . . . non siamo andati al mare quest' anno, abbiamo preso una casa in campagna.** | *Yes . . . it was a holiday that was a bit different from usual . . . we didn't go to the seaside this year, we took a house in the country.* |
| Teresa | **E cosa avete fatto in campagna?** | *And what did you do in the country?* |
| Maria | **Io ho fatto delle lunghe passeggiate, Giovanni ha letto molto libri, e non abbiamo visto nessuno.** | *I went for long walks, Giovanni read lots of books, and we didn't see anyone at all.* |
| Teresa | **E i bambini? Si sono divertiti?** | *And the children? Did they enjoy themselves?* |
| Maria | **No. I bambini si sono lamentati perché per tre settimane non hanno potuto guardare la televisione.** | *No. The children complained because for three weeks they couldn't watch any television.* |

## A visit to England

| | | |
|---|---|---|
| Franco | **Lei è mai stata in Inghilterra?** | *Have you ever been to England?* |
| Teresa | **Ci sono stata una sola volta, nel 1979. Ho fatto un corso d'inglese a Londra.** | *I've only been once, in 1979. I did an English course in London.* |
| Franco | **Come ha trovato la vita inglese?** | *How did you find English life?* |
| Teresa | **Molto interessante. Mi sono piaciuti molto i musei e le gallerie d'arte.** | *Very interesting. I really liked the museums and art galleries.* |
| Franco | **Ha visitato anche altre città?** | *Did you visit other towns?* |
| Teresa | **Sono stata a Cambridge e a Canterbury, ma ho avuto poco tempo. Non ho visitato nè Oxford nè York, per** | *I went to Cambridge and Canterbury, but I didn't have very much time. I didn't visit Oxford or York, for example.* |

> **esempio. Spero comunque**    *I hope to go back one day,*
> **di tornare un giorno.**    *however.*

**La passeggiata**: *the walk*. (Also refers to the nightly promenade up and down the main street, piazza, or sea front to be seen in any Italian town.)

Note the following verbs taken from the dialogues above, with their meaning and the **passato prossimo**:

| Infinitive | Meaning | Passato prossimo |
|---|---|---|
| fare | *to do* | ho fatto |
| piacere | *to please* | è piaciuto* |
| rilassarsi | *to relax* | mi sono rilassato |
| sedersi | *to sit down* | mi sono seduto |
| incontrarsi | *to meet* | ci siamo incontrati |
| lamentarsi | *to complain* | mi sono lamentato |

\* This verb is used mainly in the third person, singular or plural. See unit 16. When used in the perfect tense, it is used with **essere** and the past participle (**piaciuto**) has to agree.

> Mi è piaciuta la casa.    *I liked the house*
> Mi **sono** piaciuti i tortellini.    *I liked the tortellini.*

———————— **In aggiunta** ————————

## 1 The historic past

The perfect tense (**passato prossimo**) is the tense generally used in spoken Italian when talking about an action in the past, especially if it is somehow related to the present context:

> Non ho ancora mangiato.    *I haven't eaten yet.*
> Ieri è andata in centro e ha    *Yesterday she went to the centre*
> comprato una maglia.    *and bought a sweater.*

But speakers in the south will sometimes use the historic past (**passato remoto**) used elsewhere in Italy only to describe a historic event (e.g. the Romans invading Britain), or a completed action in the past with no link to the present day. Here is an example of how the past historic might be used in written Italian:

| | |
|---|---|
| Mary Regina della Scozia **nacque** nel 1542, **sposò** giovane il futuro Re della Francia e **morì** decapitata nel 1587 per ordine della Regina Elisabetta d'Inghilterra. | *Mary Queen of Scots was born in 1542, married very young the future King of France and died beheaded by Elizabeth Queen of England.* |

Although it is unlikely that you will want to use the **passato remoto** (also known as the past absolute or past definite) its forms are supplied in the Grammar Section on page 203.

## 2 Pronouns

The subject pronouns (**io, tu, lui**, etc.) can be used when wanting to emphasise or contrast two different actions by two people:

| | |
|---|---|
| **Io** ho telefonato. | *I phoned.* |
| **Lui** non ha telefonato. | *He didn't phone.* |
| **Io** sono stata in Italia; **tu** non ci sei mai stata. | *I have been to Italy, but you have never been there.* |

# 12

## — Describing the past —

**Le funzioni**

In this unit you will learn how to:
Describe how things were in the past • Describe actions which happened regularly in the past • Describe actions which were in the process of taking place when an event or incident occurred • Describe events which had already taken place when an action or event occurred

**Le strutture**

The imperfect tense • Using the imperfect tense with the perfect tense • The pluperfect tense • The past anterior

## Nota introduttiva

**Describing how things were in past**

Il cielo **era** azzurro, e il sole **splendeva**.

*The sky was blue, and the sun was shining.*

**Regular action in past**

Quando **lavoravo** a Londra **prendevo** la metropolitana.

*When I worked in London, I took the tube.*

**Describing actions that were taking place when another event occurred**

**Camminava** lungo la strada quando **ha visto** una cosa stranissima.

*He was walking along the street when he saw something very odd.*

**Describing events which had already taken place when an action or event occurred**

**Eravamo** appena entrati

*We had just come in when the*

| | |
|---|---|
| quando **ha suonato** il telefono. | *telephone rang.* |

---

## Analisi della grammatica

---

### 1 Imperfetto: *the imperfect tense*

When talking about the past, the **passato prossimo** (*perfect tense*) is used to talk about an *action* or an *event*, while the **imperfetto** (*imperfect tense*) is used to describe a *state* or *condition*:

| | |
|---|---|
| Nell' Ottocento le case **erano** grandi e difficili da pulire ma tutti **avevano** la cameriera. | *In the 19th century, the houses were big and difficult to clean, but everyone had maids.* |
| Ieri faceva molto caldo e non avevo voglia di mangiare. | *Yesterday it was very hot and I didn't feel like eating.* |
| La ragazza era alta, bionda e aveva gli occhi azzurri; sembrava svedese. | *The girl was tall, blonde and had blue eyes; she looked Swedish.* |

You can also use the **imperfetto** to talk about an action that occurred *regularly* in the past:

| | |
|---|---|
| Quando era bambina, abitavo a Milano. Frequentavo una scuola vicino a casa mia e andavo a scuola a piedi. | *When I was a child I lived in Milan. I attended a school near my house and I went to school on foot.* |
| Quando i miei amici erano a Firenze, pranzavano in una piccola trattoria e tutti i giorni mangiavano lo stesso piatto. | *When my friends were in Florence they went to eat in a little restaurant and every day they ate the same dish.* |

### 2 *Combination of* passato prossimo *and* imperfetto

Lastly, you use the **imperfetto** to talk about an action which was never completed (in other words *imperfect*) because something else happened meanwhile. The *something else* is usually expressed with the **passato prossimo**:

| | |
|---|---|
| Camminavo lungo la strada quando mi è caduto un mattone in testa. | *I was walking down the road when a brick fell on my head.* |
| Parlavamo con i nostri amici quando è arrivato un vigile che ci ha fatto la multa perché c'era divieto di sosta. | *We were talking to our friends when along came a traffic warden who fined us because it was a 'no parking' area.* |

It is also possible to have two actions happening simultaneously over a length of time, such as *I was eating supper as I watched television*; in this case, use two verbs in the **imperfetto**:

| | |
|---|---|
| **Guardavo** la televisione e **mangiavo** le patatine. | *I was watching the television and eating crisps.* |
| Mentre **preparava** la cena, **cantava**. | *While she was cooking the supper, she was singing.* |

It is not always clear from the English sentence which tense ought to be used in Italian; the English past *I went* can be translated in two different ways. Look at these two examples:

**Imperfetto** in Italian:

| | |
|---|---|
| Quando ero piccola, **andavo** a scuola tutti i giorni. | *When I was little, I went to school every day.* |

**Passato prossimo** in Italian:

| | |
|---|---|
| Ieri, **sono andata** al cinema. | *Yesterday, I went to the cinema.* |

## 3 *Trapassato prossimo*: the pluperfect tense

### (a) How to form

The pluperfect tense is formed by combining the imperfect of the verb **avere** and the past participle of the appropriate verb:

| | | |
|---|---|---|
| (io) | **avevo** mangiato | *I had eaten* |
| (tu) | **avevi** mangiato | *you had eaten* |
| (lui) | **aveva** mangiato | *he had eaten* |
| (lei) | **aveva** mangiato | *she had eaten* |
| (Lei) | **aveva** mangiato | *you had eaten (polite)* |
| (noi) | **avevamo** mangiato | *we had eaten* |
| (voi) | **avevate** mangiato | *you had eaten* |
| (loro) | **avevano** mangiato | *they had eaten* |

In the case of the verbs that use **essere** (mainly verbs of motion such as **andare, venire**, see unit 11), the imperfect tense of **essere** – not **avere** – is used with the past participle. The past participle then has to agree with the number and gender of the subject:

| (io) | **ero** arrivato/-a | I had arrived |
|---|---|---|
| (tu) | **eri** arrivato/-a | you had arrived |
| (lui) | **era** arrivato/-a | he had arrived |
| (lei) | **era** arrivata | she had arrived |
| (Lei) | **era** arrivato/-a | you had arrived (polite) |
| (noi) | **eravamo** arrivati/-e | we had arrived |
| (voi) | **eravate** arrivati/-e | you had arrived |
| (loro) | **erano** arrivati/-e | they had arrived |

## (b) When to use

The pluperfect tense is used to describe an action or event which takes place *before* another past event or action in the past:

> **Eravamo** appena **arrivati** in Italia quando mio marito si è ammalato.
>
> *We had just arrived in Italy when my husband fell ill.*

It can also be used alone to express an action or event which had (or had not) already taken place:

> Mia moglie non **aveva** mai **visto** Venezia.
>
> *My wife had never seen Venice.*

This tense is often used with one of the following phrases of time:

| appena | as soon as, no sooner (had . . .) than, just |
|---|---|
| mai | never |
| non ancora | not yet |
| già | already |
| prima | earlier, before |
| quando | when |
| dopo che | after |
| siccome | since |
| perché | because |

> Avevo **appena** cominciato i miei studi all' università quando è morto mio padre.
>
> *I had just begun my studies at university when my father died.*

> I miei cugini non avevano **mai** visitato Londra.
>
> *My cousins had never visited London.*

| | |
|---|---|
| **Non** avevamo **ancora** cominciato la riunione quando è andata via la luce. | *We had not yet started the meeting when the light went off.* |
| Mario era **già** stato all'estero molte volte. | *Maro had already been abroad many times.* |
| **Dopo che** tu eri andata via, è venuta Carla con il fidanzato. | *After you had left, Carla came with her boyfriend.* |
| I bambini erano stanchi **perché** avevano fatto un viaggio molto lungo. | *The children were tired because they had had a very long journey.* |

### Trapassato remoto: the past anterior

The past anterior is formed by combining the past historic of the verb **avere** or **essere** (see unit 11) with the past participle. This tense is similar to the pluperfect except that it is used when the main verb is in the past historic and is therefore much less commonly found in everyday use. It is never found alone in a main clause, but is always introduced by the phrases **dopo che**, **appena**, **quando**.

| | |
|---|---|
| **Dopo che** ebbero mangiato, misero a letto i bambini. | *After they had eaten, they put the children to bed.* |
| **Appena** furono tornati a casa, arrivò un amico da Milano. | *They had just got back home when a friend arrived from Milan.* |
| **Quando** ebbero finito di studiare, uscirono. | *When they had finished studying, they went out.* |

## In contesto

### *Life one hundred years ago*

**Cento anni fa, il mondo era molto diverso. Non c'erano tante automobili e tante grandi città. Le case erano molto più semplici.**

*One hundred years ago, the world was very different. There weren't so many cars or so many big towns. The houses were much simpler.*

## My childhood

Quando ero bambina, abitavo al mare. Andavo a scuola tutti i giorni. La sera, leggevo dei libri e, di notte, dormivo.

*When I was a child, I lived by the sea. I went to school every day. In the evening, I read books and, at night, I slept.*

## Why my wife was angry

Andavo a casa lunedì sera quando ho incontrato Marco. Marco andava al bar e così ho deciso di accompagnarlo e prendere qualcosa anch'io. Mia moglie intanto mi aspettava a casa e quando sono tornato a casa con tre ore di ritardo, mi ha fatto la predica.

*I was going home on Monday evening when I met Marco. Marco was going to the bar and so I decided to go with him and have a drink too. Meanwhile my wife was waiting for me at home and when I got home three hours late, she read me the riot act.*

Per l'anniversario del matrimonio, mio marito aveva promesso di portarmi a Parigi. Io non c'ero mai stata. Avevamo già preso i biglietti quando la signora che aveva offerto di prendersi cura dei bambini si è ammalata e così abbiamo dovuto portare anche i bambini. È stata una gita poco romantica!

*For our wedding anniversary my husband had promised to take me to Paris. I had never been there. We had just got the tickets when the lady who had offered to take care of the children fell sick and so we had to take the children too. It was not a very romantic trip.*

---

# In aggiunta

---

## 1 Stare *plus gerund*

In the examples given on page 84 for the **imperfetto** with the **passato prossimo**, the **imperfetto** can be replaced by **stare** plus the gerund. In unit 6, you saw how **stare** was used to express the idea of continuous action in the present; in the same way, **stare** can be used in the imperfect tense (**stavo**) plus the gerund (**parlando**, **mettendo**, **dormendo**) to express the idea of an ongoing action.

> **Stavamo guardando** il telegiornale quando è andata via l'elettricità.
>
> *We were watching the news on TV when the electricity was cut off.*

> Cosa **stavi facendo** lì per terra?
>
> *What were you doing there on the ground?*

## 2 Stare *plus* per

**Stare** can also be used with the preposition **per** to say what you were on the point of doing:

> **Stavo per** uscire quando è arrivato il postino.
>
> *I was about to go out when the postman arrived.*

> **Stavo** proprio **per** telefonarti.
>
> *I was just about to phone you.*

There are a few special (idiomatic) ways in which the **imperfetto** is used in Italian; these are known as 'idiomatic' because they are very much part of the spoken language (idiom). See points 3, 4 and 5.

## 3 To express politeness

> **Voleva**, signora?
>
> *Can I help you Madam? (Lit. What did you want?)*

> **Volevo** vedere qualche maglia.
>
> *I would like to see a few sweaters. (Lit. I wanted to see a few sweaters.)*

## 4 To replace the conditional in the past

Informally, in spoken Italian, the **imperfetto** can be used to replace the past conditional. (See unit 22 for examples of sentences which normally use the past conditional.)

> **Potevi** telefonarmi. (Avresti potuto telefonarmi)
>
> *You could have phoned me.*

> **Dovevi** farmi sapere. (Avresti dovuto farmi sapere.)
>
> *You should have let me know.*

Era meglio se tu gli
**telefonavi** subito.
(Sarebbe stato meglio se tu
gli avessi telefonato subito)

*It would have been better if you
had phoned him straightaway.*

**Se venivi** a casa mia, ti
portavo in giro.
(Se tu fossi venuto a casa mia,
ti avrei portato in giro)

*If you had come to my house, I
would have shown you round.*

## 5 Used with da to express the pluperfect

As you saw in unit 11, **da** can be used with the present tense to express
what one *has* been doing for some time (and is still doing):

Studio l'italiano **da** tre anni.

*I have been studying Italian for
three years (and I am still
studying it).*

In the same way, it can be used with the **imperfetto** to express what
one *had* been doing:

**Imparavo** l'italiano **da** tre
anni quando il direttore mi
ha mandato in Italia.

*I had been studying Italian for
three years when the director
sent me to Italy.*

**Stavamo** a Oxford già **da** un
anno quando abbiamo
comprato questa casa.

*We had been at Oxford for one
year already when we bought
this house.*

Quando Silvia è venuta a casa
mia, non **fumava da** più di
un mese.

*When Silvia came to my house she
hadn't smoked for more than a
month.*

# 13

# – Talking about the future –

**Le funzioni**

In this unit you will learn how to:
Talk about future plans and intentions ● Use the future to express probability

**Le strutture**

The future tense ● The present tense with future meaning ● The future perfect ● The future to express probability

## Nota introduttiva

| | |
|---|---|
| Domani **andrò** al mercato. | *Tomorrow I'll go to the market.* |
| L'anno prossimo **andrà** a Roma. | *Next year he'll go to Rome.* |
| Stasera **andiamo** al cinema. | *Tonight we're going to the cinema.* |
| Fra un anno, **avrete finito** di studiare. | *In a year, you will have finished studying.* |
| Marco e Carla **saranno** già a casa. | *Marco and Carla will be home already.* |

## Analisi della grammatica

### 1 Future tense and present tense to express the future

#### (a) When to use

As in English, the future is used to talk about what you are going to do that evening, tomorrow or in the more distant future. As in English, it is often replaced by the present tense:

| | |
|---|---|
| Domani **andrò a visitare** il museo. | *Tomorrow I'll go and visit the museum.* |
| Domani **vado a visitare** il museo. | *Tomorrow I'm going to visit the museum.* |
| La settimana prossima **andremo** negli Stati Uniti. | *Next week we will go to the USA.* |
| La settimana prossima **andiamo** negli Stati Uniti. | *Next week we're going to the USA.* |

Sometimes the future tense contains the idea of a promise:

| | |
|---|---|
| Te lo **porterò** domani. | *I'll bring you it tomorrow.* |
| Ti **telefonerò** la settimana prossima. | *I'll call you next week.* |

## (b) Form of the future

The future is formed by taking the infinitive of the verb (such as **parlare**), removing the ending **-are**, **-ere**, or **-ire** and adding the future endings, as seen below.

Here are all the forms of the future tense:

### -are verbs

| | | | | | |
|---|---|---|---|---|---|
| (io) | parler**ò** | *I will speak* | (noi) | parler**emo** | *we will speak* |
| (tu) | parler**ai** | *you will speak* | (voi) | parler**ete** | *you will speak* |
| (lui) | parler**à** | *he will speak* | (loro) | parler**anno** | *they will speak* |
| (lei) | parler**à** | *she will speak* | | | |
| (Lei) | parler**à** | *you will speak (polite)* | | | |

### -ere verbs

| | | | | | |
|---|---|---|---|---|---|
| (io) | legger**ò** | *I will read* | (noi) | legger**emo** | *we will read* |
| (tu) | legger**ai** | *you will read* | (voi) | legger**ete** | *you will read* |
| (lui) | legger**à** | *he will read* | (loro) | legger**anno** | *they will read* |
| (lei) | legger**à** | *she will read* | | | |
| (Lei) | legger**à** | *you will read (polite)* | | | |

| **-ire verbs** | | | | | |
|---|---|---|---|---|---|
| (io) | partirò | *I will leave* | (noi) | partiremo | *we will leave* |
| (tu) | partirai | *you will leave* | (voi) | partirete | *you will leave* |
| (lui) | partirà | *he will leave* | (loro) | partiranno | *they will leave* |
| (lei) | partirà | *she will leave* | | | |
| (Lei) | partirà | *you will leave (polite)* | | | |

There are very few verbs whose future tense is irregular; these few include:

(i) Verbs in which the **e** of the future is dropped: **potere (potrò)**, **dovere (dovrò)**, **sapere (saprò)**, **vedere (vedrò)**: **andare (andrò)**.

(ii) Verbs in the which **e** or **i** is dropped, but which then undergo a further change: **volere (vorrò)**; **rimanere (rimarrò)**, **venire (verrò)**, **tenere (terrò)**.

(iii) Those with an already contracted (shortened) infinitive such as **bere** (*to drink*) whose future tense has a double **rr** like the verbs listed above (**berrò**).

(iv) Verbs with a **c** or **ci** or **gi** beginning the last syllable, which undergo spelling changes:

| **Infinitive** | **Future** |
|---|---|
| cominciare | comincerò |
| lasciare | lascerò |
| cercare | cercherò |
| mangiare | mangerò |
| pagare | pagherò |

## 2 Future expressing probability

Often, in English, you say *he'll be in London by now* using a future form to express the present with the meaning of probability. You sometimes use the future, in Italian, in the same way:

| **Sarà a** Londra. | *He must be in London.* |
| **Sarai** stanca. | *You must be tired.* |
| **Avrete** fame. | *You must be hungry.* |

## 3 Future perfect

The future perfect (future in the past) is used when you talk about the future, but in fact you are talking about what you *will have done* by then rather than what you *will do*.

| | |
|---|---|
| Per martedì **avrà finito** il libro. | *He will have finished the book by Tuesday.* |
| La settimana prossima **sarà tornata** in Italia. | *She will have gone back to Italy by next week.* |
| **Saremo morti** di fame. | *We will have died from starvation.* |

## 4 Future perfect expressing probability

Like the future this tense can be used to express probability (*what people must have done by the moment in time at which we are speaking*):

| | |
|---|---|
| Gli **sarà successo** qualcosa. | *Something must have happened to him.* |
| **Avrà lasciato** il numero di telefono, spero. | *She'll have left her phone number, I hope.* |
| **Avrai** già **fatto** le valigie, immagino? | *You must have packed already, I imagine?* |

## 5 Future after quando and se

In English, the future tense is **not** used after **when** or **if**. In Italian, either the future or the future perfect should be used after **quando** and **se** when there is a future in the main part of the sentence:

| | |
|---|---|
| **Quando** arriveremo al mare, i bambini vorranno fare subito un bagno. | *When we arrive at the seaside the children will want to have a swim straightaway.* |
| **Se** lo vedrò, gli dirò qualcosa. | *If I see him, I'll say something to him.* |
| **Quando** arriverete a Napoli, dovrete cercare un albergo. | *When you arrive in Naples, you will have to look for a hotel.* |
| **Quando** avrò trovato la lettera, te la farò vedere. | *When I have found the letter, I'll show you it.* |

In the last example, the future perfect **avrò trovato** can be replaced by one of the following tenses:

Future: Quando **troverò** la lettera, te la farò vedere.
Present: Quando **trovo** la lettera, te la faccio vedere.

---

# In contesto

---

## Conversation between students

| | | |
|---|---|---|
| Franca | **Cosa farai l'anno prossimo, quando sarai laureata?** | *What will you do next year when you will have graduated?* |
| Teresa | **Penso di andare a lavorare all'estero. Se non trovo un posto qui, andrò in Spagna. E tu?** | *I'm thinking of going to work abroad. If I can't find a job here, I'll go to Spain. And you?* |
| Franca | **Mio padre ha un' impresa a Milano. Forse andrò a lavorare con lui. Mi pagherà bene, e non dovrò lavorare troppo.** | *My father has a firm in Milan. Maybe I'll go and work with him. He'll pay me and I won't have to work too hard.* |
| Teresa | **Vedrai che fra dieci anni avrai già fatto i primi miliardi!** | *You'll see, in ten years you'll already have made your first million!* |
| Franca | **E tu fra dieci anni avrai già sposato uno spagnolo e avrai fatto tre figli!** | *And you, in ten years, will have married a Spaniard and had three children!* |

## Next year's holidays

| | | |
|---|---|---|
| Franco | **Dove farete le vacanze l'anno prossimo?** | *Where will you go on holiday next year?* |
| Maria | **Abbiamo intenzione di andare negli USA. Forse andremo a trovare qualche parente. Mio marito non vuole andare in Italia come abbiamo fatto quest' anno.** | *We intend going to the USA. Maybe we'll go and visit some relatives. My husband doesn't want to go to Italy, like we did this year.* |

| Franco | **Sarete stufi di andare in Italia ormai, e sempre in Calabria. Avrete visto tutta la Calabria, no?** | *You must be fed up with going to Italy by now, and always to Calabria. You must have seen all of Calabria, haven't you?* |
| Maria | **Beh, tutta no, ma forse basterà per adesso!** | *Well, not all of it, but perhaps it'll be enough for now!* |

## In aggiunta

### Phrases of time

Here are some of the most common phrases of time used with the future:

| | |
|---|---|
| fra poco | *soon, in a short time* |
| fra alcuni giorni | *in a few days* |
| fra qualche giorno | *in a few days* |
| fra un mese | *in a month* |
| l'anno prossimo | *next year* |
| il mese prossimo | *next month* |
| la settimana prossima | *next week* |
| stasera | *this evening* |
| domani | *tomorrow* |
| dopodomani | *the day after tomorrow* |
| allora | *then, at that time* |

## 2 Intention

To say what you intend doing in the future, you can also use:

| | |
|---|---|
| aver intenzione di | *to intend (doing)* |
| pensare di | *to think of (doing)* |

| L'anno prossimo penso di lavorare in Italia. | *Next year I think I might work in Italy.* |
| L'estate prossima ho intenzione di venire a trovarti. | *Next summer I intend coming to see you. (Lit. to find you even if one knows where the person is!)* |

## 3 Translating the English 'going to'

In English and other languages, you frequently use the verb *to go* to express the future:

> *I'm going to have problems with this luggage.*
> *He's going to get his degree next year.*

In Italian, you can *not* use the verb **andare** (*to go*) in this sense. **Andare** only expresses the idea of physically going to a place to do something. The future tense must be used instead.

# 14

## – Talking about wants and – preferences

**Le funzioni**

In this unit you will learn about:
Expressing a wish or desire ● Expressing a preference

**Le strutture**

Present tense, **voglio**, to express an immediate want ● Conditional **vorrei** to express a wish ● Verb plus infinitive **voglio andare**/other verbs plus infinitive ● Preferire

## Nota introduttiva

**Voglio plus the object**

| | |
|---|---|
| **Voglio dei soldi.** | *I want some money.* |

**Voglio plus the direct object pronouns**

| | |
|---|---|
| **Li voglio** subito. | *I want them straightaway.* |

**Voglio plus the infinitive**

| | |
|---|---|
| **Voglio uscire** stasera. | *I want to go out tonight.* |

**Vorrei (conditional)**

| | |
|---|---|
| **Vorrei** vedere il film di Fellini. | *I should like to see the film by Fellini.* |
| **Vorrei** una bistecca con insalata verde. | *I would like a steak with green salad.* |

**Preferisco plus the infinitive**

**Preferisco viaggiare** in
aereo.

*I prefer travelling by plane.*

**Voglio with che and the subjunctive**

Non **voglio che** mio figlio
**giochi** fuori.

*I don't want my son to play
outside.*

---

## Analisi della grammatica

### 1 Voglio *plus the direct object pronouns*

**Volere** (*to want*) is an irregular verb: it does not follow the pattern of the
-ere verbs (see unit 5). The forms of the present tense are as follows:

| | | | |
|---|---|---|---|
| (io) | **voglio** | (noi) | **vogliamo** |
| (tu) | **vuoi** | (voi) | **volete** |
| (lui/lei) | **vuole** | (loro) | **vogliono** |
| (Lei) | **vuole** | | |

**Volere** can be used with an object or a person:

**Voglio** un panino con salame.  *I want a roll with salami.*
**Vuole** la mamma.  *He wants his mummy.*

You can also use **volere** with the direct object pronouns **lo, la, li, le**
(*it/them*). In unit 4, you saw the direct object pronouns **lo, la, li, le** used
with **ecco, eccolo** (*here it is*), etc. These pronouns can also be used with
**volere, preferire**, etc. to say *I want it* or *I prefer it*, etc.

The direct object pronouns (**lo, la, li, le** and **mi, ti, ci, vi**) go *before* the
verb, but there are exceptions. (See Grammar Section).

Whether we use **lo** or **la, li** or **le** depends on whether the object in
question is masculine or feminine, singular or plural.

Non prendi il caffè, Sandra?  *Aren't you having coffee, Sandra?*
No, non **lo voglio**, grazie.  *No. I don't want it, thanks.*
Vuoi la marmellata?  *Do you want jam?*
Sì, **la voglio** sul pane.  *Yes, I want it on bread.*

| | |
|---|---|
| Volete i fagiolini? | *Do you want beans (long green ones)?* |
| No, non **li vogliamo**. | *No, we don't want them.* |
| Volete le patatine? | *Do you want crisps?* |
| Sì, **le vogliamo**. | *Yes, we want them.* |

## 2 Ne

When the noun has **dei**, **delle**, etc. (*some*) or **un**, **uno**, **una** rather than **i**, **le**, etc. (*the*) the correct pronoun to use is **ne . . .**, etc. which means *of it*, *of them*, etc.

| | |
|---|---|
| Vuole delle melanzane, signora? | *Would you like some aubergines, Madam?* |
| Sì, **ne vorrei** un chilo. | *Yes, I would like a kilo (of them).* |
| Vuoi un biscotto? | *Do you want a biscuit?* |
| Sì, **ne vorrei** due. | *Yes, I would like two (of them).* |

All these pronouns can, of course, be used not just with **volere**, but with *any* verb that takes a direct object:

| | |
|---|---|
| Hai scritto le cartoline? | *Have you written the postcards?* |
| No, **le scriverò** stasera. | *No, I'll write them tonight.* |
| Hai mangiato la pasta con i tartufi? | *Have you eaten pasta served with truffles?* |
| No, non **l'ho** mai **mangiata**. | *No, I've never eaten it.* |

When the pronouns come before a **passato prossimo**, the past participle must change its ending according to whether the pronoun is masculine or feminine, singular or plural. More examples are in the Grammar Section on page 182.

## 3 Vorrei

A less abrupt way of saying or asking what one wants is to use the conditional (**vorrei**, etc.) the forms of which are given, in full, in unit 20:

| | |
|---|---|
| **Vorrei** parlare con il direttore, per favore. | *I would like to speak to the manager, please.* |
| **Vorrebbe** vedere qualche modello, signora? | *Would you like to see a few styles, Madam?* |

| | |
|---|---|
| **Vorremmo** una camera matrimoniale con bagno. | *We would like a double room with bath.* |
| **Desidererebbero** vedere la camera? | *Would you like to see the room?* |

Waiters, hotel personnel, etc. may use the **loro** form to address more than one person rather than using **voi**.

## 4 Voglio *plus the infinitive*

In English, you frequently join verbs such as *I want* or *I begin* to a second verb which is usually expressed in its infinitive form (e.g. *to go*, *to study*) to form sentences such as *I want to go* or *I begin to study*. Sometimes, the second verb is expressed in the gerund or *-ing* form; such as *I stop smoking*. (The gerund is fully explained in unit 6).

In Italian, you usually join verbs by using a combination of verb and infinitive (the **-are/-ere/-ire** form); sometimes these are joined by the preposition **a**, sometimes they are joined by **di** and sometimes they need no preposition at all, as in the case of **voglio**:

| | |
|---|---|
| **Voglio diventare** ricca e famosa. | *I want to become rich and famous.* |
| **Desidero iscrivermi** al corso. | *I want to enrol for the course.* |
| **Preferisco prendere** il treno. | *I prefer to take the train.* |

### (a) Examples of verbs joined with 'a'

| | |
|---|---|
| Comincio **a** capire. | *I begin to understand.* |
| Imparo **ad** andare in windsurf. | *I'm learning to windsurf.* |

### (b) Examples of verbs joined with 'di'

| | |
|---|---|
| Smetto **di** fumare. | *I stop smoking.* |
| Finisco **di** lavorare alle cinque. | *I stop working at 5pm.* |

A list of verbs and the prepositions that follow them is found in the Grammar Section on pages 204–6.

### (c) Verb with 'che' and the subjunctive

When there are two people involved, for example when you are ordering or wishing someone else to do something, (I want him to come), you have to use a different construction from the one shown above. Use **volere** with **che** and a special verb form known as the subjunctive.

| | |
|---|---|
| **Voglio che** Franco **venga**. | *I want Franco to come.* |
| **Vuole che** io **paghi**. | *He wants me to pay.* |

For a fuller explanation of this construction after **volere** see unit 20.

## 5 Preferire

**Preferire** (*to prefer*) can be used with an object or person:

| | |
|---|---|
| Chi preferisci dei due? | *Who do you prefer of the two?* |
| **Preferisco Nino**. | *I prefer Nino.* |
| | |
| Preferisci la birra o il vino? | *Do you prefer beer or wine?* |
| **Preferisco il vino**. | *I prefer wine.* |

When **preferire** is used with *two* different objects or persons, the English *to* is translated by **a**:

| | |
|---|---|
| Preferisco il caffè **al** tè. | *I prefer coffee to tea.* |
| Preferisco Londra **a** Roma. | *I prefer London to Rome.* |

Like **volere** or **desiderare**, the verb **preferire** can be used with a direct object or direct object pronoun:

| | |
|---|---|
| Come **lo preferisci**? | *How do you prefer it?* |
| **Lo preferisco** con latte. | *I prefer it with milk.* |

**Preferire** can also be used with a verb:

| | |
|---|---|
| **Preferisci andare** al cinema o pattinare? | *Do you prefer going to the cinema or ice skating?* |
| **Preferisco pattinare**. | *I prefer skating.* |

---

# In contesto

---

### Have a coffee

| | | |
|---|---|---|
| Maria | **Vuoi un caffè, Sandra?** | *Do you want a coffee, Sandra?* |
| Sandra | **No, grazie non lo prendo mai dopo cena. Non avresti mica un po' di succo di frutta, per caso?** | *No, thanks, I never have it after supper. You wouldn't have a little bit of fruit juice, by any chance?* |

| | | |
|---|---|---|
| Maria | **Ne ho un po' in frigo – lo vuoi? Aspetta, vado a a prenderlo.** | *I've got a little bit in the fridge – do you want it? Wait, I'll go and get it.* |
| Sandra | **Grazie!** | *Thanks!* |

## How would you like it?

| | | |
|---|---|---|
| Cameriere | **Desidera?** | *What would you like?* |
| Cliente | **Un bicchiere di vino, per favore.** | *A glass of wine, please.* |
| Cameriere | **Come lo vuole – rosso o bianco?** | *How would you like it – red or white?* |
| Cliente | **Bianco.** | *White.* |
| Cameriere | **Lo preferisce secco o dolce?** | *Do you prefer it dry or sweet?* |
| Cliente | **Secco.** | *Dry.* |
| Cameriere | **Lo prende fresco o a temperatura ambiente?** | *Will you have it chilled or at room temperature?* |
| Cliente | **Basta! Preferisco prendere un caffè.** | *That's enough! I prefer a coffee.* |
| Cameriere | **Espresso o cappuccino?** | *Espresso or cappuccino?* |

---

# In aggiunta

---

## 1 Volere: *to want*

**Volere** in the perfect tense (**passato prossimo**) normally takes **avere**; but if the verb that follows is a verb that takes **essere** in the perfect tense (**andare**, etc) then **volere** can also form the **passato prossimo** with **essere**; (**avere** is equally acceptable nowadays).

> **Ho** voluto vedere la mostra.    *I wanted to see the exhibition.*
> **Sono** voluto andare a letto presto.    *I wanted to go to bed early.*

*or*

> **Ho** voluto andare a letto presto.

## 2 Ci vuole: *it takes*

**Ci vuole** is a phrase that means *it takes* (referring to time); the plural form – i.e. for more than one hour – is **ci vogliono**:

| | |
|---|---|
| Da Londra a Oxford **ci vuole un'** ora. | *From London to Oxford it takes one hour.* |
| Da Londra a Edimburgo **ci vogliono sei** ora in treno. | *From London to Edinburgh it takes six hours by train.* |

In the **passato prossimo**, this verb must take **essere**:

| | |
|---|---|
| Da Roma a Reggio Calabria **ci sono volute** sette ore. | *From Rome to Reggio Calabria it took seven hours.* |

## 3 Voler bene a: *to love*

**Voler bene a** is an expression meaning *to love*: **bene** is an adverb (i.e. it describes the verb) and does not change.

| | |
|---|---|
| A chi **vuoi bene**? | *Who do you love?* |
| **Voglio bene al** mio cane. | *I love my dog.* |

## 4 Tenses of volere

### Imperfect/*passato prossimo*

There tends to be a difference of meaning between these two tenses: **volevo** means *I wanted to* (but I couldn't) and **ho voluto** means *I wanted to* (and I did):

| | |
|---|---|
| **Volevo** andare in banca, ma era chiusa. | *I wanted to go to the bank, but it was shut.* |
| **Ho voluto** andare in banca per cambiare soldi. | *I wanted to go to the bank to change money (and I did).* |

### Conditional

While the present conditional **vorrei** means *I would like*, the past conditional **avrei voluto** means *I would have liked*. There are two ways of translating the same sentence in English:

| | |
|---|---|
| **Avrei voluto** vedere quel film. | *I would have liked to see that film.* *I would like to have seen that film.* |

# 15

# Describing processes and procedures

**Le funzioni**

In this unit you will learn to:
Say how something is done • Say how something ought to be done

**Le strutture**

The passive using **essere** and the past participle (**è fatto**) • The passive using **venire** (**viene fatto**) • The passive using **andare** (**va fatto**) • The passive using **si passivante**

---

## Nota introduttiva

---

La cena **è servita**.

*Dinner is served.*

La cena **viene servita** alle otto.

*Dinner is served at 8 o'clock.*

La cena **va servita** alle otto.

*Dinner should be served at 8 o'clock.*

**Si** serve la cena alle otto.

*Dinner is served (one serves dinner) at 8 o'clock.*

---

## Analisi della grammatica

---

## 1 Active and passive verbs

In a normal sentence, the subject of the sentence is the person or thing carrying out the action. The verb is therefore called an *active* verb. The *passive* means that the person or thing that is the subject of the sentence is not the *doer*, but is having something *done* to him or it. The verb is then described as *passive*.

## 2  Passive with essere

To form the passive use the verb **essere** (*to be*) and the past participle e.g. **parlato, bevuto, capito** (*eaten, drunk, understood*). The endings of the past participle have to change according to whether the subject (the person or thing having the action done to them) is masculine or feminine, singular or plural. (See unit 11 for the forms of the past participle.) Here are some examples of passive sentences with **essere**:

| | |
|---|---|
| I vestiti Benetton **sono venduti** in tutta l'Italia. | *Benetton clothes are sold thoughout Italy.* |
| La bistecca **è cotta** ai ferri. | *The steak is cooked on the grill.* |

## 3  Passive with venire

When the action is carried out regularly, **venire** is often used instead of **essere**:

| | |
|---|---|
| In Italia gli spaghetti **vengono mangiati** spesso. | *In Italy, spaghetti are eaten often. (See note on page 113.)* |
| Il vino **viene bevuto** a tutti i pasti. | *Wine is drunk at all meals.* |

## 4  Passive with andare

When something *ought to be done*, or *must be done*, **andare** should be used instead of **essere**:

| | |
|---|---|
| Gli spaghetti **vanno cotti** al dente. | *Spaghetti should be cooked 'al dente' (not soggy).* |
| Il vino bianco **va servito** fresco. | *White wine should be served cool.* |

## 5  Si passivante

Lastly, you can make the verb passive by adding the **si passivante** (Lit. the **si** that makes the verb passive!) to the 3rd person singular or plural (the *he*, *she*, *they* form) of the verb.

If the person or object which is having the action done to it (or him, her or them) is singular, the verb will be *singular*:

In Inghilterra, **si legge** il Times.   *In England, one reads the Times.*

A Milano, **si mangia** il risotto alla milanese.   *In Milan, one eats risotto milanese.*

If there is more than one person or object involved, the verb must be *plural*:

In Inghilterra, **si leggono** molti libri.   *In England, one reads lots of books (lots of books are read).*

D'estate, **si noleggiano** le biciclette da montagna.   *In summer, mountain bikes are hired out.*

D'inverno, **si noleggiano** gli sci.   *In winter, skis are rented out.*

## 6  Other tenses

Any tense or mood which can normally be used with an active verb can also be used with a passive one:

### Imperfetto

In quei giorni il burro **veniva fatto** in casa.   *In those days butter **was made** at home.*

### Futuro

L'uva non **verrà raccolta** prima di ottobre.   *The grapes **will not be picked** until October.*

### Condizionale

Questo vino **andrebbe servito** fresco.   *This wine **should be served** chilled.*

### Passato prossimo

Non **è stato fatto** niente.   *Nothing **has been done**.*

### Trapassato

La camera non **era stata** ancora **preparata**.   *The room **had not been prepared** yet.*

The past participle changes according to whether the subject is masculine or feminine, singular or plural. In the last two tenses, the past participle of **essere (stato)** must change as well.

---
## In contesto
---

### How to serve pasta

In Italia, si mangia molta pasta. La pasta viene mangiata all'ora di pranzo, soprattutto al centro e al sud del paese. Al nord, invece, si mangiano più spesso il riso e la polenta. La pasta è servita con sugo di pomodoro o di carne. Va servita al dente, e quindi non troppo cotta.

A Bologna, le tagliatelle sono spesso servite con prosciutto e panna mentre, in Sicilia, gli spaghetti vengono serviti con le melanzane.

**English translation**

In Italy, lots of pasta is eaten. Pasta is eaten at lunchtime, especially in the centre and the south of the country. In the north, on the other hand, rice and polenta are more often eaten. Pasta is served with tomato or meat sauce. It should be served 'al dente' and therefore not over-cooked.

In Bologna, tagliatelle is often served with ham and cream whereas in Sicily the spaghetti comes served with aubergine.

### Quotes from famous personalities (Oggi, agosto 1991)

| | |
|---|---|
| Intervistatrice | **Sei mai stata lasciata? E tu hai mai lasciato?** |
| Diva | **Sì, sono stata lasciata e ho lasciato. Lasciare è doloroso, essere lasciati dolorosissimo.** |

**English translation**

| | |
|---|---|
| Interviewer | *Have you ever been left? And have you ever left (someone)?* |
| Star | *Yes, I've been left and I've left (someone). Leaving (someone) is painful, being left is very painful.* |

## To cook or not to cook? Advice from a dietician on vegetables

Domanda    Mi è stato detto che tutti i benefici effetti delle verdure si disperdono con la cottura. È vero?

Risposta    La perdita delle vitamine nelle verdure, quando si cuociono, dipende da come vengono cotte, e se vengono cotte a vapore o se vengono cotte in acqua. Quindi un consiglio: le verdure non vanno cotte molto a lungo, e non va usata molta acqua.

**English translation**

Question    *I've been told that all the beneficial effects of vegetables are lost when they are cooked. Is this true?*

Answer    *The loss of vitamins in vegetables, when they are cooked, depends how they are cooked, whether they are steamed or cooked in water. So here is some advice: green vegetables should not be cooked for very long, and very little water should be used.*

## Holiday 'musts' when staying in Versilia (by Contessa Ripa di Meana)

Si ascolteranno concerti come quello di Gianni Morandi . . . al tramonto si visitano gli studi degli scultori . . . il mercoledì si va al mercato dove le più belle tovaglie, lenzuola, piatti e bicchieri attendono solo di essere comprati. Tra i colori preferiti, va incluso il bianco: camicie bianche, scarpe da tennis bianche, . . . etc. L'unica concessione verrà riservata al kaki coloniale.

**English translation**

*One will listen to concerts like Gianni Morandi's . . . at sunset one visits sculptors' studios . . . On Wednesdays, one goes to the market where the most beautiful tablecloths, sheets, plates and glasses are just waiting to be bought. Among the favourite colours, white must be included: white shirts, white tennis shoes, . . . etc. A concession can be made only for colonial khaki.*

| La polenta | *polenta (dish made out of maize)* |
| Al dente | *cooked with some 'bite' left in it!* |
| Troppo cotto/a | *over-cooked (soggy)* |
| Scotto/a | *very over-cooked! (very soggy)* |

---

# In aggiunta

## 1  Si passivante *and impersonal* si

A **si** construction such as **si fa**, as well as meaning *It is done*, can also be impersonal and express the English *one* i.e. **si fa** (*one does*).

Although the **si** passivante (the **si** which turns the verb into a passive) is *not* exactly the same as the impersonal **si** (*one*), the meaning of the sentence can be very similar.

However, the impersonal **si** is *only* used with a singular verb:

In Italia, **si pranza** all'una.   *In Italy, one dines at 1.00pm*
Non **si sa** mai.   *One never knows.*

Oddly, the adjective used with impersonal **si** is always plural: La sera **si** è stanchi. *In the evening one is tired.*

The **si** passivante, used to express the passive, can be used with singular or plural:

**Si** noleggiano biciclette.   *There are bikes for hire.*
**Si** affitta una casa.   *There is a house for rent.*

## 2  Si passivante *used to give instructions*

The **si** construction can be used to explain to someone how to do something, in which case it can be translated, in English, as *one*:

Prima, **si** taglia la cipolla, **si**   *First, one cuts the onion, one puts*
mette nel tegame, poi **si**   *it in the pan, then one adds the*
aggiungono i pomodori   *tomatoes cut into small pieces,*
tagliati a pezzetti piccoli e **si**   *and one leaves them to cook for*
lasciano cuocere per   *half an hour.*
mezz'ora.

## 3 Ci si: *one, himself, etc.*

When the impersonal **si** (*one*) meets the reflexive **si** (*himself, herself, itself*) there are problems! In theory, by combining **si** as in **si parla** (*one speaks*) with **si**, as in **si alza** (*he gets up*), you should get: **si si alza**. But to avoid that, you say: **ci si alza**.

Here are some other examples:

| | |
|---|---|
| **Ci si** veste | *one gets dressed* |
| **Ci si** vede alle cinque | *one sees one another (we see one another, we meet) at 5pm* |

## 4 Rimanere, rimasta: *to remain, was*

When emotions are involved, the verb **rimanere** (Lit. *to remain*) is used, with the past participle *or* an adjective:

| | |
|---|---|
| Sono **rimasta sorpresa**. | *I was surprised.* |
| È **rimasta delusa**. | *She was disappointed.* |
| La casa è **rimasta distrutta**. | *The house was destroyed.* |

Other examples of adjectives or past participles used with **rimanere** are:

| | | | |
|---|---|---|---|
| **offeso** | *hurt, offended* | **scandalizzato** | *shocked* |
| **contento** | *happy* | | |

The adverb **male** (hurt badly) is also used with **rimanere**, as follows:

Siamo rimasti molto **male**.    *We were very hurt (not literally).*

Italians occasionally use the word **scioccato** for *shocked*, even though this is borrowed from the English.

## 5 Indirect objects and the passive

Turning 'active' sentences into the passive, as we do in English, does not always work in Italian:

| | | |
|---|---|---|
| *He gives the book.* | → | *He is given the book. (The book is given to him.)* |
| *She sends the flowers.* | → | *She is sent the flowers. (The flowers are sent to her.)* |

It is not possible to translate the first of each pair of examples literally into Italian. The person being given the book (or the flowers) is an *indirect object* (because one gives something *to* someone) and so in Italian could not be turned round and used as the subject of the sentence. Only *direct objects* can be turned into the passive in Italian.

This is what happens if we take the examples above and try to turn them into the passive:

| | |
|---|---|
| *He gives the book.* | **(Lui) dà il libro.** |
| *He is given the book.* | Can *not* be translated literally. |
| *The book is given to him.* | **Il libro gli viene dato**: *or* |
| | **Gli si dà il libro.** |
| | |
| *She sends flowers.* | **(Lei) manda i fiori.** |
| *She is sent flowers.* | Can *not* be translated literally. |
| *Flowers are sent to her.* | **I fiori le vengono mandati**: *or* |
| | **Le si mandano i fiori.** |

# 16

## Talking about likes and dislikes

**Le funzioni**

In this unit you will learn how to:
Express your likes and dislikes ● Talk about someone else's likes and dislikes ● Ask someone about their likes and dislikes

**Le strutture**

The verb **piacere** ● The unstressed indirect object pronouns **mi, ti, gli,** etc. ● The stressed (disjunctive) pronouns **me, te, lui,** etc.

### Nota introduttiva

To say that you like something in Italian, you use **piacere** (*to please*) with the indirect pronouns **mi, ti, gli,** (*to me, to you, to him,* etc) or their emphatic forms (**a me, a te, a lui,** etc.).

When you use **piacere** you are saying *something is pleasing to me.* This *something* can be either a verb: **eating is pleasing to me** (*I like eating*) or a noun: *ice-cream is pleasing to me* (*I like ice-cream*). Look at these examples of the verb **piacere**:

**Saying whether you like or dislike something**

**Verb:**

| | |
|---|---|
| **Mi piace** guardare la televisione. | *I like watching the TV.* |
| or (more emphatic) | |
| **A me piace** ballare. | *I really like dancing.* |

**Noun:**

| | |
|---|---|
| **Mi piacciono** i bastoncini di di pesce. | *I like fish fingers.* |
| or (more emphatic form) | |
| **A me** non **piace** *il pesce*. | *I really don't like fish.* |

## Saying whether others like or dislike something

**Verb:**

| | |
|---|---|
| **A mia** figlia **piace** visitare i musei. | *My daughter likes visiting museums.* |
| **Le piace** visitare i musei. | *She likes visiting museums.* |
| or (more emphatic form) | |
| **A lei piace** visitare i musei. | *She really likes visiting museums.* |

**Noun:**

| | |
|---|---|
| Non **gli piace** la pizza. | *He doesn't like pizza.* |
| or (more emphatic form) | |
| **A lui piacciono** molto gli spaghetti. | *He likes spaghetti a lot.* |

## Asking people about their likes and dislikes

**Verb:**

| | |
|---|---|
| **Le piace** cucinare? | *Do you like cooking?* |
| **Vi piace** studiare la lingua italiana? | *Do you like studying Italian?* |

**Noun:**

| | |
|---|---|
| **Ti piace** quel ragazzo? | *Do you like that boy?* |
| **Vi piacciono** i cannelloni? | *Do you like cannelloni?* |

**Cannelloni** and **spaghetti** are plural; so are **lasagne**, **tagliatelle**, **rigatoni**, **maccheroni**: they are all forms of pasta.

## Analisi della grammatica

### 1 Piacere: to please

**Piacere** is a verb which is most commonly used in the 3rd person singular or plural (**piace** or **piacciono**). It is used with the Italian indirect object pronouns **mi**, **ti**, **gli**, etc. (*to me, to you, to him*, etc.) explained below. The indirect pronoun is usually placed *before* the verb, and always next to it, which is why these pronouns are often called *conjunctive* ('joining') pronouns. The literal meaning of **mi piace** in English is *it is pleasing to me*.

**(a)** If what is liked is a verb, i.e. doing something, then use **piace** followed by the infinitive of the verb (the **-are**, **-ere**, **-ire** part):

Mi **piace fare** delle                 *I like going for walks.*
passeggiate.

**(b)** If the person or object liked is singular, use **piace**:

Ti **piace** questa maglia?         *Do you like this sweater?*
or (Questa maglia ti **piace**?)

**(c)** If the person or object liked is plural, use **piacciono**:

Le **piacciono** queste scarpe.    *She likes these shoes.*
or (Queste scarpe le **piacciono**.)

## 2   Other tenses with piacere

**Piacere** has a full range of tenses, for example:

Future:
Vi pia**cerà** molto Firenze.      *You **will** really like Florence.*

Conditional:
Mi pia**cerebbe** andare a         *I **would** like to go skiing.*
sciare.

Imperfect:
Gli pia**ceva** tanto la cucina    *He really **used to** like Italian cooking.*
italiana.

**Passato prossimo**:
Le è pia**ciuta** la gita al       ***Did** you like the trip to the lake?*
lago?

**Piacere** is used with **essere** in the **passato prossimo**, and not with **avere**.

## 3 Mi, ti, ci, vi: *indirect object pronouns*

You have already met the direct object pronouns **mi**, **ti**, **lo**, **la**, (*me, you, him, her*) etc. in unit 4. Luckily many of the indirect object pronouns (**mi, ti, ci, vi**) are the same as the direct object pronouns. **Mi, ti, ci** and **vi**, like **mi, ti, lo, la**, normally come before the verb.

| **Singular** | | **Plural** | |
|---|---|---|---|
| **mi** | *to me* | **ci** | *to us* |
| **ti** | *to you* | **vi** | *to you* |
| **gli** | *to him* | **gli** | *to them\** |
| **le** | *to her* | | |
| **Le** | *to you (polite)* | | |

\* An older form of **gli** is **loro**. Nowadays this is less common, although you may see it in written Italian. Unlike the other pronouns, **loro** has to come after the verb:

> Abbiamo mandato **loro** un invito.  *We sent them an invitation.*

These indirect pronouns (**mi, ti, ci** and **vi**) are used not only with **piacere**, but with any verb where English might use the preposition *to* or *for* and with many other verbs. See the Grammar Section on page 179.

There are exceptions to the rule that pronouns always come *before* the verb, and these are explained in the Grammar Section.

## 4 *Stressed pronouns:* a me, a te

Often tastes differ and to express this difference, you can use an emphatic 'stressed' form of pronoun, used with the preposition **a**, instead of the normal indirect object pronouns you saw above; these pronouns are also known as disjunctive (non-joining) pronouns because they are separate from the verb. Here are some examples of how the normal unstressed form can be replaced by the emphatic form:

**(a) Unstressed indirect object pronoun**

> **Mi** piace il caldo.    *I like the heat.*
> **Ti** piace?    *Do you like it?*

## (b) Stressed (emphatic) form

| | |
|---|---|
| **A me** piace il caldo. | I *like the heat.* |
| **A te** piace? | *Do* **you** *like it?* |

Here are all the forms of the stressed pronouns:

| Singular | | Plural | |
|---|---|---|---|
| **a me** | *to me* | **a noi** | *to us* |
| **a te** | *to you* | **a voi** | *to you* |
| **a lui** | *to him* | **a loro** | *to them* |
| **a lei** | *to her* | | |
| **a Lei** | *to you (polite)* | | |

This form of pronoun is also found used:

(i) after a preposition

Sono uscita con **lui**.    I *went out with him.*

(ii) as an emphatic form of the direct object pronoun:

Vuole **me** non **te**.    *He wants* **me** *not* **you**.

For further information, see the Grammar Section on page 179.

--- **In contesto** ---

## Going to the cinema

| Anna | **Ti piace andare al cinema?** | *Do you like going to the cinema?* |
|---|---|---|
| Mara | **Sì, mi piace molto. E a te?** | *Yes. I like it a lot. And* **you***?* |
| Anna | **Sì, anche a me piace.** | *Yes, I like it too.* |
| Mara | **Che film ti piacciono?** | *What films do you like?* |
| Anna | **A me piacciono i film romantici ma a mio marito non piacciono i film di questo genere.** | I *like romantic films but my husband doesn't like films of this kind.* |
| Mara | **E a lui che tipi di film piacciono?** | *What kinds of film does* **he** *like?* |
| Anna | **Nessuno.** | *None.* |

## Making polite conversation

| Turista | Che bella casa! Quanto mi piacciono le case italiane! | *What a lovely house! How I love Italian houses!* |
|---|---|---|
| Signora | Le piace il nostro paese? | *Do you like our country?* |
| Turista | Mi piace tanto. Mi piacerebbe stare qui per sempre. | *I like it so much. I would like to stay here for ever.* |
| Signora | Cosa Le piace in particolare? | *What do you particularly like?* |
| Turista | Mi piace la cucina, mi piace il modo di vivere, e mi piacciono anche gli italiani! | *I like the food, I like the way of life, and I like the Italians, too!* |
| Signora | C'è qualcosa che non Le piace? | *Is there anything you don't like?* |
| Turista | Non mi piacciono i verbi! | *I don't like the verbs!* |

## Conversation with a teenager

| Ragazzo | Mamma, papà, vi piace questo disco? | *Mum, dad, do you like this record?* |
|---|---|---|
| Mamma, papà | Non molto, a dire la verità. A noi piace di più la musica classica. | *Not much, to be honest. We prefer classical music.* |
| Ragazzo | A voi piacciono sempre le cose vecchie . . . forse perché anche voi siete vecchi! | *You always prefer old things . . . maybe because you're old, too!* |
| Mamma, papà | Come si fa a spiegargli che a volte le cose vecchie sono le migliori! | *How can one explain to him that sometimes the old things are the best!* |

Two other uses of the disjunctive pronouns are shown here:

### (a) With 'anche'

With **anche** (*also*) you have to use the stressed form of the indirect object pronouns:

| | |
|---|---|
| anche **a me** | *(to) me, too* |
| anche **a lui** | *(to) him, too* |

anche **a me** piace la pizza.  *I like pizza, too. (Lit. Pizza pleases to me too.)*

And, also with **neanche** (*not even, neither*):

| | |
|---|---|
| neanche **a me** | *not to me either, me neither* |
| neanche **a lui** | *not to him either, him neither* |

Neanche **a lui** piacciono i funghi.  *He doesn't like mushrooms either. (Lit. Neither does he like mushrooms.)*

Don't forget that if you put **neanche** after the verb, you will have to use **non** as well:

**Non** piace **neanche** a me lavare i piatti.  *I don't like washing dishes either.*

### (b) Without a verb

The stressed pronouns, with or without **anche**, **neanche**, can be used on their own, with no verb. This avoids repeating the verb.

A me piace il mare. E **a te**?  *I like the seaside. And you?*
Sì. Anche **a me**.  *Yes. Me too.*

## In aggiunta

## 1  Gradire: *another verb 'to like'*

Another way of saying what one likes is **gradire**:

**Gradisci** una bibita fresca?  *Would you like a cold drink?*
**Gradisce** una granita di caffè?  *Would you like a coffee granita?\**

\***Una granita** is a coffee ice, made with frozen sweet coffee.

## 2  Piacere: *1st and 2nd persons*

You *can* use the first and second persons (*I, you*) with **piacere** when it tends to have the meaning of *to fancy someone*:

| | |
|---|---|
| **Piaci** molto a Giancarlo. | *Giancarlo really likes/fancies you.* |
| | *(Lit. You really please him.)* |
| Dimmi, ti **piaccio** veramente? | *Tell me, do you really like me?* |
| | *(Lit. Do I really please you?)* |

But it is more common to express the idea of liking a person with **volere bene a** (*to love, like a lot*) or **amare** (*to love*):

| | |
|---|---|
| **Vuoi bene a** Franco? | *Do you love Franco?* |
| Gli **vuoi bene**? | *Do you love him?* |
| **Amo** soltanto mio marito. | *I only love my husband.* |
| **Amo** l'Italia. | *I love Italy.* |

# 17

## Asking and giving an opinion

---

**Le funzioni**

In this unit you will learn about:
Giving an opinion ● Asking someone else's opinion

**Le strutture**

**Sembrare, parere** and **pensare, credere** ● With **che** plus the subjunctive ● With **di** plus the infinitive ● Phrases used to express opinion

---

## Nota introduttiva

There are many ways of giving an opinion in Italian. One is to use the indirect object pronouns **mi**, **ti**, **gli** (*to me, to you, to him*, etc. see unit 16) with the verbs **sembrare** or **parere** (*to seem*). Another way is to use the verbs **pensare** or **credere** (*to think*). When you use these verbs you often need to use a special verb form known as the *subjunctive*, which is explained below.

Study these examples and their English translation before going on:

*Sembrare* **to seem, used personally (I, you, he, she, etc.):**

| | |
|---|---|
| Come **ti sembra** questa proposta? | *What do you think of this proposal? (Lit. How does this proposal seem to you?)* |
| Questa ragazzo non **mi sembra** molto intelligente. | *This boy doesn't seem very bright to me.* |

**Sembrare, parere, pensare, credere used impersonally (it seems) followed by che plus subjunctive:**

| | |
|---|---|
| Mi pare **che sia** fattibile. | *It seems to me that it is feasible.* |
| Credo **che sia** una buona idea. | *I think it is a good idea.* |
| Luigi pensa **che** l'albergo **sia** caro. | *Luigi thinks the hotel is dear.* |

**Sembrare, parere, pensare, credere used impersonally (it seems) followed by di plus the infinitive:**

| | |
|---|---|
| Mi sembra **di aver** già visto questo programma. | *I think I have seen this programme already.* |
| Mi pare **di conoscere** questo signore. | *I think I know this gentleman.* |
| Penso **di essere** in ritardo. | *I think I am late.* |
| Crede di aver sbagliato. | *He thinks he has made a mistake.* |

## ——— Analisi della grammatica ———

## 1 The subjunctive

The subjunctive is a form of the verb used in certain circumstances. The subjunctive is almost extinct in English but like the dinosaur a few remnants of it can be found. For example: *I wish he **were** here* (where **were** replaces the usual verb form **was**). In Italian, it is far from extinct. In fact it is difficult to express a feeling or opinion, doubt or uncertainty, without using it. Units 17, 18, 19 and 20 illustrate different situations in which the subjunctive is used.

It is rarely found on its own (except for expressing an order, see unit 9), but is almost always used in a subordinate clause, i.e. a clause or part of a sentence which depends on the first or main part of the sentence. Usually the second half of the sentence (the subordinate clause) is introduced by **che**, or another joining word. Look at these examples and the English translation:

**Normal (indicative) form of verb**

| | |
|---|---|
| Donatella è simpatica. | *Donatella is nice.* |

**Subjunctive form of verb**

Non penso **che** Donatella **sia** simpatica.    *I don't think Donatella is nice.*

**Normal (indicative) form of verb**

Marco è antipatico.    *Marco is unpleasant.*

**Subjunctive form of verb**

Mi pare **che** Marco **sia** antipatico.    *I think Marco is unpleasant.*

The forms of the present tense of the subjunctive are as follows:

| **Parlare**, *to speak* | | | |
|---|---|---|---|
| Che | (io) | **parli** | *that I may speak* |
| | (tu) | **parli** | *that you may speak* |
| | (lui) | **parli** | *that he may speak* |
| | (lei) | **parli** | *that she may speak* |
| | (Lei) | **parli** | *that you (polite) may speak* |
| | (noi) | **parliamo** | *that we may speak* |
| | (voi) | **parliate** | *that you may speak* |
| | (loro) | **parlino** | *that they may speak* |

| **Mettere**, *to put* | | | |
|---|---|---|---|
| Che | (io) | **metta** | *that I may put* |
| | (tu) | **metta** | *that you may put* |
| | (lui) | **metta** | *that he may put* |
| | (lei) | **metta** | *that she may put* |
| | (Lei) | **metta** | *that you (polite) may put* |
| | (noi) | **mettiamo** | *that we may put* |
| | (voi) | **mettiate** | *that you may put* |
| | (loro) | **mettano** | *that they may put* |

| **Partire**, *to leave* | | | |
|---|---|---|---|
| Che | (io) | **parta** | *that I may leave* |
| | (tu) | **parta** | *that you may leave* |
| | (lui) | **parta** | *that he may leave* |
| | (lei) | **parta** | *that she may leave* |
| | (Lei) | **parta** | *that you (polite) may leave* |
| | (noi) | **partiamo** | *that we may leave* |
| | (voi) | **partiate** | *that you may leave* |
| | (loro) | **partano** | *that they may leave* |

| Capire, *to understand* | | | |
|---|---|---|---|
| Che | (io) | **capisca** | *that I understand* |
| | (tu) | **capisca** | *that you may understand* |
| | (lui) | **capisca** | *that he may understand* |
| | (lei) | **capisca** | *that she may understand* |
| | (Lei) | **capisca** | *that you (polite) may understand* |
| | (noi) | **capiamo** | *that we may understand* |
| | (voi) | **capiate** | *that you may understand* |
| | (loro) | **capiscano** | *that they may understand* |

The other uses of the subjunctive are covered in units 18, 19 and 20.

## 2 Irregular verbs and the subjunctive

There are several verbs for which the form of the subjunctive is slightly different from what you might expect. These are listed on page 196. Sometimes the 1st, 2nd and 3rd person singular (**io, tu, lui/lei**) and the 3rd person plural (**loro**) are irregular; while the 1st and 2nd person plural (**noi, voi**) are regular.

The most common are the following:

| | | | | | |
|---|---|---|---|---|---|
| **andare** | *to go* | che io | **vada** | che noi | **andiamo** |
| **essere** | *to be* | che io | **sia** | che noi | **siamo** |
| **avere** | *to have* | che io | **abbia** | che noi | **abbiamo** |
| **fare** | *to do* | che io | **faccia** | che noi | **facciamo** |
| **dire** | *to say* | che io | **dica** | che noi | **diciamo** |
| **dare** | *to give* | che io | **dia** | che noi | **diamo** |
| **stare** | *to be* | che io | **stia** | che noi | **stiamo** |
| **venire** | *to come* | che io | **venga** | che noi | **veniamo** |
| **dovere** | *to have to* | che io | **debba** | che noi | **dobbiamo** |
| **volere** | *to want to* | che io | **voglia** | che noi | **vogliamo** |
| **potere** | *to be able to* | che io | **possa** | che noi | **possiamo** |

## 3 Sembrare, parere: to seem, to appear

**(a) Used personally:** *I, you, he seems, etc.*

**Sembrare** can be used *personally*, i.e. with a subject other than *it* as in the examples below:

Come **ti sembra** il corso?      *How does the course seem to you?*
Mi sembra ben organizzato.      *It seems well-organised to me.*

| | |
|---|---|
| **Mi sembri** stanca. | *You seem tired to me.* |
| Sì. Non ho dormito ieri sera. | *Yes. I didn't sleep last night.* |

Italians use **come** (*how*) where the English would sometimes say *What (is it) like?*.

## (b) Used impersonally (*it seems*)

To express an opinion, Italian often uses the verb **sembrare** or the verb **parere** (*to seem, to appear*). They are often used impersonally (*it seems*), in their 3rd person forms **sembra, pare** with the indirect pronouns **mi, ti, gli** (*to me, to you, to him*, etc.):

| | |
|---|---|
| **Ti sembra** che **sia** una buona idea? | *Does it seem that it is a good idea to you?* |
| Non **mi pare** che **sia** molto utile. | *It doesn't seem to me that it's very useful.* |

**Sembrare** and **parere** can be used in two ways:

### (i) Same subject in both parts of the sentence: follow by 'di' plus infinitive

If the subjects are the same, i.e. if the person expressing an opinion in the first part of the sentence is the same person carrying out the action in the second part of the sentence, the two parts of the sentence can be linked with **di**; the second verb will be in the infinitive form:

| | |
|---|---|
| Mi sembra **di sognare**. | I *think* I*'m dreaming.* |
| Gli sembra **di sbagliare**. | He *thinks* he *is making a mistake.* |

The infinitive can also be in the past; this is done by combining **avere** or **essere** with the past participle:

| | |
|---|---|
| Mi sembra di **aver** già **visto** questo film. | I *think* I*'ve seen this film already.* |
| Mi pare di **essere arrivata** troppo tardi. | I *think* I *have arrived too late.* |

Note that the final **e** of **avere** or **essere** is often dropped.

### (ii) Different subject for each part of the sentence: follow it by 'che' plus the subjunctive

If on the other hand there is a different subject in each part of the sentence, the two parts of the sentence must be linked by the conjunction **che** (*that*) which should be followed by a verb in the subjunctive:

Mi sembra **che** lui sia un po' pigro.   I *think* **he** *is a bit lazy*.

Gli sembra **che** lei sia offesa.   **He** *thinks that* **she** *is offended*.

Note that in English the word *that* can be omitted, but in Italian **che** can *not* be omitted.

## 4 Pensare, credere: *to think, to believe*

Another way of expressing an opinion is to use the verbs **pensare** or **credere**. Like the verbs above, they can be followed, when the subject is the same, by a simple **di** and the infinitive. When the subject is different, the two parts of the sentence must be linked with **che** and the second verb must be a subjunctive:

### (i) Same subject

Penso **di** sognare.   I *think* **I'm** *dreaming*.

Pensa **di** vincere.   **He** *thinks* **he** *will win*.

### (ii) Different subject

Pensa **che** tu stia sognando.   **He** *thinks* **you're** *dreaming*.

Penso **che** Venezia sia la città più bella del mondo.   I *think* **Venice** *is the most beautiful city in the world*.

## 5 Phrases expressing opinion

Here are some of the most common phrases of opinion:

| | |
|---|---|
| a mio parere | *in my opinion* |
| per me | *in my opinion* |
| a mia opinione | *in my opinion* |
| per quanto mi riguarda | *as far as I am concerned* |

These phrases can just be added on to the rest of the sentence; they do not need to be followed by **che** and the subjunctive:

**A mio parere** è un po' caro.   *In my opinion it's a little dear.*

**Per quanto mi riguarda,** non vale la pena vederlo.   *As far as I am concerned, it's not worth the trouble of seeing it.*

# In contesto

## Going to the restaurant

| | | |
|---|---|---|
| Anna | Come ti sembra questo ristorante? | *How does this restaurant seem to you?* |
| Luca | Be'. Non c'è male. E tu che cosa ne pensi? | *Well, not bad, And what do you think of it?* |
| Anna | Ma . . . io ho mangiato bene. A dire la verità la pasta mi sembrava un po' cruda, forse. | *Well, I ate well. To tell the truth, the pasta seemed to me a little underdone, perhaps.* |
| Luca | Anche a me. Comunque non mi sembra molto caro. | *(It seemed so to) me too. However it doesn't seem very dear to me.* |
| Anna | A me sembra di aver pagato molto. | *I think I've paid a lot.* |
| Luca | Infatti. Hai pagato tutto tu! | *That's right! You've paid for everything!* |

## Discussing a TV programme

| | | |
|---|---|---|
| Gianna | Hai visto quel nuovo programma ieri sera? Quello con la presentatrice americana? Cosa ne pensi? | *Did you see that new programme yesterday evening? The one with the American presenter? What do you think of it?* |
| Pino | Per me, è sciocca quell' attrice. Non credo che sia tanto brava come presentatrice; magari può avere successo negli Stati Uniti, ma qui no. | *In my opinion, that actress is silly. I don't think she's very good as a presenter; she may be successful in the USA, but not here.* |
| Gianna | Sì, ma a me pare stupido anche il programma, non credo che sia tutta colpa dell'attrice. | *Yes, but I think the programme's stupid too, I don't think it's all the fault of the actress.* |
| Pino | Geniale però l'idea di trovare una presentatrice che non parla l'italiano! | *A stroke of genius, though, the idea of finding a presenter who doesn't speak Italian!* |

| la presentatrice | presenter (female) |
|---|---|
| il presentatore | presenter (male) |
| sciocca | silly |
| bravo/a | good, clever |
| magari | perhaps, maybe |
| avere successo | to be successful |
| la colpa | blame, fault |
| geniale | brilliant (as in stroke of genius) |

## (a) Pensare di

To express an opinion, you use **pensare di** (*to think of*):

| Cosa **pensi di** questa maglietta? | *What do you think of this shirt?* |
|---|---|
| Cosa *ne* **pensi**? | *What do you think of it?* |
| Cosa **pensi di** questi sandali? | *What do you think of these sandals?* |
| Cosa *ne* **pensi**? | *What do you think of them?* |

## (b) Magari

**Magari** usually means *maybe* or *perhaps*; sometimes it means a little bit more. Used at the beginning of a sentence (where it is followed by the imperfect subjunctive) or on its own it can express a hope that something might come about:

| **Magari** lui sa dov'è. | *Maybe he knows where it is.* |
|---|---|
| **Magari** avessi la possibilità ... | *If only I had the chance ...* |

| Pensate di comprare una nuova macchina quest'anno? | *Are you thinking of buying a new car this year?* |
|---|---|
| **Magari!** | *I wish we were!/I wish we could! (The meaning implied is that it is very unlikely to happen.)* |

## —————— In aggiunta ——————

## 1  Opinion or rumour

Often when an opinion is expressed or rumour is voiced, Italians use the conditional (see unit 20) to express the present tense:

| | |
|---|---|
| Secondo la stampa, l'Italia **sarebbe** al quinto posto nella graduatoria dei paesi industrializzati. | *According to the Press, Italy **is in** fifth place in the league table of the industrialised nations.* |

## 2 Sembra di sì, sembra di no: *I think so, I think not*

To express the English *I think so* or *I think not* Italians say:

| | |
|---|---|
| Mi sembra di sì. | *I think so.* |
| Mi pare di sì. | |
| Penso di sì. | |
| Credo di sì. | |
| | |
| Mi sembra di no. | *I think not.* |
| Mi pare di no. | |
| Penso di no. | |
| Credo di no. | |

## 3 Other tenses of the subjunctive

The subjunctive is found in a variety of tenses, not only in the present tense (**Credo che *sia* stanco**) illustrated above.

Here are some examples of its other tenses:

**The imperfect**

| | |
|---|---|
| Credevo che **fosse** stanco. | *I thought he was tired.* |

**The perfect**

| | |
|---|---|
| Credo che **sia arrivato** ieri. | *I think he arrived yesterday.* |

**The pluperfect**

| | |
|---|---|
| Credevo che **fosse** già **arrivato**. | *I thought he had already arrived.* |

The imperfect and the pluperfect subjunctive can be found in greater detail in units 20 and 21.

## 4 How to form the perfect subjunctive

Use the present subjunctive of the verb **avere** (**abbia**, etc.), or the verb **essere** (**sia**, etc.) in the case of verbs taking **essere** (see unit 11), with

the past participle of the verb required (e.g. **comprato**) to form the
perfect tense of the subjunctive:

Non credo che lui mi **abbia**    *I don't think he has bought me a*
    **comprato** un regalo.    *present*
Non mi pare che lei **sia**    *I don't think she has left.*
    **partita**.

## 5 When to use the perfect subjunctive

The perfect subjunctive should be used anywhere you would use the
perfect tense in a *normal* sentence, i.e. to describe an action which has
already taken place. It generally comes in a sentence where the main
verb is in one of the following tenses: *present, future* and (very
occasionally) *perfect*:

Non credo che il treno **sia** già    *I don't think the train has left*
    **partito**.    *already.*

Visiteremo gli scavi a meno    *We will visit the excavations unless*
    che i tombaroli non **abbiano**    *the grave-robbers have taken*
    **portato** via tutto.    *everything away.*

It is much more common for a perfect tense such as **non mi è sembrato**
to be followed by the imperfect or pluperfect subjunctive.

# 18

## Expressing obligation and need

**Le funzioni**

In this unit you will learn about:
Expressing obligation ● Expressing one's needs ● Expressing a necessity

**Le strutture**

**Dovere** ● **Aver bisogno di** ● **Bisogna** ● **C'è bisogno di** ● **È necessario/essenziale**, etc. ● **Occorre** followed by: (a) infinitive; (b) **che** plus the subjunctive

---
### Nota introduttiva
---

Like the English *to have to*, *to need to*, the Italian verb **dovere** is used to express obligation (something we have to do) and need (something we need to do). Study these examples:

Maria **deve** studiare di più.     *Maria must study more.*
                                    *(Maria needs to study more.)*
                                    *(Maria has to study more.)*
**Devo** andare a casa. È tardi.     *I must go home. It's late.*

The English verb *to need* can be used with a verb, when talking about something you have to do, or with a noun, talking about an object or objects you need.

In Italian, the phrase **aver bisogno di** can be used for either verb or noun, while the verb **bisogna** can only be used with a verb (infinitive)

and has a general or impersonal meaning (*one needs, it is necessary*), i.e. not referring to any one person in particular:

| | |
|---|---|
| **Ho bisogno di** andare in bagno. | *I need to go to the toilet.* |
| **Hanno bisogno di** soldi. | *They need money.* |
| **Bisogna portare** una maglia. | *One must bring a sweater.* |
| **Bisogna pagare** il supplemento. | *One must pay a supplement.* |

**Bisogna** can be substituted by the phrase **c'è bisogno** as in:

| | |
|---|---|
| Non **c'è bisogno** di restare. | *There's no need to stay.* |

## —— Analisi della grammatica ——

### *1* Dovere: *to have to*

**Dovere** is a mildly irregular verb which means *must* or *have to*:

| | | |
|---|---|---|
| (io) | **devo** | *I must* |
| (tu) | **devi** | *you must* |
| (lui, lei) | **deve** | *he/she must* |
| (noi) | **dobbiamo** | *we must* |
| (voi) | **dovete** | *you must* |
| (loro) | **devono** | *they must* |

Used in the conditional (see unit 20) **dovere** can also means *should* or *ought to*:

| | |
|---|---|
| **Dovrei** andare a trovare gli amici inglesi. | *I ought to go and visit my English friends.* |
| **Dovresti** visitare la cattedrale. | *You ought to visit the cathedral.* |

To talk about the past, either the imperfect tense or the **passato prossimo** can be used, depending on whether the action happened regularly or once only:

| | |
|---|---|
| **Dovevo andare** a scuola a piedi. | *I had to go to school on foot.* |
| Ieri **ho dovuto comprare** una nuova gomma. | *Yesterday I had to buy a new tyre.* |

To say what one should have done, use the past conditional:

**Avresti dovuto** telefonargli. *You should have called him.*

## 2 Aver bisogno di: to need

As mentioned above, the phrase **aver bisogno di** (*to need*) can be used either with a verb or a noun. Its literal translation, in English, is **to have need of**:

**Ho bisogno di** una mano. *I need a hand.*
**Avevo bisogno di** telefonare. *I needed to telephone.*

The verb **avere** (*to have*) changes according to the person speaking, but **bisogno** does not alter.

## 3 Bisogna: it is necessary

**Bisogna** is an impersonal verb which is generally used when no one particular person is implied; it is then followed by a verb in the infinitive:

**Bisogna stare** attenti. *One must be careful.*
**Bisogna pagare** alla cassa. *One must pay at the cash desk.*

It is, however, possible to 'personalise' **bisogna** by adding **che** and the subjunctive (see unit 17) and mentioning the person or people who must carry out the action:

**Bisogna che** i ragazzi **stiano** *It is necessary for the children to*
attenti. *be careful. (The children must be careful.)*

**Bisogna che** Lei mi **dica** la *It is necessary that you tell me the*
data di partenza. *date of departure.*

## 4 C'è bisogno: there is need of

In certain situations, **bisogna** can be replaced by **c'è bisogno**. This too is impersonal (*there is need of*) and does not refer to one particular person. It can followed by:

### (a) di plus the infinitive

Non **c'è bisogno di** firmare, *There's no need to sign, is there?*
vero?

or it can be 'personalised' by using:

**(b)** *che* **plus the subjunctive**

> Non **c'è bisogno che** Lei mi *There isn't any need for you to*
> **dia** il passaporto. *give me your passport.*

## 5 È necessario/essenziale: *it is necessary/ essential*

This is another impersonal expression, which can be followed by:

**(a) the infinitive**

> È **necessario fare** il *It is necessary to buy a ticket.*
> biglietto.

or 'personalised' by using:

**(b)** *che* **plus the subjunctive**

> È **necessario che** tutti i *It is necessary that all visitors buy*
> visitatori **facciano** il *a ticket.*
> biglietto.

## 6 Occorre: *it is necessary*

**Occorre** can replace **bisogna**, meaning *it is necessary*, when used with:

**(a) a verb followed by the infinitive**

> **Occorre prendere** il treno. *It's necessary to take the train.*

**(b)** *che* **followed by the subjunctive**

> **Occorre** che voi **siate** pronti *You must be ready at 10 o'clock.*
> per le dieci.

Any of the expressions listed above can, of course, be replaced simply by using the verb **dovere**, for example:

> Tutti i visitatori **devono** *All visitors must buy a ticket.*
> comprare il biglietto.
> I ragazzi **devono** stare attenti. *The children must be careful.*

**(c) With an object**

**Occorre, occorrono**, when used with an object rather than a verb, can also mean *to be needed*. The object needed becomes the *subject* of the verb: so if the object needed is single, the verb must be single; if plural the verb must be plural:

Per l'Inghilterra **occorre** un
francobollo da L.750.

*For England, one needs a L.750
stamp.*

Per telefonare a Roma,
**occorrono** dieci gettoni.

*To telephone Rome, one needs ten
gettoni (telephone tokens).*

In this last example **occorre** can be substituted by **ci vogliono**:

Per telefonare a Roma, **ci
vogliono** dieci gettoni.

*To phone Rome, one needs ten
gettoni (tokens).*

**Occorre** can be personalised by adding an indirect object pronoun such
as **mi**, **ti**, **gli**, etc. (*to me, to you, to him*, etc.):

**Mi occorrono** cinque
francobolli.

*I need five stamps.*

**Gli occorre** la macchina.

*He needs the car.*

Quante uova ti **occorrono**?

*How many eggs do you need?*

---

# In contesto

---

## At the railway station

| | | |
|---|---|---|
| Impiegato | **Buongiorno. Desidera?** | *Good morning. What can I do for you?* |
| Viaggiatore | **Un biglietto di andata a ritorno per Roma, per favore. Prima classe.** | *A return ticket to Rome, please. First class.* |
| Impiegato | **A che ora vuole partire?** | *What time do you want to leave?* |
| Viaggiatore | **Devo essere a Roma per le cinque di sera. Che treno bisogna prendere?** | *I have to be in Rome for 5 o'clock this evening. What train does one have to take?* |
| Impiegato | **Se Lei ha bisogno di essere a Roma per le cinque, dovrebbe prendere il treno delle 12.35, che arriva a Roma alle 16.30. È un rapido, però, bisogna pagare anche il supplemento.** | *If you need to be in Rome for 5 o'clock, you should take the 12.35 train, which gets to Rome at 4.30pm. It's a 'rapido', however, one has to pay the supplement.* |
| Viaggiatore | **Va bene. Quant'è?** | *All right. How much is it?* |

| Impiegato | Sono L.39.700 andata e ritorno, compreso il supplemento. | *It's L.39.700 return, including the supplement.* |
| Viaggiatore | Ecco. | *Here you are.* |
| Impiegato | Grazie. Ecco il Suo biglietto, ed ecco L.300 di resto. Ha bisogno di altre informazioni? | *Thanks. Here's your ticket, and here's L.300 change. Do you need any other information?* |
| Viaggiatore | Ah, da quale binario parte il treno? | *Ah, what platform does the train leave from?* |
| Impiegato | Parte dal binario numero tre. Le conviene usare il sottopassaggio. | *It leaves from platform 3. It's best (for you) to use the subway.* |

## Dialogo: vacanze al mare

| Moglie | Caro, quest' anno prima di andare al mare, dobbiamo comprare dei costumi da bagno nuovi ai bambini. | *Dearest, this year, before we go to the seaside, we must buy some new swimming costumes for the children.* |
| Marito | Ce n'è proprio bisogno? | *Is there really any need?* |
| Moglie | Sì, Marina ha bisogno di un costume intero e Marcello ha bisogno di un costume più grande perché quello dell' anno scorso è diventato troppo piccolo. | *Yes, Marina needs a one-piece costume, and Marcello needs a bigger costume because last year's has become too small.* |
| Marito | Meno male che non c'è bisogno di prendergli anche le pinne, perché le abbiamo prese già l'anno scorso in svendita. | *Just as well there isn't any need to buy them flippers as well, because we got them last year in a sale.* |
| Moglie | Mi spiace deluderti, ma occorre ricomprarle, perché le abbiamo prese tre anni fa, non l'anno scorso. | *I'm sorry to disappoint you, but we do have to buy them again, because it was three years ago that we got them, not last year.* |
| Marito | Mah! | *Hmmm . . .* |
| Moglie | Bisogna che tu chieda a quel tuo amico che vende articoli sportivi, se ti fa lo sconto. | *You must ask that friend of yours who sells sports goods, if he'll give you a discount.* |

| Marito | **Sì, ma è necessario che venga anche tu, perché tu sei esperta di queste cose.** | *Yes, but you'll have to come too, because you're the expert in these things.* |

| il sottopassaggio | *the underpass (e.g. under a railway)* |
| un biglietto di andata e ritorno | *return ticket* |
| il supplemento | *supplement (payable on **rapido** trains)* |
| il costume da bagno | *swimming costume* |
| a due pezzi | *two piece (bikini)* |
| intero | *one-piece, whole* |

## In aggiunta

### 1 More impersonal expressions: with verbs

Like **bisogna**, and **occorre**, there are many other 'impersonal' verbs, i.e. verbs that are used mainly in the third person (*it is necessary*). Some of these can be used with the indirect object pronouns **mi**, **ti**, **gli**, etc. (*to me, to you, to him*, etc. See unit 16) to 'personalise' them. Most of these verbs can be followed either by the infinitive, as in English (*it is necessary to go*), or by **che** plus the subjunctive (see unit 17).

Some of the most common are:

| Basta . . . | *It is enough to . . .* |
| Basta guadare! | *One only has to look!* |
| Basta che voi me lo chiediate. | *All you have to do is ask me.* |
| | *(It is enough that you ask me.)* |
| Pare, sembra, | *It appears, it seems,* |
| Mi pare di sentire qualcosa. | *I think I can hear something.* |
| | *(Lit. It seems to me to hear something.)* |
| Mi pare che tu non sia convinto. | *It seems to me that you aren't convinced.* |
| Conviene. | *It is best. It is convenient. It is worth it.* |
| Mi conviene. | *It is best for me.* |
| Conviene prendere il treno. | *It's best to take the train.* |
| Ti conviene prendere il treno. | *It is best for you to take the train.* |
| Non mi conviene andare in albergo. | *It's not worth me going to a hotel.* |
| Può darsi.* | *It may be. It is possible.* |
| Può darsi che lei sia la persona più brava del mondo. | *It may be that she is the cleverest person in the world.* |

\* Can *not* be followed by the infinitive.

## 2  More impersonal expressions: with essere (to be) plus adjectives

As well as the 'impersonal' verbs shown above, there are some similar 'impersonal' expressions formed by **essere** (*to be*) and various adjectives, such as **è necessario** already mentioned above.

Like the verbs above, most of these expressions can be followed by (a) the infinitive or (b) **che** plus the subjunctive. Here are some further examples:

| | |
|---|---|
| È possibile | *It's possible.* |
| È impossibile. | *It's impossible.* |
| È probabile. | *It's probable.* |
| È improbabile. | *It's unlikely.* |
| È necessario. | *It's necessary.* |
| È essenziale. | *It's essential.* |
| È importante. | *It's important.* |
| È facile. | *It's easy. It's likely.** |
| È difficile. | *It's difficult. It's unlikely.** |
| È utile. | *It's useful.* |
| È inutile. | *It's useless.* |
| È bello. | *It's nice.* |
| È bene. | *It's good.* |
| È male. | *It's bad.* |
| È meglio. | *It's better.* |
| È peggio. | *It's worse.* |
| È preferibile. | *It's preferable.* |
| È naturale. | *It's natural.* |
| È strano. | *It's strange.* |

| | |
|---|---|
| **È possibile andare** in pullman. | *It's possible to go by coach.* |
| **È importante conservare** lo scontrino. | *It is important to keep the receipt.* |
| **È facile sbagliare.** | *It's easy to make mistakes.* |
| **È bello stare** al mare. | *It's nice being at the seaside.* |
| **È strano vedere** Roma d'inverno. | *It's strange seeing Rome in winter.* |
| **È molto** peggio **andare** in campeggio che dormire in un ostello. | *It's much worse camping than sleeping in a hostel.* |
| **È possibile che** lui sia ancora in Italia. | *It's possible that he's still in Italy.* |
| **È probabile che** noi partiamo sabato. | *It's likely that we'll leave on Saturday.* |

È **naturale che** tu abbia voglia di
tornare.

*It's natural that you should
want to return.*

È **strano che** loro non abbiano
telefonato.

*It's odd that they haven't
telephoned.*

È **meglio che** Lei non torni tardi.

*It's better that you don't come
back late.*

*È **facile** and È **difficile** followed by **che** and the subjunctive tend to
mean *It's likely, it's unlikely* rather than their literal meaning.

È **facile che** ti scotti **se** non
metti la crema.

*It's easy/likely that you will burn if
you don't put cream on.*

È **difficile che** ci **siano**
ritardi.

*It's unlikely that there will be
delays.*

# 19

# Expressing emotions and uncertainty

**Le funzioni**

In this unit you will learn how to:
Express emotion, hope, doubt, fear, etc. ● Express possibility and uncertainty

**Le strutture**

The subjunctive after verbs of hoping, fearing, and other emotions ● Other situations in which the subjunctive is used ● The subjunctive versus the indicative

## Nota introduttiva

In Italian, you need to use the subjunctive whenever you wish to express an opinion or when something is only a possibility and not a definite event. It is used after certain verbs or verb phrases some of which you have already seen in units 17 and 18. These include verbs expressing emotion (hope, fear, sorrow, etc.):

| | |
|---|---|
| Puoi venire stasera? | *Can you come tonight?* |
| Spero che tu **possa** venire. | *I hope you can come.* |
| Michele è in ritardo. | *Michele is late.* |
| Temo che Michele **sia** in ritardo. | *I am afraid Michele is late.* |
| Sono contenta che Lei si **sia** divertito. | *I am glad that you have enjoyed yourself.* |

In each of the examples above, the first statement or question contains the 'normal' (indicative) form of the verb; the second has the subjunctive form, used after **spero** (*I hope*), **temo** (*I fear*) and **sono contenta** (*I am glad*).

## ———— Analisi della grammatica ————

### 1 When to use the subjunctive

Here are the most common situations in which the subjunctive must be used, with examples. By far the largest groups of examples are those explained in the first two sections.

### 2 After certain verbs or verb phrases

In the examples that follow, in English you would use just a normal verb form, but in Italian you must use the subjunctive. As you can see, the verb in the subjunctive always depends on a main verb or verb phrase (the verb which is found in the main part of the sentence) and is introduced by **che**:

#### (a) Emotion or feeling

After any verb or phrase expressing emotion: *hope, fear, pleasure, sorrow, anger, surprise, regret*:

| | |
|---|---|
| **Temo che** lui **abbia** troppo da fare. | *I'm afraid he has too much to do.* |
| **Mi dispiace che** tu **sia** impegnato stasera. | *I'm sorry that you're busy tonight.* |
| **È un peccato che** i bambini non **possano** venire. | *It's a pity that the children can't come.* |

#### (b) Doubt or uncertainty

After any verb expressing *doubt* or *uncertainty*:

| | |
|---|---|
| Non so se **facciano** bene. | *I don't know if they're doing the right thing.* |
| Non credo che **costi** troppo. | *I don't think it costs too much.* |
| Dubito che il treno **parta** in orario. | *I doubt if the train will leave on time.* |

Some verbs are followed by the subjunctive *only* when they are negative:
**sapere, credere, vedere, dire**:

| | |
|---|---|
| So che **ha** una macchina. | *I know she has a car.* |
| Non so se **abbia** una macchina. | *I don't know if she has a car.* |
| Dico che **è** bravissimo. | *I say he's very clever.* |
| Non dico che **sia** stupido. | *I'm not saying he's stupid.* |

### (c) Wishing, requesting

After verbs such as **volere, chiedere, ordinare**, when the subject of the first half (e.g. 'I') is different from that of the second (e.g. *he*):

| | |
|---|---|
| Voglio che lui **stia** più attento. | *I want him to be more careful.* |
| Vorrebbe che i bambini **facessero** meno rumore. | *He would like the children to make less noise.* |

Vorrei tends to be used with the imperfect tense of the subjunctive and can be studied in more detail in unit 20.

### (d) Allowing, forbidding, denying

After verbs such **negare, permettere, vietare, impedire**:

| | |
|---|---|
| Non permette che i bambini **giochino** fuori. | *She does not allow the children to play in the street.* |
| Nega che il cane **sia** pericoloso. | *She denies that the dog is dangerous.* |

### (e) Waiting, expecting

After verbs such as **aspettare, aspettarsi**:

| | |
|---|---|
| Mi aspetto che tu **sia** puntuale. | *I expect you to be punctual.* |
| Aspetto che **arrivino** loro per cominciare. | *I am waiting for them to arrive before starting.* |

### (f) Verbs that introduce an indirect question

A question which is introduced by a phrase such as *I ask, I wonder why*:

| | |
|---|---|
| Mi chiedo perché lui **sia** così nervoso. | *I wonder why he's so edgy.* |

## (g) Impersonal verbs or expressions ('it' verbs)

The subjunctive should be used after any impersonal verb (e.g. **bisogna**) or impersonal phrase (**essere** plus the adjective), i.e. phrases beginning with *it* in English. For full details of these, see unit 18.

# 3  After certain conjunctions (joining words)

Often the subjunctive will be introduced by a conjunction, or joining word, which links up the two halves of the sentence:

| | |
|---|---|
| perché, affinché | *in order that* |
| di modo che, in maniera che | *in such a way that* |
| purché, a condizione che, a patto che | *on condition that* |
| benché, sebbene, quantunque | *although* |
| comunque | *however* |
| a meno che | *unless* |
| prima che | *before* |
| nel caso che, qualora, caso mai | *if, in case* |
| nonostante che, malgrado che | *despite* |
| come se | *as if* |

| | |
|---|---|
| Vengo **a condizione che** tu inviti anche Edoardo. | *I'll come on condition that you ask Edward.* |
| Me ne vado **a meno che** voi non mi lasciate in pace. | *I'm going unless you all leave me in peace.* |
| Se ne va **senza che** lo salutiamo. | *He goes off without us saying goodbye to him.* |
| Sposto la macchina **perché** loro possano uscire. | *I'll move the car so that they can get out.* |
| **Nonostante** avessimo sonno, non volevamo perdere la festa. | *Although we were sleepy, we didn't want to miss the party.* |
| È **come se** non capisse niente. | *It's as if he didn't understand anything.* |
| **Nel caso** veniate in Inghilterra, vi lascio il mio indirizzo. | *If you were to come to England, I'll leave you my address.* |

# 4  After a superlative (the most, etc.)

After a superlative adjective (the most, the best, the fastest, etc.) or an adjective such as **primo** (*first*), **ultimo** (*last*) or **unico** or **solo** (*only*) the subjunctive is used in the relative clause (the *who, which, that* clause) which follows it:

| | |
|---|---|
| È la cosa più bella che io **abbia** mai visto. | *It's the most beautiful thing I've ever seen.* |
| È l'unico paese che lui non **abbia** mai visitato. | *It's the only country that he's never visited.* |
| È il libro meno interessante che io **abbia** mai letto. | *It's the least interesting book I've ever read.* |

## 5 *After certain negatives*

After the following negative expressions, the subjunctive is used:

| | |
|---|---|
| Non è che lui **abbia** tanti soldi. | *It's not that he's got lots of money.* |
| Non c'è nessuno che **sappia** fare questo. | *There's nobody who knows how to do this.* |
| Non c'è niente che **desideri** di più. | *There is nothing I would like better.* |

## 6 *In 'restricted' relative clauses*

Clauses like this usually start with the words *who* or *which*. They are general statements which are then 'limited' or 'restricted' by the relative clause, i.e. the clause beginning with *who* or *which* or *that*.

| | |
|---|---|
| (a) Cerco una ragazza inglese. | *I am looking for an English girl.* |
| (b) Cerco una ragazza **che ami** i bambini. | *I'm looking for a girl who loves children.* |
| (c) Mary è una ragazza inglese **che ama** i bambini. | *Mary is an English girl who loves children.* |

In (a), there is a generalisation: *any* English girl will do.

In (b), a restrictive clause is added: any girl *who loves children*. This requires the subjunctive.

In (c), one specific girl is mentioned: this does *not* require the subjunctive.

| | |
|---|---|
| (i) Cerco un registratore a cassette per la macchina. | *I'm looking for a cassette player for the car.* |
| (ii) Cerco un registratore a cassette **che** non **costi** troppo. | *I'm looking for a cassette player which doesn't cost too much.* |

(iii) Cerco il registratore a     *I'm looking for the cassette*
cassette **che** ho comprato     *recorder that I bought*
ieri.     *yesterday.*

In (i) any cassette player for the car is being sought.

In (ii), it is *any cassette player that doesn't cost too much*. This restricted
type of clause needs the subjunctive.

In (iii) a specific cassette recorder is mentioned so no subjunctive is
necessary.

The subjunctive can also be found after **qualcuno**:

C'è **qualcuno** che **sappia**     *Is there anyone who can speak*
parlere cinese?     *Chinese?*

## 7 After indefinite adjectives or pronouns

| | |
|---|---|
| qualunque | *whatever, whichever* |
| chiunque | *whoever* |
| comunque | *however* |
| qualsiasi | *whatever, whichever* |

**Qualunque** cosa faccia, è     *Whatever he does, he's still my*
sempre figlio mio.     *son.*
**Chiunque** tu sia, non ti     *Whoever you are I won't allow you*
permetto di entrare in casa     *to come in to my house.*
mia.
**Comunque** siano le cose, non     *However things are, I won't*
cambio idea.     *change my mind.*
**Qualsiasi** cosa organizzi,     *Whatever he organises, he always*
sbaglia sempre.     *makes mistakes.*

## 8 When the subordinate or dependent clause comes before the main clause

When the two parts of the sentence are in reverse order, the subjunctive
is needed:

Si **sa** che non è perfetto.     *Everyone knows it isn't perfect.*
Che non **sia** perfetto si sa già.     *That it isn't perfect, everyone*
    *knows already.*

Normally the subjunctive is found in a subordinate clause (one that depends on something else), but there are a few situations, in Italian, in which the subjunctive is found in a *main* clause.

## 9 *As an imperative (order of command)*

To issue a polite request or instruction to someone you are on formal terms with, use the subjunctive (**Lei** form, plural **Loro**). This is covered in detail in unit 9.

| | |
|---|---|
| Venga qui! | *Come here!* |
| Faccia presto! | *Be quick!* |
| Dica! | *Tell me! (what you want)* |
| Dicano, signori! | *Tell me, ladies and gentlemen.* |

## In contesto

### *Dialogo 1*

| | | |
|---|---|---|
| Chiara | **A che ora partono Michele e Caterina?** | *What time are Michele and Caterina leaving?* |
| Luciana | **È probabile che partano verso le sette. Anzi, è difficile che partano prima delle sette, perché vogliono che i bambini salutino i nonni prima.** | *They're probably going around 7.00. In fact, it's unlikely that they'll go before then, because they want the children to say goodbye to the grandparents.* |
| Chiara | **Sono contenta che abbiano trovato bel tempo, e che si siano rilassati un po'.** | *I'm glad that they found nice weather and that they relaxed a bit.* |

### *Animali abbandonati*

(*Adapted from* Corriere della Sera)

**Vacanze, tempo di abbandoni. Ogni estate si stima che oltre 25.000 cani e migliaia di altri animali domestici vengano lasciati morire. 'In Valtellina – spiega Anna Tosi, volontaria del**

canile Enpa – riceviamo centinaia di richieste da persone che vogliono che i loro cani vengano tenuti nel nostro Centro.'

A meno che la situazione non migliori, il randagismo diventerà un pericolo sia per gli uomini che per il bestiame. Qualsiasi provvedimento sia stato varato finora, non ha ottenuto risultati incoraggianti.

'La nuova legge appena approvata – aggiunge l'onorevole socialista Dino Mazza – si spera che faccia perdere l'abitudine agli italiani di mettere il cane a dicembre sotto l'albero e ad agosto sull'autostrada.' Ma è difficile che questo problema sia risolto facilmente.

### English translation

Holidays, a time of desertion. Every summer, it is estimated that over 25,000 dogs and thousands of other domestic animals are left to die. 'In Valtellina,' explains Anna Tosi, a voluntary worker at the Enpa kennels, 'we receive hundreds of requests from people who want their dogs to be looked after in our Centre.'

Unless the situation improves, the stray dog phenomenon will become a danger both to man and livestock. Any measures taken up until now have not achieved encouraging results.

'It is to be hoped that the new law, which has just been approved,' adds the Socialist M.P., Dino Mazza, 'will ensure that the Italians kick their habit of putting a dog under the tree at Christmas and out on the motorway in August.' But it is unlikely that this problem will be resolved easily.

## —————— In aggiunta ——————

## 1 How to avoid using the subjunctive

If, despite having read units 17, 18 and 19, you still prefer to avoid using the subjunctive, note the following:

### (a) Verbs with the same subject

Many verbs, or verb phrases, can be followed directly by the infinitive (-are, -ere, -ire), but only if the person in the main part of the sentence is the same person as in the subordinate (dependent) clause. Some examples of this have already been seen in units 17 and 18.

    (i) *Same subject in both parts of sentence:*
        **Credo di** vedere il treno.   *I think I can see the train.*
    (ii) *Different subject:*
        **Teresa crede che io**      *Teresa thinks that I have too*
         abbia troppe scarpe.      *many shoes.*

## (b) Impersonal verbs

In the case of *impersonal* verbs (see unit 18), where the subject is in fact *it*, the subjunctive can be avoided if no specific person is mentioned, i.e. if it is a general statement that applies to everyone. If the statement is 'personalised' then **che** plus the subjunctive has to be used.

    (i) *Impersonal:*
        Conviene partire presto.   *It's best to leave early.*
    (ii) *Specific person:*
        Conviene **che voi**      *It's best if you leave early.*
        **partiate** presto.

# 20

## Expressing wishes or polite requests

**Le funzioni**

In this unit you will learn how to:
Express a wish involving someone or something else ● Make a polite request

**Le strutture**

The conditional **vorrei**: to express a wish or request ● **Vorrei** plus **che** plus the imperfect subjunctive ● The conditional: to express polite request ● Other uses of the conditional ● Other uses of imperfect subjunctive

### Nota introduttiva

**Expressing a wish for oneself**

| | |
|---|---|
| **Vorrei mangiare** fuori stasera. | *I should like to eat out tonight.* |

**Expressing a wish for others**

| | |
|---|---|
| **Vorrei che lui** non fosse cosi ostinato. | *I wish he were not so stubborn.* |

**Expressing a polite request using the conditional**

| | |
|---|---|
| Le **dispiacerebbe** aprire la finestra? | *Would you mind opening the window?* |

**Making a request using verb plus the infinitive**

Ci **chiede** di non **fumare**.    *She asks us not to smoke.*

--------- **Analisi della grammatica** ---------

## 1   Wishing: the conditional plus the subjunctive

In units 17, 18 and 19, you saw how the subjunctive was used after verbs of emotion, hoping, or fearing; it must also be used after verbs of wishing, (e.g. **volere**) and requesting (e.g. **chiedere**) where another person is involved. If you are expressing a wish for yourselves, **voglio** or **vorrei** can be followed directly by the infinitive (see unit 14 for further examples.) But when we are wishing that *someone else* would do something, **voglio** or **vorrei** have to be followed by **che** then the subjunctive. Look at these two examples:

Domani **voglio lavare** la macchina.    *Tomorrow I want to wash the car.*

Domani **voglio che** mio marito lavi la macchina.    *Tomorrow I want my husband to wash the car.*

Frequently verbs of wishing are expressed in the conditional form (*I would like*, etc.) and are followed by the *imperfect* tense of the subjunctive rather than the *present* tense:

Vorrei che tu mi **portassi** fuori ogni tanto.    *I would like you to take me out every so often.*

Vorrebbe che Lei gli **telefonasse**.    *He would like you to telephone him.*

When a wish is expressed that the action had or hadn't taken place, the *pluperfect* tense of the subjunctive is used:

Desidererei che non fosse mai successa questa cosa.    *I would like for this thing never to have happened.*
*(I wish this had never happened.)*

(See unit 21 for further examples of this.)

## 2 How to form the conditional

The conditional, in English, is expressed by the words *would* or *should*. It is called 'conditional' because the statement will only become fact *on condition that something happens*. The equivalent forms, in Italian, of the **condizionale**, are given below. The **condizionale** varies little from verb to verb. It is formed by using the infinitive (**-are, -ere, -ire**), dropping the final **e**, and adding the conditional endings. In the case of **-are** verbs, one must change the **a** of **-are** to **e**.

**Conditional endings**

-ei, -esti, -ebbe, -emmo, -este, -ebbero.

---

### Verbs ending in -are: *parlare*

| (io) | parler**ei** | *I would speak* |
| (tu) | parler**esti** | *you would speak* |
| (lui) | parler**ebbe** | *he would speak* |
| (lei) | parler**ebbe** | *she would speak* |
| (Lei) | parler**ebbe** | *you would speak (polite)* |
| (noi) | parler**emmo** | *we would speak* |
| (voi) | parler**este** | *you would speak* |
| (Loro) | parler**ebbero** | *they would speak* |

---

### Verbs ending in -ere: *mettere*

| (io) | metter**ei** | *I would put* |
| (tu) | metter**esti** | *you would put* |
| (lui) | metter**ebbe** | *he would put* |
| (lei) | metter**ebbe** | *she would put* |
| (Lei) | metter**ebbe** | *you would put (polite)* |
| (noi) | metter**emmo** | *we would put* |
| (voi) | metter**este** | *you would put* |
| (Loro) | metter**ebbero** | *they would put* |

---

### Verbs ending in ire: *partire*

| (io) | partir**ei** | *I would leave* |
| (tu) | partir**esti** | *you would leave* |
| (lui) | partir**ebbe** | *he would leave* |
| (lei) | partir**ebbe** | *she would leave* |
| (Lei) | partir**ebbe** | *you would leave (polite)* |
| (noi) | partir**emmo** | *we would leave* |
| (voi) | partir**este** | *you would leave* |
| (Loro) | partir**ebbero** | *they would leave* |

## 3 When to use the conditional

### (a) To express a wish

| | |
|---|---|
| **Vorrei** un panino con prosciutto. | *I would like a ham sandwich.* |

(More examples can be found in unit 14.)

### (b) To express a request more politely

| | |
|---|---|
| Le **dispiacerebbe passarmi** la valigia? | *Would you mind passing me my suitcase?* |
| **Potrei venire** più tardi? | *Could I come later?* |
| **Potrebbe prestarmi** il suo orario? | *Could you lend me your timetable?* |
| Mi **farebbe** una cortesia? | *Could you do me a favour?* |

The phrase **fare una cortesia** can be replaced by **fare un piacere** or **fare un favore**.

### (c) To make a statement sound less categorical

| | |
|---|---|
| **Dovrei mandare** delle cartoline. | *I ought to send some postcards.* |

Compare this with:

**Devo mandare** delle cartoline. *I must send some postcards.*

### (d) To express rumour, hearsay or report

The conditional is often used to tell us what someone said, or what was written in the Press. It is translated by a straightforward present tense in English.

| | |
|---|---|
| Secondo la stampa, il governo **sarebbe** contrario. | *According to the Press, the government is against it.* |
| Secondo Gianni, Maria **avrebbe** più di 40 anni. | *According to Gianni, Maria is over 40.* |

### (e) When a condition is implied or stated:

You use the conditional when an action is dependent on certain conditions being fulfilled; sometimes these conditions are stated;

sometimes they are just implied. (See unit 22 for further examples of conditional sentences.)

| | |
|---|---|
| Andrei in vancanza ma non ho soldi. | *I would go on holiday, but I don't have any money.* |
| Io partirei subito. | *I would leave straightaway. (An 'if' condition is implied – such as* **if I were you, if I were able***.* |
| Se avessi i soldi, comprerei una macchina nuova. | *If I had the money, I would buy a new car.* |

**(f) Indirect, reported speech or after a verb of saying, thinking, etc.**

| | |
|---|---|
| **Dice che verrebbe** domani. | *He says he would come tomorrow.* |
| **Penso che sarebbe** meglio partire domani. | *I think it would be better to leave tomorrow.* |

(To see what happens when the sentence is in the past tense, see unit 21.)

## 4  How to form the imperfect subjunctive

The imperfect subjunctive is formed by taking the stem of the infinitive, i.e. the infinitive without the final **-are**, **-ere**, **-ire**, then adding a set of endings, e.g. **parl**are – **parlassi**.

When giving the subjunctive forms, we usually start with the word **che** since it is rare for the subjunctive to stand on its own. Here are the forms of the imperfect subjunctive for the three main groups of verbs:

---

**Parlare: (e.g. Che parlassi.)**

| | | | | | |
|---|---|---|---|---|---|
| (io) | parl**assi** | *I spoke* | (noi) | parl**assimo** | *we spoke* |
| (tu) | parl**assi** | *you spoke* | (voi) | parl**aste** | *you spoke* |
| (lui) | parl**asse** | *he spoke* | (loro) | parl**assero** | *they spoke* |
| (lei) | parl**asse** | *she spoke* | | | |
| (Lei) | parl**asse** | *you spoke (polite)* | | | |

---

**Mettere: (e.g. Che mettessi.)**

| | | | | | |
|---|---|---|---|---|---|
| (io) | mett**essi** | *I put* | (noi) | mett**essimo** | *we put* |
| (tu) | mett**essi** | *you put* | (voi) | mett**este** | *you put* |
| (lui) | mett**esse** | *he put* | (loro) | mett**essero** | *they put* |
| (lei) | mett**esse** | *she put* | | | |
| (Lei) | mett**esse** | *you put (polite)* | | | |

---

---

**Partire: (Che partissi.)**

| (io) | partissi | I left | (noi) | partissimo | we left |
|------|----------|--------|-------|------------|---------|
| (tu) | partissi | you left | (voi) | partiste | you left |
| (lui) | partisse | he left | (loro) | partissero | they left |
| (lei) | partisse | she left | | | |
| (Lei) | partisse | you left | | | |

---

There are few verbs which vary from this pattern (irregular). They include the following:

---

| bere | to drink | (che) io **bevessi** |
|------|----------|---------------------|
| essere | to be | (che) io **fossi** |
| stare | to be | (che) io **stessi** |
| fare | to do | (che) io **facessi** |
| dire | to say | (che) io **dicessi** |
| dare | to give | (che) io **dessi** |

---

## 5  When to use the imperfect subjunctive

The imperfect subjunctive is often used after the following tenses in the main clause: *imperfect, conditional*, but can also be used after the **passato remoto**, the *perfect* or *pluperfect* tense, the *past conditional* and occasionally after the *present*.

### (a) After the imperfect

Mio marito **aveva paura** che l'albergo fosse troppo caro.

*My husband was afraid that the hotel was too dear.*

### (b) After the conditional

Sarebbe meglio che tu non mi **chiedessi** questo.

*It would be better if you didn't ask me this.*

### (c) After the passato remoto

Il terrorista si lanciò dalla finestra perché la polizia non lo **prendesse**.

*The terrorist threw himself out of the window so that the police would not get him.*

### (d) After the perfect

La signora ci ha chiesto se ci **trovassimo** bene in Italia.

*The lady asked us if we were enjoying Italy.*

#### (e) After the pluperfect

L'impiegata ci aveva chiesto se **volessimo** un biglietto di andata e ritorno.

*The ticket clerk had asked us if we wanted a return ticket.*

#### (f) After the past conditional

Non avrei mai pensato che tu **potessi** fare una cosa del genere.

*I should never have thought that you could do a thing like that.*

#### (g) After the present

Penso che l'autista **avesse** qualche problema.

*I think the driver had some problem or other.*

---------------- **In contesto** ----------------

## Equal rights (a dialogue in the tu form): expressing a polite request

Moglie **Sono stufo di stare in casa. Stasera vorrei andare al cinema.**

*I'm bored staying at home. Tonight I'd like to go to the cinema.*

Marito **Anch'io vorrei uscire ma ho da lavorare. Ti dispiacerebbe mettere i bambini a letto?**

*I'd like to go out too, but I've got work to do. Would you mind putting the children to bed?*

Moglie **No, affatto. Ma vorrei che tu lavassi almeno i piatti.**

*No, not at all. But I would like you to at least wash the dishes.*

| | |
|---|---|
| avere da lavorare | to have work to do |
| da (plus) verb | express something that can be or has to be done |
| qualcosa da mangiare | something to eat |
| qualcosa da fare | something to do |

## Let sleeping sofas lie!

| Carla | Senta, mi potrebbe fare una piccola cortesia? | *Listen, could you do me a little favour?* |
| --- | --- | --- |
| Franco | Sì, certo. Cosa vuole che (io) faccia? | *Yes, of course. What do you want me to do?* |
| Carla | Avrei intenzione di spostare quel divano nell'angolo, ma è un po' pesante. | *I intend* (Lit. Would intend.) *moving that sofa into the corner, but it's a bit heavy.* |
| Franco | Lo farei volentieri; ma per me, il divano starebbe bene così com'è adesso! | *I'd do it willingly; but, in my opinion, the sofa would be all right left as it is now!* |

## In my grandmother's bed: using the imperfect subjunctive

**Era strano quel che succedeva quando dormivo con mia nonna . . . quando mi risvegliavo, mi ritrovavo nella stessa posizione . . . Penso che mia nonna si svegliasse molto prima di me e mi risistemasse nella stessa posizione, ma era bello immaginare che avessimo dormito in quella posizione per tutta la notte. In ogni caso era bellissimo che lei facesse di tutto per farmelo credere.**
Lara Cardella *Volevo i pantaloni.*

### English translation

*It was strange what happened when I slept with my grandmother . . . when I woke up, I found myself in the same position . . . I think that my grandmother woke up a good bit before me and put me back in the same position, but it was nice to imagine that we had slept in that position for the whole night. Anyway it was really nice that she did everything possible to make me believe it.*

| succedere | to happen |
| --- | --- |
| fare di tutto | to do everything (possible) |

## Details of my past

**Ogni tanto andavo a casa di Bruno ed era facile che restassimo fino alle due di notte a chiacchierare, perché era l'unica persona con cui io potessi parlare liberamente. Lui voleva che**

io gli parlassi in inglese, perché stava studiando la lingua, ma io non mi sentivo più a mio agio nonostante fosse la mia madre lingua. Mia madre non mi chiedeva mai con chi uscissi e lasciava che io prendessi la macchina senza farmi domande di nessun tipo.

### English translation

*Every so often I went to Bruno's house, and it was quite easy for us to stay chatting until two in the morning, because he was the only person I could talk to freely. He wanted me to speak to him in English because he was studying the language, but I didn't feel happy speaking it any longer, despite it being my native language. My mother never asked who I was going out with, and let me take the car without asking me any questions at all.*

| | |
|---|---|
| fino a | *until (time or place)* |
| a mio agio | *at my ease* |
| di nessun tipo | *of any kind (Lit.)* |

## In aggiunta

There are other ways in which you can ask someone to do something without using the subjunctive. Generally these are combinations of verb plus the person being asked plus the infinitive to express what they are being asked to do, with or without prepositions linking these different elements.

## 1 Verb plus *a* plus the person being asked plus *di* or *a* and a verb in the infinitive

Chiedo **al** cameriere **di** portare il menù. *I'll ask the waiter to bring the menu.*

I tedeschi hanno ordinato **alla** cameriera **di** portare la birra. *The Germans ordered the waitress to bring the beer.*

The person who is being asked can also be indicated by using the indirect pronouns **mi, ti, gli,** etc. (*to me, to you, to him,* etc.) instead of the name or person. The examples above would then become:

**Gli** chiedo **di** portare il menù.  *I'll ask him to being the menu.*
**Le** hanno ordinato **di** portarla  *They ordered her to bring it*
subito.  *straightaway.*

Apart from the verbs of requesting illustrated above, there are several other verbs which are followed by **a** (plus the person) then **di** (plus the infinitive). Here are the most common:

| | |
|---|---|
| comandare | *to command* |
| dire | *to say, to tell* |
| domandare | *to ask* |
| permettere | *to permit* |
| proibire | *to forbid* |
| vietare | *to forbid* |
| impedire | *to prevent* |
| suggerire | *to suggest* |
| ricordare | *to remind* |
| promettere | *to promise* |
| consigliare | *to advise* |

Cosa ci **consigli** di fare?  *What do you advise us to do?*
Non **permette** agli ospiti di  *He doesn't allow the guests to use*
usare la doccia.  *the shower.*
Il padrone del ristorante ha  *The owner of the restaurant told*
**detto** ai clienti di scegliere  *the customers to choose what*
quello che volevano.  *they wanted.*

In addition, there are a few verbs which are followed by **a** (plus the person) then **a** (plus the infinitive):

Ti **insegno ad andare,** in  *I'll teach you to go on the windsurf*
windsurf.  *(board).*

## 2  Verb plus the person plus a plus the infinitive

The verbs below are followed *directly* (i.e. without a) by the person being given the instruction, then by 'a' and the infinitive.

| | |
|---|---|
| consentire | *to allow* |
| invitare | *to invite* |
| convincere | *to persuade* |
| persuadere | *to persuade* |
| obbligare | *to oblige* |
| costringere | *to force* |
| forzare | *to force* |
| aiutare | *to help* |

| | |
|---|---|
| Hanno **invitato** mio marito a fare una conferenza. | *They have asked my husband to give a lecture.* |

In this case, the pronoun if used must be the *direct* object pronoun: **mi**, **ti**, **lo**, **la**, **ci**, **vi**, **li** and **le**:

| | |
|---|---|
| **Mi** ha invitata a venire al mare con lui. | *He invited me to come to the seaside with him.* |
| **Ti** ha convinta a comprare quella borsa? | *Did he persuade you to buy that bag?* |

## 3 Verb plus the person and infinitive

Other verbs can be followed directly by the person and then directly by the infinitive. Again the pronoun, if used, must be a direct object pronoun and the participle must agree with it:

| | |
|---|---|
| lasciare | *to allow* |
| fare | *to allow or to make someone do something* |

| | |
|---|---|
| **La** lascia salire sul treno senza biglietto. | *He lets her get on the train without a ticket.* |
| **Mi** ha fatto salire senza biglietto. | *He let me get on without a ticket.* |

| | |
|---|---|
| sentire | *to hear* |
| vedere | *to see* |

| | |
|---|---|
| **Li ho visti** salire sul treno. | *I saw them get on the train.* |
| **L'ho sentita** entrare. | *I heard her come in.* |

Finally, look at the difference between the following examples; in some cases (a) the verb can be followed directly by the infinitive – in others (b) **che** plus the subjunctive has been used:

(a) Chiedo a Marco di **venire** con noi. — *I ask Marco to come with us.*

(b) Chiedo **che** Marco **venga** con noi. — *I ask (someone, not necessarily Marco himself) that Marco should come with us.*

(a) Marco mi chiede di **pagare**. — *Marco asks me to pay.*

(b) Marco chiede **che** io **paghi**. — *Marco asks that I pay.*

(a) Non permette a suo marito di **uscire** la sera. — *She doesn't allow her husband to go out in the evening.*

(b) Non permette **che** suo marito **esca** la sera. — *She doesn't allow her husband to go out in the evenings.*

# 21

## Expressing regrets

---

**Le funzioni**

In this unit you will learn about:
Expressing regrets • Saying you are sorry

**Le strutture**

**Vorrei** plus **che** plus the pluperfect subjunctive • Other ways of using the pluperfect subjunctive

---

## Nota introduttiva

---

When a wish is expressed that the action had or hadn't taken place, the *pluperfect* tense of the subjunctive is used:

### After the conditional

Desidererei che non fosse mai successa questa cosa.

*I wish that this had never happened. (Lit. I would like that this had never happened.)*

Preferirebbe che io l'avessi avvertito.

*He would prefer me to have warned him. (Lit. He would prefer that I had warned him.)*

Vorrei che non fossimo mai venuti.

*I wish that we had never come. (Lit. I would like that we had never come.)*

### After the past conditional

Avrei voluto che non fossimo mai venuti.

*I would have wished that we had never come.*

> Avrebbe preferito che la
> mamma gli avesse regalato
> una pistola

*He would have preferred his mum*
*to have given him a (toy) pistol.*

Both conditional and past conditional can also be followed directly by the infinitive:

> Avrei voluto non **esserci**.
> Avrei voluto **vederlo**.
> **Preferirei** non **essere** qui
> in questo momento.

*I would have liked not to be there.*
*I would like to have seen it.*
*I would prefer not to be here right*
*now.*

---

## Analisi della grammatica

---

### 1 How to form the pluperfect subjunctive

The pluperfect subjunctive is formed by combining the imperfect subjunctive of the verb **avere**, or the verb **essere** (whichever the verb normally takes), and the past participle, e.g. **mangiato, bevuto** and **partito**:

---

**Vorrebbe che . . .**

| (io) | avessi mangiato | (noi) | avessimo mangiato |
|------|-----------------|-------|-------------------|
| (tu) | avessi mangiato | (voi) | aveste mangiato |
| (lui) | avesse mangiato | (loro) | avessero mangiato |
| (lei) | avesse mangiato | | |
| (Lei) | avesse mangiato | | |

---

**Vorrebbe che . . .**

| (io) | fossi venuto/a | (noi) | fossimo venuti/e |
|------|----------------|-------|------------------|
| (tu) | fossi venuto/a | (voi) | foste venuti/e |
| (lui) | fosse venuto/a | (loro) | fossero venuti/e |
| (lei) | fosse venuto/a | | |
| (Lei) | fosse venuto/a | | |

---

## 2 When to use the pluperfect subjunctive

The pluperfect subjunctive is generally used in a dependent clause where in a 'normal' sentence you would use the pluperfect indicative (**avevo mangiato, ero venuto**, etc.), i.e. to express something that someone *had* or *hadn't* done.

Look at these pairs of examples: in the *first* example of each pair, the pluperfect *indicative* (the normal verb form ) is used; in the *second* of each pair, the *pluperfect subjunctive* is used:

**Avere** verb

> **Avevi** già assaggiato la pasta con le vongole?     *Had you already tried pasta with clams?*
>
> Pensavo che tu **avessi** già **assaggiato** la pasta con le vongole.     *I thought you had already tried pasta with clams.*

**Essere** verb

> **Eri** già **stata** a Pompei?     *Had you already been to Pompei?*
>
> Pensavo che tu **fossi** già **stata** a Pompei.     *I thought you had already been to Pompei.*

## 3 How to form the past conditional

In unit 20, we saw how the conditional was used, often to express a wish or to put a request more politely. The past conditional is used in a similar way.

Whereas the conditional is expressed in English by the words *would* or *should*, the past conditional is expressed by the words *would have* or *should have*. It is formed, in Italian, by using the conditional of **avere** (or **essere**, in the case of verbs that use **essere** in the past) with the past participle (the **-ato, -ito, -uto** form):

---

**Verbs in -are:**

| | |
|---|---|
| avrei mangiato | *I would have eaten* |
| avresti mangiato | *you would have eaten* |
| avrebbe mangiato | *he/she/you would have eaten* |
| avremmo mangiato | *we would have eaten* |
| avreste mangiato | *you would have eaten* |
| avrebbero mangiato | *they would have eaten* |

---

| **Verbs in -ere:** | |
|---|---|
| avrei potuto | *I would have been able to* |
| avresti potuto | *you would have been able to* |
| avrebbe potuto | *he/she/you would have been able to* |
| avremmo potuto | *we would have been able to* |
| avreste potuto | *you would have been able to* |
| avrebbero potuto | *they would have been able to* |

| **Verbs in -ito:** | |
|---|---|
| avrei dormito | *I would have slept* |
| avresti dormito | *you would have slept* |
| avrebbe dormito | *he/she/you would have slept* |
| avremmo dormito | *we would have slept* |
| avreste dormito | *you would have slept* |
| avrebbero dormito | *they would have slept* |

| **Verbs that take *essere*, e.g. *andare* (to go):** | |
|---|---|
| sarei andato/a | *I would have gone* |
| saresti andato/a | *you would have gone* |
| sarebbe andato/a | *he/she/you would have gone* |
| saremmo andati/e | *we would have gone* |
| sareste andati/e | *you would have gone* |
| sarebbero andati/e | *they would have gone* |

In the case of verbs that take **essere**, the participle must change ending depending on whether the subject is masculine or feminine, singular or plural.

## 4  When to use the past conditional

### (a) To express a wish

Avrei preferito una granita.　　*I would have preferred a granita (water ice).*

### (b) When a condition is implied or stated

Use the past conditional when the action would have taken place if certain conditions had been fulfilled. Sometimes these conditions are stated; at other times they are just implied.

Sarei andato in vancanza, ma　*I would have gone on holiday, but*
non avevo i soldi.　　　　　　*I didn't have the money.*

| Io non avrei comprato quella casa. | *I wouldn't have bought that house.* (The condition implied is: 'If it had been me . . .' |

### (c) Indirect or reported speech, or after a verb of saying, thinking, etc.

In Italian, when the verb in the main part of the sentence is in the *past*, the conditional also has to be in the past:

| **Ero sicura** che ti **sarebbe piaciuto.** | *I was sure that you would have liked it.* |

Even when, in English, you use the present tense (*I **would** come*), in Italian, you *must* use the past tense if the first (main) verb is in the past:

| Mi ha detto che **sarebbe venuto.** | *He told me he would come.* |
| Gli ho detto che ci **avrei pensato.** | *I told him I would think about it.* |

### (d) To express rumour or hearsay

In unit 20, you saw how the conditional is used to express hearsay, (e.g. in a newspaper report). The past conditional can also be used in this way and translated in English as a past tense:

| Secondo il giornalista, l'economia inglese **sarebbe migliorata** in questo periodo. | *According to the journalist, the English economy has improved recently.* |
| Stando alle statistiche, gli italiani **avrebbero comprato** più beni di lusso negli anni '90. | *According to statistics, the Italians have bought more luxury goods in the nineties.* |

## ———— In contesto ————

## Dialogo

Andrea   Ciao, Nando, pensavo che tu fossi già partito per la Spagna.

Nando   No, invece, abbiamo avuto dei problemi con la

macchina. Il meccanico ci aveva fatto la manutenzione e ha detto che era tutto a posto ma è impossibile che l'abbia controllata per bene, perché dopo neanche duecento metri si è fermata e non è più partita. Magari non l'avessimo mai portata da lui!

Andrea  Ma vi fidavate di questo meccanico? Lo conoscevate già?

Nando  Noi non sapevamo se fosse bravo o no. Dei nostri amici avevano portato la macchina da lui, e ci avevano detto che era bravo, benchè avesse fatto pagare un prezzo un po' salato. E poi ci ha riparato la macchina subito, senza che dovessimo aspettare.

Andrea  Era meglio invece se aveste aspettato!

**English translation**

Andrea  *Hi, Nando. I thought you had left for Spain already?*

Nando  *No, we had problems with the car. The mechanic had serviced it for us and he said everything was OK, but it's impossible that he checked it well (he couldn't have checked it well) because after not even 200 metres it stopped and wouldn't go again. I wish we had never taken it to him.*

Andrea  *But did you trust this mechanic? Did you know him already?*

Nando  *We didn't know if he was any good or not. Some friends of ours had taken their car to him and had told us he was good, although he had charged a high price. And also he repaired the car for us straightaway, without us having to wait.*

Andrea  *Instead of which it would have been better if you had waited!*

---

prezzo salato   *high price (Lit. salty!)*

---

## Soggiorno a Venezia

La vita è piena di sbagli. Noi avevamo prenotato l'albergo a Venezia su consiglio di un'amica. Non sapevamo che lei non fosse mai stata a Venezia, e che il nome dell'albergo l'avesse trovato su una vecchia guida turistica. Sarà stato bello cinquanta anni fa, ma non più.

E il ristorante poi . . .! Morivamo di sete! Nonostante avessimo detto al cameriere tre volte di portare del vino rosso, ha portato solo acqua minerale. Peccato poi che il cuoco abbia dimenticato di togliere lo spago prima di servire l'arrosto . . . mi chiedevo poi perché mio marito avesse deciso di mangiarlo; ma lui, poveretto, aveva pensato che il cuoco avesse preparato una specialità tipica e che lo spago ne fosse una parte essenziale. Avremmo mangiato meglio alla mensa degli studenti e avremmo anche speso di meno.

### English translation

*Life is full of mistakes. We had booked the hotel in Venice on the advice of a friend. We didn't know that she had never been to Venice, but had found the name in an old guide book. It might have been nice 50 years ago but no longer.*

*And the restaurant . . .! We were dying of thirst. Despite the fact that we had asked the waiter three times to bring us some red wine, he brought only mineral water. A pity too that the chef forgot to take off the string around the roast before serving it. I wondered why my husband had decided to eat it, but he, poor thing, thought the chef had prepared some typical local speciality and that the string was an essential part of it. We would have eaten better at the student canteen, and we would have spent less too.*

## In aggiunta

### 1 Other expressions of regret

| | |
|---|---|
| Che peccato! | *What a pity! What a shame!* |
| Che peccato che lui non abbia potuto finire il corso di laurea. | *What a pity that he couldn't finish his degree course.* |
| Che peccato che voi non siate potuti venire/abbiate potuto venire. | *What a shame that you couldn't come.* |
| Mi dispiace. | *I am sorry.* |
| Mi dispiace che non ci siamo più visti. | *I'm sorry that we haven't seen each other again.* |
| Sono desolato. | *I'm really sorry.* |
| Sono desolato che lui non ti abbia più telefonato. | *I'm really sorry that he hasn't rung you anymore.* |

# 22

## — Expressing conditions —

## ——— Nota introduttiva ———

Study these different examples of conditional sentences before reading
the grammar explanation:

**Conditions that might well be met and simple statements of fact**

| | |
|---|---|
| Se ho tempo, scrivo delle cartoline. | *If I have time, I write postcards.* |
| Se verrà Marco, andremo al cinema. | *If Marco comes, we will go to the cinema.* |

**Conditions that could still be met, but are unlikely to be met**

| | |
|---|---|
| Se fossi ricca, comprerei una Rolls Royce. | *If I were rich, I would buy a Rolls Royce.* |

| | |
|---|---|
| Se avessimo tempo, andremmo a visitare la cattedrale. | *If we had time, we would go and visit the cathedral.* |

### Conditions that cannot now be met

| | |
|---|---|
| Se avessi sposato un italiano avrei dovuto imparare l'italiano. | *If I had married an Italian, I would have had to learn Italian.* |
| Se avessimo comprato la guida non avremmo avuto tanti problemi per trovare un buon ristorante. | *If we had bought the guide we would not have had so many problems finding a good restaurant.* |

## —— Analisi della grammatica ——

When we start a sentence with *if* in English, we are laying down a condition (*If* you do or don't do something, then something will or won't happen).

Sometimes, it is a straightforward statement of fact:
*If you stay up late, you will be tired tomorrow.*

Sometimes, the condition is one which can easily be met:
*If we have time, we will go and see the Duomo.*

Sometimes, it is unlikely ever to happen, in other words it is hypothetical:
*If I were to become rich, I would buy a Rolls Royce.*

And sometimes, it can no longer happen because the time or opportunity has passed:
*If I had had more time, I would have gone to see the museum.*

Here is how these different ideas are expressed in Italian:

## 1 Conditions that can or might be met and simple statements of fact

In this type of sentence where a straightforward statement of facts is involved, the indicative (the normal verb form) is used, in a variety of tenses:

**Present**

| | |
|---|---|
| Se Lei mi dà L.100.000, io Le do il resto. | *If you give me L.100.000, I'll give you the change.* |

**Future**

| | |
|---|---|
| Se andrete a Roma, potrete vedere il Colosseo. | *If you go to Rome, you will be able to see the Colosseum.* |

**Past tenses:**

| | |
|---|---|
| Se aveva paura, non lo dimostrava. | *If she was afraid, it didn't show.* |

**Mixture of tenses**
**The present plus the the future:**

| | |
|---|---|
| Se non fai il bravo, non andrai al mare domani. | *If you're not good, you won't go to the seaside tomorrow.* |

**The perfect plus the future perfect:**

| | |
|---|---|
| Se hai parlato con lui, avrai capito come stanno le cose. | *If you have spoken to him, you will have understood how things are.* |

**The present plus the imperative:**

| | |
|---|---|
| Se vieni, fammi sapere. | *If you come, let me know.* |

## 2 Conditions that are unlikely to be met

Where a condition is expressed that is unlikely to be fulfilled, the *if* clause (conditional clause) is expressed by **se** and the imperfect subjunctive, while the event which *would* happen (the main clause) is expressed by the present conditional. Because it is purely hypothetical, it is called, in Italian, the **periodo ipotetico**.

| | |
|---|---|
| Se l'albergo non fosse cosi caro, resteremmo più di una notte. | *If the hotel were less dear, we would stay more than one night.* |
| Se avessimo più soldi, andremmo a mangiare al ristorante. | *If we had more money, we would go and eat in a restaurant.* |
| Se gli italiani quidassero con più attenzione, non ci sarebbero tanti incidenti. | *If the Italians drove more carefully, there wouldn't be so many accidents.* |

## 3 Conditions that can not now be met

When a condition or hypothesis is expressed that can *not* now be fulfilled because the opportunity has passed, the *if* clause uses **se** and the pluperfect subjunctive, while the main clause (the event which *would have* happened) is expressed in the past conditional:

*If clause:*

**Se** io non **avessi perso** il portafoglio . . .     *If I had not lost my wallet . . .*

*Main clause:*

. . . non **avrei avuto** tutti questi problemi.     *. . . I wouldn't have had all these problems.*

*If clause plus a main clause:*

**Se fossimo venuti** in treno, **saremmo arrivati** prima.     *If we had come by train, we would have got here sooner.*

**Se** tu **avessi guidato** con più prudenza, non **saremmo andati** a finire contro il muro.     *If you had driven more carefully, we would not have ended up crashing into the wall.*

The forms and uses of the pluperfect subjunctive were given in unit 21.

The past conditional can also be used after a gerund (**-ando**, or **-endo**) where the idea of *if* is implied:

**Sapendo** questo, non **sarei andata** con lui.     *If I had known this, I wouldn't have gone with him.*

## 4 Phrases expressing condition

A few conjunctions (joining words) that express condition are:

| | |
|---|---|
| a condizione che | *on condition that* |
| a meno che | *unless* |
| purchè | *provided that* |

All these conjunctions are followed by a verb in the subjunctive (see unit 19):

Io ti ci accompagno a
condizione che tu **paghi** la
benzina.

*I'll take you there on condition
that you pay for the petrol.*

Potete uscire purchè non
**rientriate** troppo tardi.

*You can go out so long as you
don't come back too late.*

Possiamo andare al mare a
meno che Lei non **preferisca**
andare in campagna.

*We can go to the seaside unless
you prefer to go to the country.*

---

## In contesto

| | | |
|---|---|---|
| Carla | **Ciao, Maria. Come mai non sei venuta stasera?** | *Hi, Maria. How come you didn't come this evening?* |
| Maria | **Sarei venuta se non avessi avuto tante altre cose da fare.** | *I would have come if I hadn't had so many other things to do.* |
| Carla | **Peccato. Se tu fossi venuta, ti avrei fatto conoscere mio cugino.** | *Pity. If you had come, I would have introduced you to my cousin.* |
| Maria | **Pazienza! Sarà per la prossima volta. Se lui viene per Natale, fammi sapere.** | *Never mind! Next time! If he comes for Christmas, let me know.* |
| Carla | **Non mancherò. Intanto se tu non fossi sempre così impegnata, ti inviterei a cena.** | *I wouldn't fail to. Meanwhile if you weren't always so busy, I would invite you to dinner.* |
| Maria | **Se mi inviti, accetto volentieri!** | *If you invite me, I accept with pleasure!* |

---

> **pazienza!**   *(Lit. patience!) Never mind! Can't be helped.*

---

## In aggiunta

### 1  Past conditional replaced by the imperfect

Often, in hypothetical sentence such as that seen in 3, both conditional
and imperfect subjunctive are replaced by a simple imperfect tense
(indicative) in spoken Italian:

Se lo **sapevo**, non **venivo**   *If I had known, I wouldn't have*
stasera.                          *come this evening.*

Occasionally, only the hypothetical part of the sentence (the *if* clause) is replaced by an imperfect:

Se lo **sapevo**, non sarei venuta   *If I had known, I wouldn't have*
stasera.                            *come this evening.*

# Grammatica
## *Grammar Notes*

## Irregular nouns

### (a) Nouns with the same form for both singular and plural

Nouns ending in an accented vowel:

| | | | |
|---|---|---|---|
| il caffè | *coffee* | i caffè | *coffees* |
| il lunedì | *Monday* | i lunedì | *Mondays* |

Nouns ending in **-ù** or **-à** are usually feminine and express an abstract quality:

| | | | |
|---|---|---|---|
| la virtù | *virtue* | le virtù | *virtues* |
| la città | *the city* | le città | *the cities* |

Nouns ending in **-i**:
These are mainly feminine:

| | | | |
|---|---|---|---|
| la crisi | *the crisis* | le crisi | *the crises* |

But note:

| | | | |
|---|---|---|---|
| il brindisi | *the toast* | i brindisi | *the toasts* |
| *(e.g. to bride and groom)* | | | |

Feminine nouns ending in **-ie**:

| | | | |
|---|---|---|---|
| la serie | *the series* | le serie | *the series* |

But note:

| | | | |
|---|---|---|---|
| la moglie | *the wife* | le mogli | *the wives* |

Abbreviated words:

| | | | |
|---|---|---|---|
| la bici(cicletta) | *the bike* | le bici | *the bikes* |
| il cinema(tografo) | *the cinema* | i cinema | *the cinemas* |

Words of foreign origin (mainly ending in a consonant)

| | | | |
|---|---|---|---|
| il night | *the nightclub* | i night | *the nightclubs* |
| il toast | *toasted sandwich* | i toast | *toasted sandwiches* |

## (b) Nouns with masculine singular form -o, and feminine plural form -a

| | | | |
|---|---|---|---|
| il paio | *the pair* | le paia | *the pairs* |
| l'uovo | *the egg* | le uova | *the eggs* |
| il migliaio | *thousand* | le migliaia | *thousands* |

Some nouns have regular plural form **-i** *and* irregular plural form **-a**.

Often the regular plural has a figurative meaning, while the irregular plural has a literal meaning:

| | | | |
|---|---|---|---|
| il braccio | *the arm* | le braccia | *the arms (of a person)* |
| | | i bracci | *the arms (e.g. of a chandelier)* |

But in some cases there is no difference in meaning:

| | | | |
|---|---|---|---|
| il lenzuolo | *the sheet* | le lenzuola | *the sheets* |
| | | *or* i lenzuoli | |

## (c) Nouns that change in the plural

Masculine nouns ending in **-co** and **-go**:

Nouns where the stress falls on the second last syllable form their plural in **-chi** or **-ghi** keeping the hard 'g' sound:

| | | | |
|---|---|---|---|
| il luo**go** | *the place* | i luo**ghi** | *the places* |
| il fi**co** | *the fig* | i fi**chi** | *the figs* |

Unfortunately there are many exceptions:

| | | | |
|---|---|---|---|
| l'ami**co** | *the friend* | gli ami**ci** | *the friends* |

Words where the stress generally falls *before* the second last syllable, form their plural in **-ci** and **-gi** with a soft 'g':

| | | | |
|---|---|---|---|
| l'aspara**go** | *asparagus* | gli aspara**gi** | *asparagus* |
| il medi**co** | *doctor* | i medi**ci** | *doctors* |

But again there are very many exceptions:

| | | | |
|---|---|---|---|
| il catalo**go** | *catalogues* | i catalo**ghi** | *catalogues* |

Feminine nouns ending in **-ca** and **-ga**:

Plural in **-che** and **-ghe**:

| | | | |
|---|---|---|---|
| l'ami**ca** | *the friend* | le ami**che** | *the friends* |

Feminine nouns ending in **-cia** or **-gia**:

Plural in **-cie** or **-gie** if there is a vowel before the -cia, or -gia:

| | | | |
|---|---|---|---|
| la farma**cia** | *the chemist's* | le farma**cie** | *the chemists'* |

| la vali**gia** | *the suitcase* | le vali**gie** | *the suitcases* |

Plural in **-ce** or **-ge**, if there is a consonant before the **-cia** or **-gia**:

| la spia**ggia** | *the beach* | le spia**gge** | *the beaches* |
| la man**cia** | *the tip* | le man**ce** | *the tips* |

Other nouns ending in **-io**:

If the stress falls on the i, the i is doubled:

| lo **zio** | *the uncle* | gli **zii** | *the uncles* |

Otherwise it is not:

| lo studio | *the study* | gli studi | *the studies* |

Compound nouns

Nouns made up of two different words stuck together sometimes have rather unusual plural forms:

| il capostazione | *station master* | i capistazione | *station masters* |
| il fuoribordo | *motor boat* | i fuoribordo | *motor boats* |

Since the rules, and the exceptions, are numerous, it is safer to use a good dictionary to check the plural of such nouns.

## —— Bello, buono, grande, santo ——

The adjective **bello** when placed before the noun has the same forms as the definite article **il, lo, la**, etc.:

| un **bel** fiore | *a beautiful flower* |
| un **bello** specchio | *a beautiful mirror* |
| una **bella** casa | *a beautiful house* |
| una **bell'**automobile | *a beautiful car* |
| dei **bei** ragazzi | *some nice-looking boys* |
| dei **begli** alberi | *some lovely trees* |
| delle **belle** cose | *some beautiful things* |

**Grande** can change form before masculine singular words but this is optional:

un **gran** capitano/un grande capitano   *a great captain*

Before feminine nouns, or before vowels or **z, ps, x, gn, s** with a consonant, use **grande**:

| un **grande** albergo | *a great hotel* |
| un **grande** scultore | *a great sculptor* |
| una **grande** sorpresa | *a big surprise* |

**Buono** in the singular has the same forms as un, una etc.:

| | |
|---|---|
| un **buon** ristorante | *a good restaurant* |
| un **buono** studente | *a good student* |
| una **buona** donna | *a good woman* |
| una **buon**'idea | *a good idea* |

**Santo** (feminine **Santa**) meaning *saint* (e.g. Santo Stefano) before a masculine singular name not beginning with **z** or **s** with a consonant is shortened to **San**. Before names beginning with a vowel it can be shortened to **Sant'**.

## ——— Comparison of adjectives ———

### Più (*more*): meno (*less*)

When making a comparison, *than* is expressed by **di**, or **che** if *than* comes directly between the two things or people which are compared:

| | |
|---|---|
| Lui è meno bravo **di** te. | *He is less clever than you.* |
| Marco è più simpatico **di** Giuliano. | *Marco is nicer than Giuliano.* |
| Fa meno freddo oggi **che** ieri. | *It is less cold today than yesterday.* |
| Adesso si mangia più pesce **che** carne. | *Nowadays one eats more fish than meat.* |

The **di** (*than*) sometimes combines with **il**, **lo**, or **la**:

| | |
|---|---|
| Gli italiani sono più simpatici **degli** inglesi. | *The Italians are nicer than the English.* |

The adjectives below have their own special form of comparative as well as the regular form:

### Buono, più buono *or* migliore

| | |
|---|---|
| I gelati francesi sono **buoni**, ma i gelati italiani sono **più buoni.** | *French ice-creams are good, but Italian ice-creams are better.* |
| Quest' albergo è **buono**, ma l'altro è **migliore**. | *This hotel is good, but the other is better.* |

### Cattivo, più cattivo *or* peggiore

| | |
|---|---|
| Questo vino è **cattivo**, ma l'altro è ancora **più cattivo**. | *This wine is bad, but the other is even worse.* |
| Questa pensione non è buona, ma l'altra è **peggiore**. | *This hotel isn't good, but the other is worse.* |

### *Grande*, più grande (*physical size*), maggiore (*older, greater in importance*)

| | |
|---|---|
| Milano è **più grande** di Torino. | *Milan is bigger than Turin.* |
| La mia sorella **maggiore** si chiama Rosa. | *My older sister is called Rosa.* |

### *Piccolo*, più piccolo (*physical size*), minore (*younger, lesser in importance*)

| | |
|---|---|
| La nostra camera è **più piccola** della vostra. | *Our room is smaller than yours.* |
| Questo è di **minore** importanza. | *This is of less importance.* |

**Maggiore** and **minore** have plural forms: **maggiori** and **minori**.

### Tanto . . . quanto: così . . . come

| | |
|---|---|
| La pensione di seconda categoria può essere **tanto** comoda **quanto** l'albergo di lusso. | *A Category 2 hotel can be just comfortable as a luxury hotel.* |

Così and tanto are sometimes omitted.

### Il più (most) . . . Il meno (least)

| | |
|---|---|
| È **il** ristorante **meno** caro della città. | *It's the least expensive restaurant in town.* |
| È **la** chiesa **più** bella di Venezia. | *It's the most beautiful church in Venice.* |

The common adjectives can also come before the noun:

| | |
|---|---|
| È **il più** bel ragazzo della classe. | *He's the best-looking boy in the class.* |

Again **buono, cattivo, grande, piccolo** have the two different forms mentioned above:

| | |
|---|---|
| Gli incidenti stradali sono **la maggiore** causa di morte in Italia. | *Road accidents are the biggest cause of death in Italy. (greatest)* |
| La 126 è **la** macchina **più piccola** di tutte. | *The 126 is the smallest car of all. (physical size)* |

When *no* comparison is being made, use **molto** or **estremamente** or **veramente**:

I bambini erano **veramente** stanchi.

*The kids were really tired.*

Or add the suffix **-issimo** on the end:

Questi fiori sono **bellissimi**.

*These flowers are very beautiful.*

## Comparison of adverbs

### Più (*more*) or meno (*less*):

Gianfranco cammina **più** velocemente.

*Gianfranco walks faster.*

Gianfranco cammina **meno** velocemente.

*Gianfranco walks less quickly.*

### Bene (meglio), male (peggio), molto (più), poco (meno)

Giuliana guida bene, ma Mariangela guida **meglio**.

*Giuliana drives well, but Mariangela drives better.*

Franco cucina male, ma Giovanni cucina **peggio**.

*Franco cooks badly, but Giovanni cooks worse.*

**Più** imparo questa lingua **più** difficile la trovo.

*The more I study this language the more difficult I find it.*

Marco studia molto, ma Monica studia **di più**.

*Marco studies a lot, but Monica studies more.*

**Meno** lavoro fai, **meno** guadagni.

*The less work you do the less you earn.*

Arabella lavora poco, ma Marina lavora **di meno**.

*Arabella works little, but Marina works less.*

### Tanto . . . quanto; così . . . come

Sandra guida **così** male **come** sua sorella.

*Sandra drives just as badly as her sister.*

### Il più possibile/molto/-issimamente

Guidava **il più** lentamente **possibile**.

*He drove very slowly.*

Guidava **molto** lentamente.

*He drove very slowly.*

Guidava lent**issimamente**.

*He drove very slowly.*

Lo vedo **il meno possibile**.

*I see him as little as possible.*

When there is no comparison, use **benissimo, malissimo, moltissimo** or **pochissimo**:

| | |
|---|---|
| Ha sciato **benissimo**. | *She skied very very well.* |
| L'ha fatto **malissimo**. | *He did it very very badly.* |
| Hai studiato **pochissimo**. | *You've studied very very little.* |

The first two have alternative forms: **ottimamente** and **pessimamente**.

---
## Pronouns
---

The forms **mi, ti, gli, le, Le, ci, vi, gli/loro** are used with any verb that takes an *indirect* object:

When something is given *to* someone:

| | |
|---|---|
| **Vi** porto il conto? | *Shall I bring (to) you the bill?* |
| **Ti** ha dato il resto? | *Did he give (to) you the change?* |

Or done *for* someone:

| | |
|---|---|
| **Mi** compreresti il giornale? | *Would you buy the newspaper for me?* |
| **Ti** preparo un caffè? | *Shall I make (for) you a coffee?* |

### Combined pronouns me lo, te lo, glielo, etc:

Look what happens when direct object (**mi, ti, lo, la,** etc. see Unit 14) meets indirect object (**mi, ti, gli, le,** etc.):

| Indirect | Direct | Combined | Singular |
|---|---|---|---|
| mi | lo | me lo | *it to me* |
| ti | lo | te lo | *it to you* |
| gli | lo | glielo | *it to him* |
| le | lo | glielo | *it to her* |
| Le | lo | glielo | *it to you (polite)* |
| | | | **Plural** |
| ci | lo | ce lo | *it to us* |
| vi | lo | ve lo | *it to you* |
| gli | lo | glielo | *it to them* |

The same pattern is repeated whatever the direct object pronoun: **mi** plus **li** = **me li**; **mi** plus **le** = **me le**; etc. (The exception is **loro** which is always after the verb and does not combine with the other pronouns.)

This is how they are used:

> Come si apre questa bottiglia? *How does one open this bottle?*
> **Te la** apro io. *I'll open it for you.*
> I ragazzi hanno lasciato questo *The kids have left behind this*
> libro. *book.*
> **Glielo** mandiamo per posta. *We'll send it to them by mail.*

**Glielo** means *it to him* or *it to her* or *it to them*.

To avoids confusion you can use **a** **a lui, a lei, a loro**:

> Lo mando **a lui**. *I send it to him.*
> Lo mando **a lei**. *I send it to her.*
> Lo mando **a loro**. *I send it to them.*

## Position of pronouns

Normally the pronouns come *before* the verb, but they come *after*:

The infinitive (the **-are, -ere, -ire** form):

> Sono andata in centro per *I went to the centre to buy it.*
> comprar**la**.
> Ho deciso di spedir**gli** una *I've decided to send him a*
> cartolina. *postcard.*
> Mi ha telefonato per *He rang me to ask for it.*
> chieder**melo**.

With **volere, dovere, sapere, potere, preferire** the pronouns can either be joined to the end of the infinitive as above, *or* come before both verbs:

> **Lo** puoi comprare al centro. *You can buy it in town.*
> *or* Puoi comprar**lo** al centro.
> Voglio parlar**gli** chiaro. *I want to speak clearly to him.*
> *or* **Gli** voglio parlare chiaro.
> Deve dir**glielo** appena *She must tell him it as soon as*
> possibile. *possible.*
> *or* **Glielo** deve dire appena
> possibile.

The gerund (**-ando, -endo** form):

| | |
|---|---|
| Telefonando**ti** di sera, risparmio parecchio. | *By phoning you in the evening, I save a lot.* |
| Riparando**telo** gratis, ti faccio un grande favore. | *Repairing it for you free, I'm doing you a big favour.* |

With **stare** plus the gerund, the pronoun can be joined to the end of the gerund as above, *or* can come before **stare**:

| | |
|---|---|
| **Lo** stavo guardando ora. | *I was just looking at it now.* |
| *or* Stavo guardando**lo** ora. | |

The **tu, noi, voi** imperative (giving an order):

| | |
|---|---|
| Chiamiamo**li**! | *Let's call them!* |
| Telefona**gli**! | *Ring him!* |
| Passate**melo**! | *Pass it to me!* |

When attached to the one-syllable imperatives such as **da'**! **fa'**! **di'**! **sta'**! **va'**! the initial consonant of the pronoun doubles:

| | |
|---|---|
| **Dallo** a tuo fratello! | *Give it to your brother!* |
| **Dammelo**! | *Give it to me!* |
| **Dimmi** cosa vuoi! | *Tell me what you want!* |
| **Facci** un piacere! | *Do us a favour!* |

Except for **gli**:

| | |
|---|---|
| Di**gli** di andare via! | *Tell him to go away!* |

The negative imperative:

| | |
|---|---|
| Non segui**rmi**! | *Don't follow me!* |
| *or* Non **mi** seguire! | *Don't follow me!* |
| Non compriamo**lo**! | *Let's not buy it!* |
| *or* Non **lo** compriamo! | *Let's not buy it!* |
| Non mangiate**li**! | *Don't eat them!* |
| *or* Non **li** mangiate! | *Don't eat them!* |

Lei (polite) form:

| | |
|---|---|
| **Lo** prenda pure! | *Please take it!* |
| Non **lo** prenda! | *Don't take it!* |

**Lo** and **la** are often abbreviated before the verb **avere** to **l'**. But the plurals **li** and **le** should *not* be abbreviated:

| | |
|---|---|
| Ce **l'ho**. | *I have it.* |
| Ce **le** ho. | *I have them.* |

## Ci

**Ci** can mean *there* or *to there*:

| | |
|---|---|
| Mi piace Londra; **ci** abito da sei anni. | *I like London; I've lived there for six years.* |
| Andando**ci** di lunedì, troverete meno gente. | *Going there on a Monday, you will find fewer people.* |

**Vi** (*there*) can replace **ci**, but is less common in spoken Italian.

**Ci** can be used after a verb such as **credere, riuscire, pensare**:

| | |
|---|---|
| Credi a quello che dice? | *Do you believe what he says?* |
| No, non **ci** credo. | *No, I don't believe it.* |

Or after a verb which normally takes **con**:

| | |
|---|---|
| Hai parlato con il direttore? | *Did you speak to the director?* |
| Sì, **ci** ho parlato ieri. | *Yes, I spoke to him yesterday.* |

With the verb **avere**, especially when there are direct object pronouns as well:

| | |
|---|---|
| Hai il giornale? | *Do you have the newspaper?* |
| No, non **ce** l'ho. | *No, I don't have it.* |

In the expression **farcela** (*to manage it, to cope*):

| | |
|---|---|
| **Ce la** fai a finire quella relazione? | *Can you manage to finish that report?* |

And with the verbs **vedere, sentire**:

| | |
|---|---|
| Non **ci** vedo. | *I can't see anything.* |
| **Ci** senti, Chiara? | *Can you hear, Chiara?* |

## Ne

**Ne** means *of it, of them*:

| | |
|---|---|
| Quanti figli hai? | *How many children do you have?* |
| **Ne** ho tre. | *I have three (of them).* |

Note the agreement when **ne** is used with a past tense and followed by a number or quantity:

| | |
|---|---|
| Hai visto dei gabbiani? | *Have you seen any seagulls?* |
| Sì, ne ho visti tre. | *Yes, I have seen three.* |

It means *some* or *any* where no quantity is mentioned:

| | |
|---|---|
| Vuoi delle patatine? | *Do you want some crisps?* |
| No, grazie. Ne ho. | *No, thanks. I have some.* |
| *or* Sì, grazie. Non ne ho. | *Yes, thanks. I haven't got any.* |

It means *of it* when the verb takes **di**:

| | |
|---|---|
| Parla dell'affare? | *Does he speak about the affair?* |
| **Ne** parla spesso. | *He often speaks of it.* |

Or **da**:

| | |
|---|---|
| Sono usciti dal ristorante? | *Have they come out of the restaurant?* |
| **Ne** escono adesso. | *They're coming out of it just now.* |

And in fixed expressions:

| | |
|---|---|
| Me ne vado. | *I'm going away.* |
| Non ne posso più. | *I can't take any more.* |
| Ne va della mia reputazione. | *It's a question of my reputation.* |

When there are other pronouns, **ne** comes after:

| | |
|---|---|
| Me ne dai un po'? | *Will you give me a bit (of it)?* |

### With past tenses (e.g. passato prossimo)

The participle (**mangiato**, **capito**, etc.) has to agree with the pronoun object:

| | |
|---|---|
| Hai visto i bambini? | *Have you seen the children?* |
| No, non li ho visti. | *No, I haven't seen them.* |
| Avevi già conosciuto Lidia? | *Had you already met Lidia?* |
| No, non l'avevo mai **vista** prima. | *No, I had never seen her before.* |

# — Qualche, alcun, ogni, ciascun, tale —

### Alcun, (*some, any*)

The singular is used only after a negative. **Alcun (alcuno/alcuna/alcun')** has the same endings as **un/uno**, etc. and means *any*:

| | |
|---|---|
| Non ho alcun' idea. | *I haven't a clue.* |
| Non c'era alcuna ragione. | *There was no reason at all.* |

## Qualunque, qualsiasi (*any, whatever*)

These are singular only.

| | |
|---|---|
| Farebbe qualunque cosa pur di vederla. | *He would do anything just to see her.* |
| Pagherebbe qualsiasi prezzo pur di avere quella macchina. | *He would pay any price just to have that car.* |

Used *after* the noun, **qualunque** and **qualsiasi** can be singular or plural and mean *any kind of/any whatever/any old*:

| | |
|---|---|
| Mettiti un vestito qualunque. | *Put on any old dress.* |
| Prendo dei biscotti qualsiasi. | *I'll take any old biscuits.* |

## Chiunque, (*anyone, whoever*)

This is singular only.

| | |
|---|---|
| Chiunque può venire. | *Anyone can come.* |

## Ogni (*every, each*)

This is singular only.

| | |
|---|---|
| Ogni cosa è possibile. | *Everything is possible.* |
| Ogni ospite paga lo stesso. | *Each guest pays the same.* |

## Ognuno (*each one, everyone*)

This is singular only.

| | |
|---|---|
| Ognuno fa quello che vuole. | *Each does what he wants.* |

## Ciascuno, (*each, each one*)

This is singular only.

**Ciascun (ciascuno/ciascuna/ciascun')** has the same endings as **un** when used as an adjective:

| | |
|---|---|
| Ci sono quattro persone a ciascun tavolo. | *There are four people at each table.* |

Used on its own, it has just two forms: **ciascuno** and **ciascuna**:

| | |
|---|---|
| Ciascuno dei bambini ha una camera separata. | *Each one of the children has a separate room.* |

### Un tale, tale/i (*such; some person/thing or other*)

Used with a noun, it means *such*:

Ha un tale complesso che non riesce neanche a parlare.
*She has such a complex that she can't even speak.*

Used on its own, it means *somebody or other*:

Ho visto un tale che vendeva delle magliette.
*I saw somebody (some bloke) selling T-shirts.*

### Altro, altro/a/i/e (*another, other*)

C'è un altro modello?
*Is there another style?*

Vuole altro?
*Do you want anything else?*

## Molto, poco, troppo, tutto, tanto, parecchio

Used as an adjective, these have different endings depending on the noun they are describing; used as noun or adverb, their ending does not change.

### Molto (*much, many, a lot*)

Ci sono molte cose da vedere.
*There are lots of things to see.*

Ho mangiato molto.
*I've eaten a lot.*

Scrive molto bene.
*He writes very well.*

### Troppo (*too much, too many*)

Ho mangiato troppo.
*I have eaten too much.*

Ieri c'era troppa gente.
*Yesterday there were too many people.*

### Poco (*little, few*)

Ci sono poche cartoline.
*There are only a few postcards.*

Sono un poco stanco.
*I am a bit tired.*

### Tutto (*all of, everything*)

I ragazzi hanno mangiato tutta la pizza.
*The boys have eaten all the pizza.*

Prendi tutto!
*Take everything!*

# Che, Cui, Il Quale

## Che, *who, what*

| | |
|---|---|
| La signora **che** lavora nel-l'ufficio turistico è di Milano. | *The lady who works in the tourist office is from Milan.* |
| Il treno **che** parte alle dieci arriva all'una. | *The train which leaves at 10 o'clock arrives at 1 o'clock.* |

## Cui, *who/whom, what*

After a preposition (**con, per, di, da, a,** etc.) **che** is replaced by **cui**:

| | |
|---|---|
| L'amico **a cui** volevo telefonare è fuori. | *The friend to whom I wanted to telephone is out.* |
| La ragione **per cui** voglio andare a casa è semplice. | *The reason for which I want to go home is simple.* |

## Il quale, *who/whom, what*

Both **che** and **cui** can be replaced by **il quale/la quale/i quali/le quali** (agreeing with the person or object referred to):

| | |
|---|---|
| Il canotto con **il quale** giocano i bambini è nostro. | *The dinghy with which the children are playing is ours.* |

Adding a preposition (**a, di, da, in, su**) produces forms such as **al quale** (**alla quale, ai quali, alle quali**); **del quale; dal quale; nel quale; sul quale**:

| | |
|---|---|
| La moglie del professore **alla quale** abbiamo telefonato è inglese. | *The wife of the teacher that we telephoned is English.* |

## Il cui, la cui, i cui, le cui, *whose*

The exact form used depends on the object *not* on the person owning it:

| | |
|---|---|
| Il ragazzo **le cui** pinne sono state rubate è inglese. | *The boy whose flippers were stolen is English.* |

## Chi

Chi is used in proverbs and generalisations:

| | |
|---|---|
| **Chi** si alza presto piglia i pesci. | *He who gets up early catches the fish. Or: The early bird catches the worm!* |

**Chi** vuole venire ad Assisi deve comprare il biglietto.

*Those who want to come to Assisi must buy a ticket.*

Colui che, colei che, coloro che (tutti) quelli che

*he who, she who, they who (all) those who*

### Ciò, che, quello che, *what*

These do *not* refer to a specific thing or person:

Faccio **quello che** mi pare.

*I'll do as I please/what I like.*

**Ciò che** bisogna fare è parlargli subito.

*What we have to do is speak to him straightaway.*

### Tutto ciò che, tutto quello che, *everything (which)*

Prendi **tutto ciò** che vuoi.

*Take everything you want.*

### Il che, *which*

**Il che** refers to a *whole* clause or part of sentence:

Mi ha portato dei fiori, **il che** mi ha fatto molto piacere.

*He brought me some flowers, which made me very happy.*

---

# Prepositions

---

## A

| | | | |
|---|---|---|---|
| a scuola | *(at school)* | a casa | *(at home)* |
| a letto | *(in bed)* | al mare | *(at the seaside)* |

Directions and distance:

| | |
|---|---|
| a destra, a sinistra | *on the right, on the left* |
| a nord, a sud (etc) | *North, south (etc)* |
| a dieci chilometri | *ten kms. away* |
| ad un'ora di strada | *an hour's drive away* |

Times and seasons

| | |
|---|---|
| A Natale, a Pasqua | *at Christmas, at Easter* |
| a domani! | *(see you) tomorrow!* |
| alle cinque, a mezzogiorno | *at five o'clock, at midday* |
| un pasto al giorno | *one meal a day* |

How things are prepared:

| | |
|---|---|
| pollo allo spiedo | *chicken on the spit* |
| fatto a mano | *handmade* |

After certain adjectives or participles:

| | |
|---|---|
| pronto a | *ready to* |
| disposto a | *prepared to* |

Some prepositions are always found with **a**:

| | | | |
|---|---|---|---|
| accanto a | *besides, next to* | davanti a | *in front of* |
| fino a | *as far as, until* | in capo a | *at the head/top of* |
| in cima a | *at the top of* | incontro a | *towards, against* |
| in fondo a | *at the bottom of* | di fronte a | *opposite* |
| in mezzo a | *in the middle of* | insieme a | *together with* |
| intorno a | *around* | quanto a | *as regards* |
| riguardo a | *on the subject of, as regards* | vicino a | *near* |
| rispetto a | *in comparison with, regarding* | | |

## DI

Possession, belonging:

| | |
|---|---|
| La regina d'Inghilterra | *the queen of England* |
| un film di Fellini | *a film by Fellini* |

Quantity, age, time (etc)

| | |
|---|---|
| un litro di vino | *a litre of wine* |
| un bambino di dieci anni | *a child aged ten* |

Composition and origin:

| | |
|---|---|
| un bicchiere di cristallo | *a crystal glass* |
| una signora di Firenze | *a lady from Florence* |

Time, seasons:

| | |
|---|---|
| d'inverno, di primavera | *in winter, in spring* |
| di mattina, di notte | *in the morning, at night* |

After certain adjectives and verbs:

| | |
|---|---|
| Sono stufo del lavoro | *I'm bored with work* |
| riempire di acqua | *to fill with water* |

Used as an adverb of manner:

| | |
|---|---|
| di nascosto | *hidden, by stealth* |
| di corsa | *in a hurry, at a rush* |

After qualcosa, niente:

| | |
|---|---|
| Non c'è niente di speciale. | *There's nothing special.* |
| Hai fatto qualcosa di bello? | *Have you done anything nice?* |

Some prepositions are always found with **di**:

| | | | |
|---|---|---|---|
| a causa di | *because of* | | |
| al di là di | *beyond (Lit. and otherwise)* | | |
| fuori di | *outside* | invece di | *instead of* |
| per mezzo di | *by means of* | prima di | *before* |

Those listed below are usually followed by **di** *only* before pronouns (**me, te, lui, lei,** etc.). (Where there is an alternative, the less common preposition is shown in brackets):

| | | | |
|---|---|---|---|
| contro il muro | *(against the wall)* | contro di noi | *(against us)* |
| dietro il muro | *(behind the wall)* | dietro di (a) me | *(behind me)* |
| dentro l'armadio | *(inside the cupboard)* | dentro di (a) me | *(inside myself)* |
| dopo la tempesta | *(after the storm)* | dopo di te | *(after you)* |
| fra/tra amici | *between friends)* | fra di noi | *(between ourselves)* |
| senza soldi | *(without money)* | senza di te | *(without you)* |
| sopra le nuvole | *(above the clouds)* | sopra di (a) noi | *(above us)* |
| sotto il letto | *(under the bed)* | sotto a lui | *(underneath him)* |
| sullo scaffale | *(on the bookshelves)* | su di noi | *(over us)* |
| verso casa | *(towards home)* | verso di loro | *(towards them)* |

## Da

By and from:

> È stato riparato dall' idraulico. *It was repaired by the plumber.*
> Il treno in arrivo da Pisa . . . *The train arriving from Pisa . . .*

Measurement, quantity, capacity, denomination:

> Un francobollo da seicento lire *A six hundred lire stamp*

At the house/shop/restaurant of:

> Andiamo da Giovanni. *We're going to Giovanni's.*
> Vado dal medico. *I'm going to the doctor's.*

Physical characteristics:

> una signora dai capelli neri *a woman with black hair*

Joining **molto, poco, niente, qualcosa** to the infinitive:

> C'è poco da mangiare. *There's not much to eat.*

Indicating manner:

> Si è comportato da pazzo. *He behaved like a madman.*
> Sono andati da soli. *They went by themselves.*

Purpose:

| | |
|---|---|
| una camera da letto | *a bedroom* |
| un costume da bagno | *a bathing costume* |

## In

Transport:

| | |
|---|---|
| in bicicletta, in aereo | *by bike, by plane* |
| in treno, in macchina | *by train, by car* |

Seasons:

| | |
|---|---|
| in primavera, in autunno | *in spring, in autumn* |

Other:

| | |
|---|---|
| Siamo in quattro. | *There are four of us.* |
| Se io fossi in te . . . | *If I were you . . .* |
| in orario, in ritardo | *on time, late* |
| in anticipo | *in advance, early* |

For dates, use the prepositions and articles combined:

| | |
|---|---|
| Mio figlio è nato nel 1979. | *My son was born in 1979.* |

## Per

For:

| | |
|---|---|
| I fiori sono per te. | *The flowers are for you.* |

Duration of time:

| | |
|---|---|
| Siamo qui per dieci giorni. | *We are here for ten days.* |

For (destination):

| | |
|---|---|
| Sono partiti per la Francia. | *They've left for France.* |

Place:

| | |
|---|---|
| Ha buttato la giacca per terra. | *He threw the jacket on the ground.* |
| Giravano per le strade. | *They were wandering around the streets.* |
| Scendiamo per le scale. | *Let's go down the stairs.* |

Means of transport:

| | |
|---|---|
| Non mandare i soldi per posta. | *Don't send money by post.* |
| Puoi ringraziarla per telefono. | *You can thank her by phone.* |

## Con

With:

| | |
|---|---|
| Sono andata con Franco. | *I went with Franco.* |

Manner:
    con mia grande sorpresa    *to my great surprise*

In expressions or phrases:
    E con questo?    *And so what?*

## Su

On or onto:
    I bambini sono saltati sul    *The children jumped on to the*
    muro.    *wall.*

Out of:
    Tre gatti su cinque    *Three out of five cats prefer fish.*
    preferiscono il pesce.

About, on (a subject or topic):
    Ha parlato sul problema della    *He spoke on the problem of drugs.*
    droga.

Expressions or phrases:
    sul giornale, sulla rivista    *in the newspaper, magazine*
    Un signore sui venti anni    *A man of around thirty.*
    sul serio    *seriously*
    su misura    *made to measure*

## Fra, tra

Between or among:
    La casa è situata tra/fra la    *The house is situated between the*
    ferrovia e la superstrada.    *railway line and the main road.*

In, within (time):
    Ci vediamo tra un'ora.    *See you in one hour.*

### Combined preposition and article

**A, da, in, di** combine with **il**, (**la, lo**, etc.) to form **al, dal, nel** (unit 4), and **del** (unit 10). So does **su** (*on*) giving the following forms: **sul, sullo, sulla, sull', sui, sugli, sulle**.

It is rare for **con** or **per** to do this, but you may see the forms **col** (**con** plus **il**) and **coi** (**con** plus **i**).

# Negatives

In Italian, a negative sentence must include **non** as well as a second negative word:

| | |
|---|---|
| Non siamo affatto stanchi. | *We're not tired at all.* |
| (Non siamo stanchi per niente.) | |
| Non viene nemmeno (neppure) Luisa. | *Luisa's not coming either.* |
| Non c'è nulla da fare. | *There's nothing to be done.* |
| Non mi piacciono né Mara né suo marito. | *I don't like either Mara or her husband.* |
| Non ci vengo più. | *I'm not coming any more/any longer.* |

**Non** comes before the verb, while the other negative comes after:

| | |
|---|---|
| Preferisce **non** vederlo **più**. | *She prefers not to see him again.* |
| **Non** fate **più** queste cose! | *Don't do these things any more!* |

But the negative can come in between **avere/essere** and the participle (**mangiato**, etc.):

| | |
|---|---|
| **Non** ho **ancora** mangiato. | *I haven't eaten yet.* |
| *or* **Non** ho mangiato **ancora**. | |
| **Non** è **più** venuto. | *He didn't come any more.* |
| *or* **Non** è venuto **più**. | |

**Nulla, niente, nessuno, per niente, alcun, né . . né** come *after* the participle:

| | |
|---|---|
| **Non** ho visto **nessuno**. | *I haven't seen anyone.* |
| **Non** mi è piaciuto **per niente**. | *I didn't like it at all.* |

You can use two or even three negative expressions in one sentence:

| | |
|---|---|
| **Non** ci vengo **mai più**. | *I'm not coming here ever again.* |
| **Non** mi regala **più niente**. | *He doesn't give me anything any more.* |
| **Non** ho **mai** detto **niente** a **nessuno**. | *I've never told anyone anything.* |

**Nessuno, niente** or **nulla, mai, né . . né, nemmeno, neppure, neanche** can all be placed at the beginning of the sentence, in which case **non** is left out. However, with the exception of **nessuno**, this word order sounds less natural and somewhat dramatic:

| | |
|---|---|
| **Nessuno** viene alla festa. | *Nobody's coming to the party.* |
| **Niente** succede in questa città. | *Nothing happens in this town.* |
| **Mai** in vita mia ho visto una cosa simile. | *Never in my life have I seen something like this.* |

Most of the negatives can stand entirely on their own:

| | |
|---|---|
| Io non ci vado stasera. | *I'm not going this evening.* |
| Neanch'io. | *Me neither.* |
| | |
| Sei mai stata in Cina? | *Have you ever been to China?* |
| Mai. | *Never.* |
| | |
| Pensate di tornare a Nocera? | *Do you think you'll go back to Nocera?* |
| | |
| Mai più! | *Never again!* |
| | |
| Credo di no. | *I don't think so.* |
| È arrivato senza niente. | *He arrived without anything.* |

## Question Words

### Quando? (*when*)

In questions:

| | |
|---|---|
| Quando partite? | *When are you going away?* |

In indirect or reported questions or statements:

| | |
|---|---|
| Non mi ha detto quando vuole venire. | *He hasn't told me when he wants to come.* |

### Che? (*what*)

**Che** is usually found with a noun, as in **Che cosa?**

| | |
|---|---|
| Che cosa vuoi? | *What do you want?* |

You can use it by itself in spoken Italian, but it is less correct:

| | |
|---|---|
| Che fai? | *What are you doing?* |

It is often used as an adjective, as a substitute for **quale?** (*which?*) as in:

| | |
|---|---|
| Che macchina hai? | *What car do you have?* |

## Perché (why)

**Perché** is used in direct questions:

| | |
|---|---|
| Perché ti sei messo quel vestito? | *Why have you put on that dress?* |

And in indirect questions and statements:

| | |
|---|---|
| Dimmi perché sei andata al cinema con Marco. | *Tell me why you went to the cinema with Marco.* |

## Come? (how)

With **stare**, to ask how someone is:

| | |
|---|---|
| Come sta, signora Rossi? | *How are you, signora Rossi?* |

With **essere** to ask what someone or something is like:

| | |
|---|---|
| Com'è Marco? | *What is Marco like?* |
| Marco è alto, bruno. | *Marco is tall, dark.* |
| Come sono le tagliatelle? | *What are the noodles like?* |
| Sono salate. | *They're over salted.* |

**Come** is abbreviated before **è** to form **Com'è**.

Note the expression **come mai** (meaning *how come*):

| | |
|---|---|
| Come mai sei venuto a piedi? | *How come you came on foot?* |

**Come, che, quanto** can also be used in an exclamation:

| | |
|---|---|
| Quanto sei bello! | *How nice you look!* |
| Come sei stupido! | *How stupid you are!* |

When used as above, **quanto** does not change its ending. But when it means *what a lot of*, it must agree with the noun:

| | |
|---|---|
| Quanti bambini! | *What a lot of children!* |
| Quanto vino hai bevuto stasera! | *What a lot of wine you've drunk tonight!* |

---

# Conjunctions (joining words)

---

Conjunctions join parts of a sentence together; two examples are **ma** (*but*) and **e** (*and*):

| | |
|---|---|
| Vorrei andare a Parigi ma non ho soldi. | *I would like to go to Paris, but I haven't any money.* |

Other simple conjunctions are:

| | |
|---|---|
| anche  *also* | inoltre  *besides* |
| o, oppure  *or, or else* | altrimenti  *otherwise* |
| piuttosto  *rather* | cioè  *that is, in other words* |
| infatti  *in fact, indeed* | insomma  *in short* |

| | |
|---|---|
| però, tuttavia  *yet, however, nevertheless* | |
| anzi  *rather, on the contrary, in fact* | |
| invece  *on the other hand, whereas* | |
| perciò, quindi, pertanto, dunque  *so, therefore* | |
| neanche, neppure, nemmeno  *not even* | |

**E** usually becomes **ed** when followed by a vowel, especially **e**.

Some conjunctions (such as **perché, benché**) are followed by the subjunctive (unit 19). Examples of conjunctions which do *not* need the subjunctive are:

(a) Connecting words such as **che** (*that*), **come** (*how, like as*):

Hai visto come era vestita?    *Did you see how she was dressed?*
È così stupido che non    *He's so stupid that he doesn't*
capisce niente.    *understand anything.*

(b) Words expressing cause: **perché** (*because*), **poiché, giacché, siccome, dal momento che** (*since*):

Dal momento che abbiamo    *Since we have only twenty minutes,*
solo venti minuti, non    *we can't do everything.*
possiamo fare tutto.

**Perché** takes the subjunctive only when it means *in order to*.

(c) Words expressing *time*: **quando** (*when*), **mentre** (*while*), **dopo che** (*after*), **ogni volta che** (*every time that*), **da quando** (*since*), **(non) appena** (*as soon as*), **finchè** (*as long as*):

Resta finchè vuoi.    *Stay as long as you like.*

**Finchè** meaning *until* needs the subjunctive (see unit 19).

(d) Words expressing *consequence*: **e così** (*and so*), **al punto che** (*to such an extent that*), **talmente . . . che** (*so much so that*):

Ero talmente stanca che non    *I was so tired that I didn't*
ci capivo più niente.    *understand anything.*

# ——— **Requiring gerunds (-*ing*)** ———

## As, while, on, in

Use the Italian **gerundio** (-ando, -endo):

| | |
|---|---|
| Entr**ando** nella stanza, ha visto suo cugino. | *As he came into the room, he saw his cousin.* |
| Studi**ando** molto, sarai promosso. | *(By) studying hard, you will pass the exam.* |

There is a past form of the gerundio, **avendo** or **essendo** used along with the past participle (-**iato**, -**ito**, -**uto** form:

| | |
|---|---|
| **Avendo** studiato il latino dall'età di 7 anni, sapeva tutti i verbi a memoria. | *Having studied Latin from the age of 7, he knew all the verbs by heart.* |
| **Essendo** nato da quelle parti, conosceva bene la zona. | *Being born around there, he knew the area well.* |

## Prima di, invece di

Use the infinitive (-**are**, -**ere**, -**ire** forms):

| | |
|---|---|
| **Primo di** uscire, ha chiuso tutte le finestre. | *Before going out, he shut all the windows.* |
| **Invece di** guardare la televisione, fai i compiti d'italiano. | *Instead of watching t.v., do your Italian homework.* |

## Dopo

Use **avere** or **essere** and the past participle:

| | |
|---|---|
| **Dopo** aver mangiato, ho lavato i piatti. | *After eating, I washed the dishes.* |

In all the examples above, the subject (person carrying out the action) *must* be the same in both parts of the sentence. Otherwise **che** will probably be needed:

| | |
|---|---|
| Ho visto Carlo **che** entrava nella stanza. | *I saw Carlo entering the room.* |

# ——— **Common irregular verbs** ———

Only the irregular parts are given. Where alternative forms are possible, these are shown in brackets. Verbs which take **essere** in the **passato prossimo** are asterisked. The **passato remoto** and subjunctive forms are given in full in the appropriate section. (*p.p.*: = past participle)

**andare**
*(to go)*

*p.p.:* andato*
*present tense:* vado, vai, va, andiamo, andate, vanno
*present subj:* vada; andiamo, andiate, vadano
*imperative:* vai (va'), vada, andiamo, andate, vadano
*future:* andrò *conditional:* andrei

**aprire**
*(to open)*

*p.p.:* aperto
*passato remoto:* aprii (apersi), apristi
*similar verbs:* coprire (*to cover*), scoprire (*to discover*)

**avere**
*(to have)*

*present:* ho, hai, ha, abbiamo, avete, hanno
*present subj:* abbia, abbiamo, abbiate, abbiano
*imperative:* abbi, abbia, abbiamo, abbiate, abbiano
*future:* avrò *conditional:* avrei
*passato remoto:* ebbi, avesti

**bere**
*(to drink)*

*p.p.:* bevuto
The parts of **bere** are derived from its original form
**bevere** using the -ere pattern. Exceptions are:
*passato remoto:* bevvi (bevetti), bevesti
*future:* berrò
*conditional:* berrei

**cadere**
*(to fall)*

*p.p.:* caduto*
*passato remoto:* caddi, cadesti
*future:* cadrò
*conditional:* cadrei
*similar verbs:* accadere, scadere

**chiedere**
*(to ask)*

*p.p.:* chiesto
*passato remoto:* chiesi, chiedesti
*similar verbs:* richiedere (*to request*)

**chiudere**
*(to shut,
to close)*

*p.p.:* chiuso
*passato remoto:* chiusi, chiudesti
similar verbs: rinchiudere, schiudere

**cogliere**
*(to gather,
to take)*

*p.p.:* colto
*present:* colgo, cogli, coglie, cogliamo, cogliete, colgono
*present subj:* colga, cogliamo, cogliate, colgano
*imperative:* cogli, colga, cogliamo, cogliete, colgano
*passato remoto:* colsi, cogliesti
*similar verbs:* raccogliere, accogliere, sciogliere

**conoscere**
*(to get to
know, to
meet)*

*p.p.:* conosciuto
*passato remoto:* conobbi, conoscesti
*similar verbs:* riconoscere

**correre**
*(to run)*

*p.p.:* corso*
*passato remoto:* corsi, corresti

|  | *similar verbs:* occorrere, percorrere, rincorrere, scorrere |
|---|---|
| **crescere** | *p.p.:* cresciuto* (sometimes) |
| *(to grow)* | *passato remoto:* crebbi, crescesti |
|  | *similar verbs:* accrescere, rincrescere |
| **dare** | *p.p.:* dato |
| *(to give)* | *present tense:* do, dai, dà, diamo, date, danno |
|  | *present subj:* dia, diamo, diate, diano |
|  | *imperative:* da' (dai, dà), dia, diamo, date, diano |
|  | *passato remoto:* diedi (detti), desti, diede (dette), demmo, deste, diedero (dettero) |
|  | *future:* darò *conditional:* darei |
|  | *imperfect:* davo |
|  | *imperfect subj:* dessi, dessi, desse, dessimo, deste, dessero |
|  | *similar verbs:* ridare (*to give back*) |
| **decidere** | *p.p.:* deciso |
| *(to give back)* | *passato remoto:* decisi, decidesti |
| **difendere** | *p.p.:* difeso |
| *(to defend)* | *passato remoto*: difesi, difendesti |
|  | *similar verbs:* offendere (*to offend*) |
| **dire** | *p.p.:* detto |
| *(to say)* | *present:* dico, dici, dice, diciamo, dite, dicono |
|  | *present subj:* dica, diciamo, diciate, dicano |
|  | *imperative:* di', dica, diciamo, dite, dicano |
|  | *passato remoto:* dissi, dicesti |
|  | *imperfect:* dicevo |
|  | *future:* dirò *conditional:* direi |
|  | *similar verbs:* benedire, maledire, contraddire |
| **discutere** | *p.p.:* discusso |
| *(to discuss)* | *passato remoto:* discussi (discutei), discutesti |
| **dividere** | *p.p.:* diviso |
| *(to divide)* | *passato remoto:* divisi, dividesti |
| **dovere** | *p.p.:* dovuto |
| *(to have to, to owe)* | *present:* devo (debbo), devi, deve, dobbiamo, dovete, devono (debbono) |
|  | *present subj:* deva (debba), dobbiamo, dobbiate, devano (debbano) |
|  | *future:* dovrò *conditional:* dovrei |
| **essere*** | *p.p.:* stato |
| *(to be)* | *present:* sono, sei, è, siamo, siete, sono |
|  | *present subj:* sia, siamo, siate, siano |
|  | *imperative:* sii, sia, siamo, siate, siano |

*future:* sarò *conditional:* sarei
*passato remoto:* fui, fosti, fu, fummo, foste, furono
*imperfect:* ero, eri, era, eravamo, eravate, erano
*imperfect subj:* fossi, foste, fosse, fossimo, foste, fossero

**fare**
*(to make,
to do)*
*p.p.:* fatto
*present:* faccio, fai, fa, facciamo, fate, fanno
*present subj:* faccia, facciamo, facciate, facciano
*imperative:* fa (fai, fa') faccia, facciamo, fate, facciano
*imperfect:* facevo
*imperfect subj:* facessi
*future:* farò *conditional:* farei
*passato remoto:* feci, facesti

**giungere**
*(to reach, to
arrive)*
*p.p.:* giunto*
*passato remoto:* giunsi, giungesti
*similar verbs:* aggiungere, raggiungere, soggiungere

**leggere**
*(to read)*
*p.p.:* letto
*passato remoto:* lessi, leggesti
*similar verbs:* reggere, correggere, proteggere

**mettere**
*(to put)*
*p.p.:* messo
*passato remoto:* misi, mettesti
*similar verbs:* ammettere, scommettere, smettere,
trasmettere

**nascere**
*(to be born)*
*p.p.:* nato*
*passato remoto:* nacqui, nascesti
*similar verbs:* rinascere

**nascondere**
*(to hide)*
*p.p.* nascosto
*passato remoto:* nascosi, nascondesti

**offrire**
*(to offer)*
*p.p.:* offerto
*passato remoto:* offrii (offersi), offristi
*similar verbs:* soffrire *(to suffer)*

**parere**
*(to appear)*
*p.p.:* parso*
*present:* paio, pari, pare, pariamo (paiamo), parete,
paiono
*present subj:* paia, pariamo, pariate (paiate), paiano
*passato remoto:* parvi, paresti
*future:* parrò
*conditional:* parrei
Commonly found used impersonally: mi pare *(it seems
to me)*

**perdere**
*(to lose)*
*p.p.:* perduto/perso
*passato remoto:* persi (perdei, perdetti), perdesti

**persuadere**
*p.p.:* persuaso

| | |
|---|---|
| *(to persuade, to convince)* | *passato remoto:* persuasi, persuadesti |
| **piacere** | *p.p.:* piaciuto* |
| *(to please)* | *present:* piaccio, piaci, piace, piacciamo, piacete, piacciono |
| | *present subj:* piaccia |
| | *passato remoto:* piacqui, piacesti |
| | *similar verbs:* compiacere, dispiacere |
| **piangere** | *p.p.:* pianto |
| *(to cry, to weep)* | *passato remoto:* piansi, piangesti |
| | *similar verbs:* compiangere, rimpiangere |
| **piovere** | *p.p.:* piovuto* (optional) |
| *(to rain)* | *passato remoto:* piovve |
| **porre** | *p.p.* posto |
| *(to place, to put)* | (The parts of **porre** are derived from its original form **ponere**.) |
| | *present:* pongo, poni, pone, poniamo, ponete, pongono |
| | *present subj:* ponga, poniamo, poniate, pongano |
| | *imperative:* poni, ponga, poniamo, ponete, pongano |
| | *passato remoto:* posi, ponesti |
| | *future:* porrò |
| | *conditional:* porrei |
| | *imperfect:* ponevo |
| | *imperfect subj:* ponessi |
| | *similar verbs:* disporre, esporre, opporre, proporre, supporre |
| **potere** | *p.p.:* potuto |
| *(to be able to)* | *present:* posso, puoi, può, possiamo, potete, possono |
| | *present subj:* possa, possiamo, possiate, possano |
| | *future:* potrò |
| | *conditional:* potrei |
| | *passato remoto:* potei (potetti), potesti |
| **prendere** | *p.p.:* preso |
| *(to take)* | *passato remoto:* presi, prendesti |
| **ridere** | *p.p.:* riso |
| *(to laugh)* | *passato remoto:* risi, ridesti |
| **rimanere** | *p.p.:* rimasto* |
| *(to remain, to stay)* | *present:* rimango, rimani, rimane, rimaniamo, rimanete, rimangono |
| | *present subj:* rimanga, rimaniamo, rimaniate, rimangano |
| | *imperative:* rimani, rimanga, rimaniamo, rimanete, rimangano |

*passato remoto:* rimasi, rimanesti
*future:* rimarrò
*conditional:* rimarrei

**rispondere**  *p.p.:* risposto
*(to reply)*  *passato remoto:* risposi, rispondesti
*similar verbs:* corrispondere

**rompere**  *p.p.:* rotto
*(to break)*  *passato remoto:* ruppi, rompesti
*similar verbs:* corrompere, interrompere

**salire**  *p.p.:* salito*
*(to go up,*  *present:* salgo, sali, sale, saliamo, salite, salgono
*to climb up)*  *present subj:* salga, saliamo, saliate, salgano
*imperative:* sali, salga, saliamo, salite, salgano

**sapere**  *p.p.:* saputo
*(to know, to*  *present:* so, sai, sa, sappiamo, sapete, sanno
*learn a fact)*  *present subj:* sappia, sappiamo, sappiate, sappiano
*imperative:* sappi, sappia, sappiamo, sapete, sappiano
*future:* saprò
*conditional:* saprei
*passato remoto:* seppi, sapesti

**scegliere**  *p.p.:* scelto
*(to choose)*  *present:* scelgo, scegli, sceglie, scegliamo, scegliete,
scelgono
*present subj:* scelga, scegliamo, scegliate, scelgano
*imperative:* scegli, scelga, scegliamo, scegliete, scelgano
*passato remoto:* scelsi, scegliesti

**scendere**  *p.p.:* sceso*
*(to descend,*  *passato remoto:* scesi, scendesti
*to get down)*  *similar verbs:* ascendere

**scrivere**  *p.p.:* scritto
*(to write)*  *passato remoto:* scrissi, scrivesti

**sedere**  *p.p.:* seduto
*(to sit)*  *present:* siedo, siedi, siede, sediamo, sedete, siedono
*present subj:* sieda (segga), sediamo, sediate, siedano
(seggano)
*imperative:* siedi, sieda, sediamo, sedete, siedano
*Exists also in reflexive form:*

**sedersi**  *p.p.:* seduto(si)*
*(to sit down)*

**stare**  *p.p.:* stato*
*(to be, to stay,*  *present:* sto, stai, sta, stiamo, state, stanno
*to stand)*  *present subj:* stia, stiamo, stiate, stiano

*imperative:* sta (stai, sta'), stia, stiamo, state, stiano
*passato remoto:* stetti, stesti
*imperfect:* stavo
*imperfect subj:* stessi, stessi, stesse, stessimo, steste, stessero

**tenere**
*(to hold)*
*p.p.:* tenuto
*present:* tengo, tieni, tiene, teniamo, tenete, tengono
*present subj:* tenga, teniamo, teniate, tengano
*imperative:* tieni, tenga, teniamo, tenete, tengano
*future:* terrò
*conditional:* terrei
*passato remoto:* tenni, tenesti
*similar verbs:* appartenere, contenere, mantenere, ritenere, sostenere, trattenere

**togliere** *(to take away, take off)*: see **cogliere**

**uscire**
*(to go out)*
*p.p.:* uscito*
*present:* esco, esci, esce, usciamo, uscite, escono
*present subj:* esca, usciamo, usciate, escano
*imperative:* esci, esca, usciamo, uscite, escano
*similar verbs:* riuscire *(to succeed)*

**vedere**
*(to see)*
*p.p.:* visto/veduto
*passato remoto:* vidi, vedesti
*future:* vedrò
*conditional:* vedrei

**venire**
*(to come)*
*p.p.:* venuto*
*present:* vengo, vieni, viene, veniamo, venite, vengono
*present subj:* venga, veniamo, veniate, vengano
*imperative:* vieni, venga, veniamo, venite, vengano
*future:* verrò
*conditional:* verrei
*passato remoto:* venni, venisti
*similar verbs:* avvenire, convenire, divenire, svenire

**vivere**
*(to live)*
*p.p.:* vissuto* (or avere)
*passato remoto:* vissi, vivesti
*future:* vivrò
*conditional:* vivrei

**volere**
*(to want to)*
*p.p.:* voluto
*present:* voglio, vuoi, vuole, vogliamo, volete, vogliono
*present subj:* voglia, vogliamo, vogliate, vogliano
*future:* vorrò
*conditional:* vorrei
*passato remoto:* volli, volesti

# Passato Remoto

Here are the forms of the **passato remoto** for each verb group:

---

**parlare** (to talk)

| | | | | | |
|---|---|---|---|---|---|
| (io) | **parlai** | I spoke | (noi) | **parlammo** | we spoke |
| (tu) | **parlasti** | you spoke | (voi) | **parlaste** | you spoke |
| (lui) | **parlò** | he spoke | (loro) | **parlarono** | they spoke |
| (lei) | **parlò** | she spoke | | | |
| (Lei) | **parlò** | you spoke (polite) | | | |

---

**vendere** (to sell)

| | | |
|---|---|---|
| (io) | **vendei/vendetti** | I sold |
| (tu) | **vendesti** | you sold |
| (lui) | **vendè/vendette** | he sold |
| (lei) | **vendè/vendette** | she sold |
| (Lei) | **vendè/vendette** | you sold (polite) |
| (noi) | **vendemmo** | we sold |
| (voi) | **vendeste** | you sold |
| (loro) | **venderono/vendettero** | they sold |

---

**dormire** (to sleep)

| | | | | | |
|---|---|---|---|---|---|
| (io) | **dormii** | I slept | (noi) | **dormimmo** | we slept |
| (tu) | **dormisti** | you slept | (voi) | **dormiste** | you slept |
| (lui) | **dormì** | he slept | (loro) | **dormirono** | they slept |
| (lei) | **dormì** | she slept | | | |
| (Lei) | **dormì** | you slept (polite) | | | |

---

There are exceptions to this pattern particularly amongst the **-ere** verbs; the irregular **passato remoto** usually follows an alternating pattern of short and long forms, for example:

---

**leggere** (to read)

| | | | | | |
|---|---|---|---|---|---|
| (io) | **lessi** | I read | (noi) | **leggemmo** | we read |
| (tu) | **leggesti** | you read | (voi) | **leggeste** | you read |
| (lui/lei) | **lesse** | he/she read | (loro) | **lessero** | they read |
| (Lei) | **lesse** | you read (polite) | | | |

---

Any common verbs which have an irregular **passato remoto** will be shown in the verb tables, with the two alternating forms.

# ——— Verbs plus the infinitive ———

An English sentence such as **I want to telephone** is translated directly into Italian by **voglio** plus the infinitive (**telefonare**).

## (a) Verbs that can be followed directly by the infinitive are:

**potere, dovere, volere, sapere, preferire**
impersonal verbs (e.g. bisogna, basta) and verb phrases (e.g. è necessario/difficile)

> Preferisci andare a piedi?  *Do you prefer to go on foot?*
> È facile imparare l'italiano!  *It's easy to learn Italian!*

## (b) Verbs of ending and many other verbs need to be linked to the infinitive by di:

> Finisco **di** mangiare poi vengo. *I'll just finish eating then I'll come.*

Phrases using **avere** plus the noun such as **avere bisogno/fretta/tempo/intenzione/paura/vergogna/voglia**:

> Hai tempo **di** parlarmi?  *Do you have time to speak to me?*

## (c) Verbs of beginning and many other verbs need to be linked to the infinitive by a:

> Comincio **a** preparare il pasto.  *I'll start preparing the meal.*

## (d) Verbs that can take more than one preposition: see unit 20

Here is a list of common verbs plus their linking words. Where the construction involves another person (**chiedo a qualcuno di fare qualcosa**) this is shown by the abbreviation qcn. (qualcuno):

| Verb | (person) | Preposition needed | |
|---|---|---|---|
| abituarsi | | **a** | *to get used* |
| accettare | | **di** | *to accept* |
| aiutare | qcn | **a** | *to help (someone)* |
| amare | | **–** | *to love* |
| ammettere | | **di** | *to admit* |
| andare | | **a** | *to go* |
| aspettare | | **di** | *to wait* |
| aspettarsi | | **di** | *to expect* |
| augurarsi | | **di** | *to hope, wish* |

| | | | |
|---|---|---|---|
| bastare | | – | *to be enough* |
| bisognare | | – | *to be necessary* |
| cercare | | **di** | *to try* |
| cessare | | **di** | *to cease* |
| chiedere | a qcn | **di** | *to ask* |
| comandare | a qcn | **a** | *to order* |
| cominciare | | **a** | *to begin* |
| consigliare | a qcn | **di** | *to advise* |
| continuare | | **a** | *to continue* |
| correre | | **a** | *to run* |
| costringere | qcn | **a** | *to force* |
| credere | | **di** | *to believe, to think* |
| decidere | | **di** | *to decide* |
| decidersi | | **a** | *to decide* |
| desiderare | | – | *to desire, to want* |
| dimenticare | | **di** | *to forget* |
| dire | a qcn | **di** | *to say* |
| divertirsi | | **a** | *to enjoy oneself* |
| domandare | a qcn | **di** | *to ask* |
| dovere | | – | *to have to* |
| fare | qcn | – | *to make* |
| fare a meno | | **di** | *to do without* |
| fare meglio | | **a** | *to do better* |
| fare presto | | **a** | *to hasten to* |
| fermarsi | | **a** | *to pause, stop* |
| fingere | | **di** | *to pretend* |
| finire | | **di** | *to finish* |
| forzare | qcn | **a** | *to force* |
| imparare | | **a** | *to learn* |
| impedire | a qcn | **di** | *to prevent* |
| incoraggiare | qcn | **a** | *to encourage* |
| insegnare | a qcn | **a** | *to teach* |
| invitare | qcn | **a** | *to invite* |
| lamentarsi | | **di** | *to complain* |
| lasciare | | – | *to let, allow* |
| mandare | qcn | **a** | *to send* |
| meravigliarsi | | **di** | *to wonder* |
| mettersi | | **a** | *to start off* |
| obbligare | qcn | **a** | *to oblige* |
| occorrere | | – | *to be necessary* |
| offrire | | **di** | *to offer* |
| ordinare | a qcn | **di** | *to order* |

| passare | | a | to stop by |
| pensare | | a | to think about |
| pensare | | di | to think of, decide to |
| permettere | a qcn | di | to allow |
| persuadere | qcn | a | to persuade |
| piacere | | – | to please |
| potere | | – | to be able |
| preferire | | – | to prefer |
| prepararsi | | a | to get ready |
| provare | | a | to try |
| ricordarsi | | di | to remember |
| rifiutarsi | | di | to refuse |
| rimanere | | a | to say |
| rinunciare | | a | to give up |
| riprendere | | a | to resume |
| riuscire | | a | to succeed |
| sapere | | di | to know, learn |
| sbrigarsi | | a | to hurry |
| sentire | | – | to hear |
| sentirsela | | di | to feel like |
| servire | | a | to be useful for |
| smettere | | di | to stop |
| sognare | | di | to dream |
| sperare | | di | to hope |
| stancarsi | | di | to tire |
| stare | | a | to stay |
| stupirsi | | di | to be amazed |
| suggerire | a qcn | di | to suggest |
| temere | | di | to be afraid |
| tentare | | di | to attempt |
| tornare | | a | to return |
| vedere | | – | to see |
| venire | | a | to come |
| vergognarsi | | di | to be ashamed of |
| vietare | a qcn | di | to forbid |
| volere | | – | to want |

# Italian–English vocabulary

This list contains all the words contained in the units and their English meaning, except for words included in the **Index**. Nouns are marked **(m)** masculine or **(f)** feminine and **(pl)** if they are plural. Verbs that take **essere** in the **passato prossimo** are asterisked. Abbreviations are p.r. = passato remoto, sing = singular.

a (al)  *to, in (the)*
abbandono (m)  *desertion*
abbandonare  *(to) abandon*
abbastanza  *enough*
abitare  *(to) live*
abitudine (f)  *habit*
accanto a  *next (to)*
accettare  *to accept*
accomodarsi  *to make oneself comfortable, come in, sit down*
acqua (f)  *water*
adesso  *now*
aereo (m)  *aeroplane*
affatto (non . . .)  *(not) at all*
affinchè  *so that, in order that*
affittare  *(to) rent*
agenzia (f)  *agency*
aggiungere  *(to) add*
aiutare  *(to) help*
albergo (m)  *hotel*
albero (m)  *tree*
alcuni  *some, a few*
allergico  *allergic*
alto  *high, tall*
altro  *other*
alzarsi*  *(to) get up*
amare  *to love*
amaro (m)  *a 'digestive' drink*
americano  *American*
amico (m)/amica (f)  *friend (male/female)*

ammalarsi*  *to get sick*
anche *also, too*
ancora (non . . . ancora)  *still (not yet)*
andare*  *to go*
angolo (m)  *corner*
anniversario (m)  *anniversary*
anno (m)  *year*
antipatico  *not nice (of a person)*
anzi  *on the contrary, in fact*
aperitivo (m)  *aperitif*
appena  *(only) just, as soon as*
aprire  *to open*
aranciata (f)  *orange squash*
arrivare*  *to arrive, to get to*
arrosto (m)  *roast (joint)*
articoli (m pl) sportivi  *sports goods*
ascoltare  *(to) listen*
aspettare  *(to) wait (for)*
assaggiare  *(to) taste*
attendere  *(to) wait (for)*
attentamente  *carefully*
attento  *careful*
attenzione (con)  *care (with)*
attraversare  *(to) cross*
autista (m/f)  *driver (m/f)*
autobus (m)  *bus*
automobile (f)  *car*
autostrada (f)  *motorway*
avere  *(to) have*

avvertire *(to) warn*
avvocato (m) *lawyer*
azzurro *blue*

bagnato *wet*
bagno (m); fare un bagno *bath, swim; to have a swim*
ballare *to dance*
bambino (m)/bambina (f) *child (m/f)*
banca (f) *bank*
banco (m) *counter*
bar (m) *bar, café*
barista (m) *barman*
basso *low*
bastare* *to be enough*
bel/bello/bella/bell'/bei/begli/belle *handsome, beautiful*
benchè *although*
beni (m pl) di lusso *luxury goods*
bene *well*
benefico (pl benefici) *beneficial*
benzina (f) *petrol*
bere *(to) drink*
bestiame (m) *cattle*
bianco *white*
bibita (f) *drink*
bicchiere (m) *glass*
bicicletta (f) *bike*
    bicicletta da montagna *mountain bike*
bimbo/a (m/f) *small child*
binario (m) *platform*
biondo *blonde, fair*
birra (f) *beer*
biscotto (m) *biscuit*
bisogna* *it is necessary to*
bisogno (m); aver bisogno di *need; to need, to have need of*
bistecca (f) *steak*
bocca (f) *mouth*
borsa (f) *bag*
borsellino (m) *purse*
borsetta (f) *handbag*
bottiglia (f) *bottle*
bravo *clever*
brioche (f) *brioche, sticky cake*
bruciarsi* *to burn oneself, get burnt*
brutto *ugly*
buon/buono/buona/buon'/buoni/ buone *good*

burro (m) *butter*

cabina (f); (e.g.: una) cabina telefonica *cabin, booth; telephone booth*
cadere* *to fall*
caffè (m) *coffee*
cagna (f) *bitch*
caldo (m); aver(e) caldo *heat; to feel hot, be hot*
calze (f pl) *stockings*
calzini (m pl) *socks*
cambiare* (or avere) *to change*
cambio (m); ufficio cambio *change; bureau de change*
camera (f) *bedroom*
cameriere (m)/cameriera (f) *waiter, waitress*
camicia (f) *shirt*
camminare *(to) walk*
camoscio (m) *chamois, suede*
campagna (in) *in the country*
campeggio (m) *campsite*
cane (m) *dog*
canile (m) *kennel*
cannelloni (m pl) *cannelloni (pasta)*
cantante (m/f) *singer*
cantare *to sing*
capire *to understand*
capelli (m pl) *hair*
cappuccino (m) *cappuccino (coffee)*
caramella (f) *sweet*
carino *pretty, sweet*
carne (f) *meat*
caro *dear, expensive*
cartolina (f) *postcard*
casa (f); a casa *house; at home*
caso (m) *by chance*
cassa (f) *cash desk, till*
cassetta (f) *cassette*
cattedrale (f) *cathedral*
cattivo *bad*
cautela (f); con cautela *care, caution; cautiously*
celibe (adj) *bachelor, unmarried*
cena (f) *dinner, supper*
centinaio (m); centinaia (f pl) *about a hundred; hundreds*
centro (m) *centre, city centre*
cercare *to look for*

certo  *certain*
che cosa  *what*
chi  *who*
chiacchierare  *(to) chat*
chiamarsi  *(to) be called*
chiaro  *clear, light*
chiedere  *to ask*
chiedersi  *to wonder*
chilo (m)  *kilo*
chiudere (chiuso)  *to close*
cielo (m)  *sky, heaven*
cioccolato (m)  *chocolate*
cioccolata (f)  *chocolate (drinking)*
cipolla (f)  *onion*
città (f), città (f pl)  *city, town*
classe (f); prima classe, seconda
  classe  *class; first, second class*
cliente (m/f)  *customer*
cognome (m)  *surname*
collega (m/f)  *colleague*
coloniale  *colonial*
colore (m)  *colour*
colpa (f); avere colpa  *blame; to be at
  fault*
comandare  *to command*
come  *as, like*
cominciare* (or avere)  *to begin*
comodo  *comfortable*
compito (m)  *homework, task*
comporre  *to compose*
comprare  *to buy*
compreso  *included*
comunque  *however*
concerto (m)  *concert*
concessione (f)  *concession*
condizione (a . . . che)  *on condition that*
conducente (m/f)  *driver*
cono (m)  *ice-cream cone*
consentire  *to allow*
conservare  *to keep*
consigliare  *to advise*
consiglio (m)  *piece of advice*
contento  *happy*
continuare  *to continue, carry on*
conto (m)  *account, bill*
contrario  *against*
controllare  *to check*
convenire  *to suit, be convenient*
convincere (convinto)  *to persuade*
coprire  *to cover*

cornetto (m)  *cake similar to croissant*
correre  *to run*
corso (m)  *course*
cortesia (f) fare una . . .  *favour, to do a
  favour*
cosa (f)  *thing*
che cosa?  *what?*
così  *thus, like this*
costare  *to cost*
costringere  *to force*
costume da bagno (m)  *swimming
  costume*
cotto (cuocere)  *cooked (to cook)*
cottura (f)  *cooking*
credere  *to think*
crudo  *raw, uncooked*
cucina (f)  *cooking, kitchen, cuisine*
cucinare  *to cook*
cugino (m)/cugina (f)  *cousin (m/f)*
cuocere  *to cook*
cuoco (m) cuoca (f)  *cook*
cura, prendere – di  *care, to take care of*

da (dal)  *from, by, at the house of (the)*
dare  *to give*
data (f)  *date*
data (f) di nascita  *date of birth*
decapitare  *to cut someone's head off*
decidere  *to decide*
del: see di
deludere (deluso)  *to disappoint*
dente (m); al dente  *tooth; with bite*
dentista (m/f)  *dentist*
desiderare  *to desire, want*
desolato  *very sorry*
destra (a)  *right (on the)*
di (del)  *of, from (the)*
dietro  *behind*
difficile  *difficult*
digestivo (m)  *'digestive' (after dinner
  drink)*
dimagrire*  *to get thin*
dimenticare  *to forget*
diminuire*  *to decrease*
dimostrare  *to show*
dire  *to say*
direttore (m), direttrice (f)  *director*
diritto (m)  *(legal) right*
diritto  *straight ahead*
disco (m)  *record*

di solito   *usually*
disperdersi*   *disperse themselves, get dispersed*
dispiacere, mi dispiace; Le dispiace?   *to be sorry, displease, I'm sorry; do you mind?*
disponibile   *available*
distruggere (distrutto)   *to destroy*
divano (m)   *sofa*
diventare*   *to become*
divenire*   *to become*
diverso   *different*
divertirsi*   *to enjoy oneself*
divieto (m) divieto di sosta   *ban, no parking*
doccia (f)   *shower*
dolce   *sweet*
doloroso   *painful*
domandare   *to ask*
dopo   *afterwards, after*
dormire   *to sleep*
dove   *where*
dovere   *to have to*
dubitare   *to doubt*
dunque   *therefore*
duomo (m)   *cathedral*

e   *and*
ecco   *here/there (it is)*
economia (f)   *economy*
educato   *well brought up*
effetto   *effect*
elenco (m) telefonico   *telephone directory*
elettricità (f)   *electricity*
entrare*   *to come in*
errore (m)   *mistake*
esempio (m); per/ad –   *example, for example*
esperto   *expert*
espresso (m)   *espresso coffee*
essere*   *to be*
estate (f)   *summer*
estero (all' . . .)   *abroad*

facile; facilmente   *easy; easily*
fagiolini (m pl)   *French beans*
fame (avere)   *hunger (to be hungry)*
famoso   *famous*
fare   *to do, to make*
fattibile   *feasible*

favore (m); per favore; fare un favore   *a favour; please; to do a favour*
fazione (f)   *faction*
felpa (f)   *sweatshirt*
ferire   *to injure*
fermarsi*   *to stop, stay*
fermata (f)   *stop (e.g. bus-stop)*
ferri (ai . . .)   *on the grill*
festa (f)   *party, festival*
fetta (f)   *slice*
fico (m), fichi (m pl)   *fig*
fidanzato/a (m/f)   *fiancé*
fidarsi*   *to trust*
figlio (m)/figlia (f)   *son, daughter*
fine (alla – )   *end (at the end)*
finestra (f)   *window*
finire   *to finish*
fiore (m)   *flower*
firmare; firmato   *to sign; designer label*
fondo (m); in fondo   *bottom; at the bottom*
fonte (f)   *source*
forse   *perhaps*
fortuna (f)   *luck*
forzare   *to force*
fra   *between, in (of time)*
fradicio   *soaking (wet)*
fragola (f)   *strawberry*
francobollo (m)   *stamp*
fratello (m)   *brother*
frequentare (una scuola, un corso)   *to attend (school, a course)*
fresco   *fresh, cool*
fretta (f)   *haste, hurry*
frigo/frigorifero (m)   *fridge, refrigerator*
fronte (di – )   *opposite*
fumare   *to smoke*
fungo (m) funghi (m pl)   *mushroom(s)*
fuori   *out (side)*
fusilli (m pl)   *pasta twists, spirals*
futuro   *future*

gallo (m)   *cock (male hen)*
galleria (f) d'arte   *art gallery*
gallina (f)   *hen (female)*
gelato (m)   *ice cream*
genere (m); genere (in)   *kind, sort; in general*
generalmente   *generally*
geniale   *brilliant, stroke of genius*

gentile *kind*
gestire *to manage*
gettone (m) (telefonico) *a (telephone) token*
già *already*
giacca (f) *jacket*
giardino (m) *garden*
giocare *to play*
giornale (m) *newspaper*
giornalista (m/f) *journalist*
giorno (m) *day*
giovane *young*
girare *to turn, to go round, to tour*
giro (m) fare un giro, andare in giro; portare in giro *to tour, go (round); to show round*
gita (f) *trip*
gomma (f) *tyre*
gonna (f) *skirt*
gradire *to like*
in grado di *able*
graduatoria (f) *league table*
grande *large, big*
granita (f) *ice, sorbet*
guardare *to look*
guida (f) *guide*
guidare *drive*

idea (f) *idea*
ieri *yesterday*
immaginare *to imagine*
imparare *to learn*
impedire *to prevent*
impegnato *busy, committed*
impiegato (m) impiegata (f) *clerk, desk worker*
impossibile *impossible*
impresa (f) *firm, company*
incidente (m) *accident*
includere (incluso) *to include*
incoraggiare, incoraggiante *to encourage; encouraged*
incredibile *incredible*
indicare *indicate*
indirizzo (m) *address*
industrializzato *industrialised*
informazioni (f pl) *information*
Inghilterra *England*
inglese *English*
ingrassare* *to get fat*

insalata (f) *salad*
insegnante (m/f) *teacher*
insegnare *to teach*
inserire *to insert*
intanto *meanwhile*
interessante *interesting*
intero *whole, one piece*
inutile *useless*
invece *instead*
invitare *to invite*
invito (m) *invitation*
ippopotamo (m) *hippopotamus*
iscriversi* *to enrol*
italiano *italian*

kaki *khaki*

lago (m) laghi (m pl) *lake(s)*
lamentarsi* *complain*
lanciarsi* *throw oneself*
lasciare *leave, let*
latte (m) *milk*
laurea (f) *degree*
laurearsi* *to graduate*
lavare *to wash*
lavorare *to work*
lavoro (m) *work*
legge (f) *law*
leggere (letto) *to read*
lento *slow*
lenzuolo (m); lenzuola (f pl) *or* lenzuoli (m pl) *sheets*
letto (m) *bed*
lezione (f) *lesson*
lì *there*
liberamente *freely*
libro (m) *book*
limonata (f) *lemonade*
lingua (f) *language*
lontano *far (off)*
luce (f) *light*
lungo *along*
lungo; a lungo *long, for a long time*
lungomare (m) *sea front*

macchina (f) *car, machine*
macchina fotografica (f) *camera*
madre (f) *mother*
maestro (m)/maestra (m) *teacher (m/f)*
magari *perhaps, hopefully, if only*

magazzino (m)  *store*
maglia (f)  *sweater*
maglietta (f)  *t-shirt*
mai (non . . . mai)  *ever (never)*
malato  *sick, ill*
male  *badly*
mancare  *to fail to, be missing*
mandare  *to send*
mangiare  *to eat*
maniera (f); in maniera che  *manner, way; in such a way that*
mano (f); mani (f pl)  *hand(s)*
manutenzione (f)  *check-up, service (car)*
marcia (f)  *gear*
mare (m)  *sea*
marito (m)  *husband*
marmellata (f)  *jam*
matrimoniale; letto matrimoniale  *matrimonial; double bed*
mattina (f)  *morning*
mattone (m)  *brick*
meccanico (m)  *mechanic*
medico (m); medici (m pl)  *doctor(s)*
meglio  *better*
mela  *apple*
melanzana (f)  *aubergine*
meno, a meno  *less, unless*
meno male  *just as well*
mensa (f)  *canteen, refectory*
mentre  *while*
menù (m)  *menu*
mercato (m)  *market*
merendina (f)  *tea, afternoon snack*
mese (m)  *month*
metà (f)  *half*
metro (m)  *metre*
metropolitana (f)  *underground*
mettere  *to put*
mettersi a\*  *to start to*
mezzo; mezz'ora (f)  *half, half-an-hour*
mica (non . . .)  *not at all*
migliaio (m) migliaia (f pl)  *thousand(s)*
migliore  *better*
migliorare\* (or avere)  *to improve*
miliardo (m)  *billion (lire)*
misurare  *to measure*
modello (m)  *style, model*
moderare  *to moderate*
modo (m); di modo che  *way, means; so that, in such a way that*

moglie (f)  *wife*
mondo (m)  *world*
morire, morto\*  *to die, dead*
mostra (f)  *show*
multa (f); fare una/la multa  *fine; to fine*
museo (m)  *museum*

nascere\* (p. nacque)  *to be born*
Natale  *Christmas*
naturale  *natural*
ne  *of it, of them*
neanche  *not even, not either*
necessario  *necessary*
negare  *to deny*
negoziante (m/f)  *shopkeeper*
negozio (m)  *shop*
nervoso  *nervous, edgy*
nessun/o/a  *nobody, no- (adj)*
niente  *nothing*
noleggiare  *to hire*
nome (m)  *name*
non  *not*
nonno (m), nonna (f), nonni (m pl)  *grandfather, grandmother, grandparents*
nonostante  *despite*
normalmente  *normally*
nostro  *our*
notte (f)/di notte  *night, at night*
nubile (adj)  *spinster, unmarried*
nuotare  *to swim*
nuovo  *new*

obbligare  *to oblige*
occhio (m)  *eye*
occorrere\*  *to be needed, be necessary to*
offendere (offeso)  *to offend, hurt*
offrire (offerto)  *to offer*
oggi  *today*
ogni  *every, each*
ogni tanto  *every so often*
ognuno  *each one, everyone*
onorevole (m/f)  *title given to MP*
ora (f)  *hour*
ora  *now*
orario (m); in orario  *timetable; on time*
ordine (m); mettere in ordine  *order; to tidy up*
organizzare  *to organise*

originale   *original, unusual*
ormai   *(by) now*
ospite (m/f)   *guest*
ostello (m)   *hostel*
ostinato   *obstinate*
ottenere   *to obtain*
Ottocento   *1800s, 19th century*

padre (m)   *father*
padrone (m)   *owner, boss*
paese (m)   *country*
pagare   *to pay*
paio (m) paia (f pl)   *pair, pairs*
pallone (m)   *football*
pane (m)   *bread*
panino (m)   *roll*
panna (f)   *cream*
panorama (m)   *panorama, view*
parcheggiare   *to park*
pare*   *it seems*
parecchio   *a lot of, several*
parente (m/f)   *relative*
parere (m)   *opinion*
parlare   *to speak*
partenza (f)   *departure*
partire*   *to leave*
passaporto (m)   *passport*
passare* (or avere)   *pass*
passeggiata (f)   *walk*
pasta (f): una pasta, la pasta   *a cake; pasta (e.g. spaghetti)*
pasto (m)   *meal*
patatine (f pl)   *crisps*
patinare   *to skate*
paura (f) avere paura   *fear, to be afraid*
peccato (m); che peccato!   *sin; what a shame!*
peggio   *worse*
pelle (f)   *skin, leather*
pena (f); valere* la pena di   *punishment; to be worth while*
pensare   *to think*
pensione (f)   *pension, boarding house*
perdere   *to lose*
perdita (f)   *loss*
perfetto   *perfect*
pericoloso   *dangerous*
permettere   *to allow*
però   *however*
persuadere   *to persuade*

pesante   *heavy*
pesca (f)   *peach*
pesce (m)   *fish*
pettinarsi*   *to comb one's hair*
pezzetto (m)   *small piece*
pezzo (m)   *piece*
piacere (m); per piacere   *pleasure; please*
piatto (m)   *plate, dish*
piazza (f)   *square*
piccolo   *small*
piede (m); a piedi   *foot; on foot*
pieno   *full*
pigro   *lazy*
pila (f)   *battery*
pinna (f)   *flipper (for swimming)*
plastica (f)   *plastic*
poco (m)   *a little, not much*
poi, in poi   *then; from then on*
polizia (f)   *police*
pomeriggio (m)   *afternoon*
pomodoro (m)   *tomato*
porta (f)   *door*
portafoglio (m)   *wallet*
portare   *to carry*
posta (f)   *post, post office*
postino (m)   *postman*
posto (m); a posto   *place, room, job; in place, in order*
potere   *to be able to*
poveretto   *poor (little) thing*
pranzare   *to dine*
pranzo (m), ora di pranzo   *dinner, dinner time*
preferibile   *preferable*
preferire   *to prefer*
prendere   *to take, get*
prenotare   *to book*
preoccuparsi*   *to worry (about)*
preparare   *to prepare*
presentare   *to present, introduce*
presentatore (m) presentatrice (f)   *presenter (m/f)*
prestare   *to lend*
presto   *quickly, early*
prezzo (m)   *price*
prima (di)   *before*
primo   *first*
problema (m)   *problem*
professore (m), professoressa (f)   *professor, lecturer, teacher*

programma (m)  *programme*
proibire  *to forbid, prohibit*
promettere  *to promise*
pronto  *ready (or Hello! on phone)*
proposta (f)  *proposal*
proprio  *own, really*
prosciutto (m)  *ham*
prossimo  *next*
provare  *to try, feel*
provvedimento (m)  *measure*
psichiatra (m/f)  *psychiatrist*
pulire  *to clean*
puntuale  *punctual*
purchè  *provided that*
pure  *also, by all means*

qualche  *some*
qualcosa  *something*
qualcuno  *someone*
quando  *when*
quanto  *how much*
qui  *here*
quinto  *fifth*

raccogliere  *to collect, gather up, harvest, pick*
raccomandarsi* (mi raccomando) *to recommend, warn*
radersi*  *to shave*
radio (f)  *radio*
ragazzo (m)/ragazza (f)  *boy, girl*
ragioniere (m) ragioniera (f) *accountant*
randagismo (m)  *straying*
rapido (m)  *fast train*
rapido  *fast*
Re (m)  *King*
regalare  *to give*
regalo (m)  *present, gift*
Regina (f)  *Queen*
registratore a cassette  *cassette recorder*
relazione (f)  *report*
restare*  *to stay, remain*
restituzione (f)  *return, giving back*
resto (m)  *change*
riattaccare  *to hang up again*
ricco  *rich*
ricevere  *to receive*
ricevitore (m)  *receiver*
richiesta (f)  *request*
ricordare  *to remember, remind*

rientrare*  *to come back in*
riguardare  *to regard, concern*
rilassarsi*  *to relax*
rimanere (rimasto)*  *to remain, to be (with emotions)*
riparare  *to repair*
riservare  *to reserve, keep*
risistemare: see sistemare  *to rearrange*
riso (m)  *rice*
risolto (risolvere)  *resolved, solved*
risparmiare  *to save*
rispondere (risposto)  *to respond, reply*
risposta (f)  *reply*
ristorante (m)  *restaurant*
risultato (m)  *result*
risvegliarsi*  *to wake up again*
ritardo (m); in ritardo  *delay, in late*
riunione (f)  *meeting*
rosso  *red*
rumore (m)  *noise*

salato  *salty (literally)* prezzi salati, un prezzo salato  *over-priced, high price(s)*
salire*  *to go up*
salutare  *to say hello/goodbye*
sandali (m pl)  *sandals*
sano  *healthy*
sapere  *to know, find out*
sarto (m)/sarta (f)  *tailor, dressmaker*
sbagliare; sbagliato  *to make a mistake; wrong*
sbaglio (m)  *a mistake*
sbrigarsi*  *to hurry*
scalzo  *barefoot*
scandalizzare  *to shock*
scarpa (f)  *shoe*
scavi (m pl)  *excavation*
scegliere  *to choose*
scendere*  *to descend*
scherzare  *to joke*
sci (m) sci (m pl); sciare  *ski, skis; to ski*
sconto (m)  *discount*
scontrino (m)  *receipt*
scontro (m)  *clash*
scorso  *last*
scottare  *to burn*
scotto  *overcooked*
scrittore (m)/scrittrice (f)  *writer*
scrivere (scritto)  *to write*

scultore (m)/scultrice (f)  *sculptor, sculptress*
scuola (f)  *school*
scusare  *to excuse*
secco  *dry*
secondo  *according to*
sedersi  *to sit down*
seguire  *to follow*
selezionare  *to select, choose*
semaforo (m)  *traffic light*
sembrare  *to seem*
semplice  *simple*
sempre  *always*
sentire  *to listen, to feel*
senza  *without*
sera (f); stasera  *evening; this evening*
servire* (or avere)  *to serve*
settimana (f)  *week*
sgarbato/a  *rude, bad mannered*
si  *one (impersonal)*
siccome  *since*
sicuro  *sure, certain*
sigaretta (f)  *cigarette*
signore (m); signora (f); signorina (f)  *Mr; Mrs; Miss*
simpatico  *likeable, pleasant*
sinistra (a)  *left, on the left*
sistemare  *to arrange*
smettere (di)  *to stop*
sognare  *to dream*
soldi (m pl)  *money*
sole (m)  *sun*
solito (di – )  *usually*
solo; da solo  *alone; by oneself*
soltanto  *only*
sonno (m); avere sonno  *sleep; to be sleepy*
sopportare  *to bear*
soprattutto  *especially*
sorella (f)  *sister*
sorprendere (sorpreso)  *to surprise*
sosta (f)  *halt, pause, stopping*
Spagna (f)  *Spain*
spagnolo/a (m/f)  *Spaniard*
spago (m)  *string*
spalmare  *spread*
spazioso  *spacious, roomy*
specchio (m)  *mirror*
speciale  *special*
specialista (m/f)  *specialist*

specialità (f)  *speciality*
spendere  *to spend*
spesso  *often*
spiaggia (f)  *beach*
spiegare  *to explain*
splendere  *to shine*
sporco  *dirty*
sportello (m)  *window, (ticket) desk*
sposare (sposato)  *to marry*
spostare  *to shift, move*
spremuta (f)  *fresh squeezed fruit juice*
spuntino (m)  *snack*
staccare  *to detach, unhook*
stadio (m)  *stadium*
stamattina  *this morning*
stampa (f)  *press*
stanco  *tired*
stanotte  *tonight*
stare  *to be (in certain circumstances)*
stasera  *this evening*
stazione (f)  *station*
stella (f)  *star*
stendere  *to lay out, stretch out*
stesso  *same*
stilista (m/f)  *fashion designer*
stimare  *to estimate*
stirare  *to iron*
stivali (m pl)  *boots*
storia (f)  *history*
strada (f)  *road, street*
straniero (m)/straniera (f)  *foreigner*
strano  *strange*
stretto  *narrow, tight*
studente (m)/studentessa (f)  *student (m/f)*
studiare  *to study*
studio (m)  *study, studio*
stufo  *bored, fed up*
su  *on, over*
subito  *immediately, suddenly*
succedere*  *to happen*
succo (m) di frutta  *fruit juice*
sugo (m)  *sauce (e.g. tomato, meat)*
suonare  *to sound, play (music), ring (bell, telephone)*
svedese  *Swedish*
svegliarsi  *to wake up*
svendita (f) in svendita  *sale, on sale*

tabaccheria (f)  *tobacconist's*

tacco (m)   *heel*
tagliare   *to cut*
tagliatelle (f pl)   *noodles*
tanto   *so much, much, so many*
tardi   *late*
tartufo (m)   *truffle*
tavolo   *table*
tè (m)   *tea*
tedesco   *German*
tegame (m)   *frying pan*
telefono (m)   *telephone*
telegiornale (m)   *tv news*
televisione (f)   *television*
temere   *to fear*
tempo (m)   *weather, time*
temperatura (f) ambiente   *room temperature*
tenere   *to hold*
terra (f); per terra   *ground; on the ground*
testa (f)   *head*
tipico   *typical*
toast (m)   *toasted sandwich*
togliere   *to remove, take off*
toilette (f)   *toilet*
tombarolo (m)   *grave robber*
tornare*   *to return*
tortellini (m pl)   *tortellini (stuffed pasta)*
tovaglia (f)   *tablecloth*
tramonto (m)   *sunset*
trattoria (f)   *little cheaper restaurant (except in London where it is chic)*
treno (m)   *train*
troppo   *too much, too many*
trovare   *to find*
trovarsi*   *to get on (How did you get on?)*
truccarsi*   *to put make up on (oneself)*
turista (m/f)   *tourist*
tutto   *all, whole of*

ubriaco   *drunk*
uccidere   *to kill*
ufficiale   *official*
ufficio (m)   *office*
ultimo   *last*
unico   *only*
usare   *to use*
utile   *useful*
uomo (m), uomini (m pl)   *man, men*
uovo (m) uova (f pl)   *egg, eggs*

uscire*   *to go out*
uva (f) (sing only)   *grapes*

vacanza (f)   *holiday*
valigia (f)   *suitcase*
vapore (m)   *steam*
varare   *to launch, pass (law)*
vecchio   *old*
vedere (visto)   *to see*
veloce   *fast*
velocità (f)   *speed*
vendere   *to sell*
venire*   *to come*
veramente   *truthfully, really*
verde   *green*
verdure (f pl)   *vegetables*
verità (f), a dir la verità   *truth, to tell the truth*
vero   *true*
verso   *towards*
vestirsi*   *to dress*
vestiti (m pl)   *clothes*
vetrina (f)   *shop window*
via (f)   *street*
via   *away*
viaggiare   *to travel*
viaggio   *journey*
viale (m)   *avenue*
vicino   *near*
vietare   *to forbid*
vigile (m)   *traffic warden*
vincere   *to win*
vino (m)   *wine*
visitare   *to visit*
visitatore (m)   *visitor*
visto: see vedere
vita (f)   *life*
vivere* (or avere) (vissuto)   *to live*
volentieri   *willingly, gladly*
volere   *to want to, wish*
volontario (m), volontaria (f) *volunteer (m/f)*
volta (f); a volte   *time; sometimes*
voltare   *to turn*
vongola (f)   *clam*

zeppo   *packed (full)*
zio (m)/zia (f)   *uncle, aunt*
zoo (m)   *zoo*
zucchero (m)   *sugar*

# Index